THE ADMINISTRATION OF JUSTICE
IN CRIMINAL MATTERS

(IN ENGLAND AND WALES)

"And earthly power doth then show likest God's,
When Mercy seasons Justice."

SHAKESPEARE.

"Justice is itself the great standing policy of civil society."

BURKE.

THE ADMINISTRATION OF JUSTICE
IN CRIMINAL MATTERS

(IN ENGLAND AND WALES)

BY

G. GLOVER ALEXANDER, M.A., LL.M.,

Formerly Scholar of Downing College, Cambridge,
and holder of an Inns of Court Studentship;
Of the Inner Temple and North Eastern Circuit,
Barrister at Law

Cambridge:
at the University Press
1915

CAMBRIDGE UNIVERSITY PRESS
Cambridge, New York, Melbourne, Madrid, Cape Town, Singapore,
São Paulo, Delhi, Dubai, Tokyo, Mexico City

Cambridge University Press
The Edinburgh Building, Cambridge CB2 8RU, UK

Published in the United States of America by Cambridge University Press, New York

www.cambridge.org
Information on this title: www.cambridge.org/9780521183482

First published 1915
Reissued with supplement 1919
First paperback edition 2010

A catalogue record for this publication is available from the British Library

ISBN 978-0-521-18348-2 Paperback

PREFACE

THE first edition of this book was published in 1911, as a volume of the *Cambridge Manuals of Science and Literature*. That edition being almost exhausted, it has been thought well to republish it in an enlarged form, as likely to prove useful to a considerable class of readers.

In its present form it is intended to serve as a first book for newly appointed Justices of the Peace, superior police officers, and law students; but it is hoped that it will also appeal to a larger class of general readers who are interested in subjects bordering on the domain of law, history, politics, and sociology. It will be seen that it has a wider scope than the ordinary law book, as it not only gives a survey of the whole field of the administration of the Criminal Law as a working system, with some comments thereon, but also shows the connection between Criminal Law and our system of government.

Another object kept steadily in view has been to show the spirit in which our Criminal Law is administered and which pervades every part of it.

It is not intended to serve as a mere text-book, or book of practice, since it deals with the broad outlines of the system and not with details; but it may possibly serve as an introduction to such old and well-established works as *Stone's Justices' Manual*, the *Magistrate's General Practice*, and *Archbold's Criminal Pleading and Evidence*, the size of which has become formidable.

The Criminal Justice Administration Act, 1914 (herein referred to as the C. J. A. Act), makes great changes in our law and practice, particularly in regard to Courts of Summary Juris-diction. By the Criminal Justice Administration (Postponement) Act, 1914, which received the Royal assent on November 27th, 1914, the operation of that Act has been postponed from December 1st, 1914, to April 1st, 1915, except sections 1, 18, 21, 22, 23, 25, 30, 31, 32, 33, 35, 36, and 37, and any repeal which is consequential on any of these sections. Section 10 (which relates to Borstal Institutions) does not come into operation until September 1st, 1915.

The attention of Justices of Peace and their Clerks is particularly directed to the new Summary Jurisdiction Rules (dated 10th March, 1915) made by the Lord Chancellor in view of the above-named Act coming into operation (which supersede all existing Rules and forms), and also to the important and lucid Home Office circular on the Act, dated 11th March, 1915.

Every care has been taken to ensure accuracy, but in a work of such a wide scope it is too much to expect that it will be found entirely free from inaccuracies; and the writer will be much obliged to any reader who will be good enough to point them out to him.

No attempt has been made to deal with the so-called Emergency Legislation, due to the European War now going on, which is quite exceptional, and which, it is hoped and believed, will be of a temporary character only.

G. G. A.

31st March, 1915.

ANALYSIS OF CONTENTS

INTRODUCTORY

PART III

THE ADMINISTRATION OF JUSTICE IN CRIMINAL MATTERS

INTRODUCTORY

CRIMINAL Justice is that part of our law which appeals most strongly to the popular imagination, which most nearly touches and concerns the average citizen, or "man in the street," since he sees it in operation in the presence of the policeman directing the traffic, or "running in" a drunk and disorderly person, arresting a notorious criminal, or assisting to keep order at a public meeting, armed with all the vague terrors of the law. Yet the blue-uniformed police officer is only the outward and visible sign of an inward and real power, the "Rule of Law," the whole force of the State at the back of the policeman, by which public law and order are maintained. Sir Robert Peel, who reorganised the police force, is reported to have said: "Behind the uplifted hand of one of my policemen stands the power of the British nation." Again, the average citizen reads in his daily newspaper full reports (too full sometimes) of police-court proceedings, of trials in the higher courts, or it may be the occasional carrying into execution of the last dread sentence of the law. Or he may himself be called upon to play his part as a citizen in the administration of this system; he may be summoned to serve as a juror at a Coroner's Inquest, at Sessions, Assizes or Central Criminal Court; or he may even be called upon, in an emergency, to assist a police officer in the execution of his duty, if, happily, he escapes the necessity of appearing in court in the rôle of a prosecutor. This is part of the price which he pays for the security of his life and limb, the protection of his property, and the enjoyment of all his rights as a citizen of a well-governed community.

A great master of our criminal law, the late Mr Justice Stephen, describes it as "an important part of our institutions, of which surely none can have a greater moral significance, or be more closely connected with broad principles of morality and politics, than those by which men rightfully, deliberately, and in cold blood, kill, enslave and otherwise torment their fellow-creatures" (*General View of the Criminal Law*, Pref. p. vi). A subject of such far-reaching importance, which affects the lives, the liberties, and the property of every member of the community, both male and female, adult and juvenile, ought to be of interest to all thoughtful citizens and not merely to lawyers and magistrates.

Historically, with the exception of the law relating to land, criminal law is the oldest part of our law; and this will be easily understood when it is remembered that the King at an early period undertook the preservation of the peace, known at first as the King's Peace, since the killing of a man meant the loss to him of a possible soldier and taxpayer. Accordingly the King at first regulated, and finally suppressed, the right of private vengeance, satisfying the injured party by the punishment of the offender. Thus, from acts of personal violence, the jurisdiction of the King was gradually extended to all other offences, on the assumption (which still lies at the root of the legal conception of every crime) that the State itself is thereby primarily injured. Although an individual may also suffer injury or loss, it is the State which punishes the offender for the sake of example and as a deterrent to others.

Those who wish to make a more intimate acquaintance with the details of criminal law, the nature and classes of the different offences known to it, and the rationale of the whole system, cannot do better than read Prof. Kenny's excellent *Outlines of Criminal Law*, a work designed for the general reader as well as the professional student, and characterised both by exact knowledge and broad philosophical and historical treatment. We are concerned here only with the working of the system.

The organs of the body politic, which we call the State, by means of which it administers justice, are the Courts of Law. These are presided over by judges of various degrees. In the higher courts the judges are assisted by juries, a characteristically

English institution, for the purpose of ascertaining and determining facts; but in the inferior courts, which deal with cases of less importance, the judges decide both the facts and the law. This distinction between law and fact, between the province of the judge and that of the jury, is a very strongly marked one; it runs throughout the whole of our system of judicature, and should never be forgotten. There can be but little doubt that the practice of calling in laymen to assist in the administration of justice has had a powerful influence upon both the judges and the jurors, and has contributed not a little to the growth of the system. The judges (except the unpaid Justices of the Peace) are trained lawyers of great experience, and to them belongs the determination of all points of law that may arise in the course of a trial. The jurors are ordinary citizens. The function of the jury is, under the guidance of the judge, to determine all disputed questions of fact, to which the judge then applies the law; yet it is well known that in the past jurors have had, and still have, considerable effect in restraining the judges, especially in criminal cases, where the political sympathies of the jurors have been with the prisoner, or where they detect, or think they detect, any unfairness towards him, either in the state of the law or in the conduct of the prosecution or of the presiding judge. Hence the jury has been belauded as the "Palladium of British Liberties," and many other similar panegyrics have been bestowed upon it. The jury will, however, be more fully considered hereafter.

*   *   *   *   *

There is no need to dwell here on the very practical character of English law. It reflects the English national character. But another matter may be mentioned, viz. the importance which English law attaches to publicity in regard to criminal proceedings. Subject to certain exceptions in the case of courts exercising a peculiar jurisdiction, e.g. the Divorce Court, which may hear cases in camerâ, where to do otherwise would tend to defeat the ends of justice, it has long been regarded in England as a settled rule that justice should be administered "in open court," especially in criminal cases. But until the recent case of *Scott* v. *Scott* [1913], A.C. 417, there was a singular lack of judicial or other authority to this effect. In this case, however,

the House of Lords affirmed the rule, and it may now be regarded
as a cardinal principle of the administration of justice in England,
not only in criminal but also in civil matters. Indeed there can
be no better security for the proper administration of justice and
the purity of national life than the vigilance and criticism of a
free and enlightened public press. This freedom of criticism
after a trial does not, however, justify comment before or during
a trial. Such comment, so far from assisting tends to defeat
the ends of justice, and amounts to gross contempt of court;
and any editor who indulges in it renders himself liable to severe
penalties. "Trial by newspaper," as it has been called, is not
desirable in the interests of justice.

Bentham, the greatest of English jurists, declared: "Where
there is no publicity there is no justice"; and "Publicity is the
very soul of justice."

PART I. JUSTICES OF THE PEACE AND THEIR WORK

I. POLICE-COURTS, OR PETTY SESSIONS

Beginning, then, at the lowest rungs of the judicial ladder,
and working our way gradually upwards, we find that the Court
of Summary Jurisdiction, popularly called the Police-Court, is
the first court with which we have to deal. This is the court
of which Sir F. Pollock says, it is "in modern times, to many
citizens, the only visible and understood symbol of law and
justice" (*Exp. of Com. Law*, p. 31).

The judges of police-courts are styled Justices of the Peace.
They are, for the most part, unpaid magistrates appointed by
the Crown on the advice of the Lord Chancellor, by commission
under the Great Seal, to keep the peace within certain districts.
They date their origin as Justices from the reign of Edward III,
A.D. 1360. Previously to that time they had been styled Con-
servators or Keepers of the Peace. Speaking of the office of
Justice of the Peace, Sir Edward Coke says: "And it is such a
form of subordinate government for the tranquillity and quiet
of the Realm, as no part of the Christian world hath the like, if

the same be duly executed" (4th *Inst.* cap. xxxi). Shakespeare, in verse, and Addison, in prose, have described the character of the Justice, and few personages are better known to English literature. Roughly speaking, in modern times, Justices of the Peace fall into two classes, (1) County Magistrates, (2) Borough Magistrates.

County Justices are much the older class. When first appointed their chief duties were, as their name implies, "to keep the peace," to prevent assaults, affrays, routs and riots, and to arrest, or issue warrants for the arrest of, offenders of all kinds, and commit them for trial. They were, indeed, at first little more than superior police officers, directing and controlling the parish constables. Lambard's *Eirenarcha, or the Office of the Justices of the Peace*, was first published in 1581. This manual, being "written in a clear and unaffected style," long remained the standard authority on the subject; and Blackstone (*Comm.* 1. c. 9) recommends the study of it. It ran through seven editions before 1610, and with the last three of these editions there was bound up *The Dueties of Constables, Borsholders, Tythingmen, and such other Lowe and Lay Ministers of the Peace*, showing how close was the connection between the Justice and the constable. But Justices have gradually acquired more and more the character of judicial officers, and on the establishment of a general system of police in 1856 they were practically stripped of their character of police officials.

County Justices are appointed by the Crown on the advice of the Lord Chancellor, usually on the recommendation of the Lord Lieutenant of a county; but the Crown is not bound to act upon such recommendation, and it may even appoint in opposition to the wishes of the Lord Lieutenant, though he is *Custos Rotulorum* of the county. Before the passing of the Justices of the Peace Act, 1906, a county Justice was required to have a certain qualification by estate or occupation, but by that Act the qualification by estate was abolished. The Act also provides that a person may be appointed a Justice for a county, although he does not reside in the county, if he resides within seven miles thereof. By the same Act a solicitor, if not otherwise disqualified, may now be appointed a Justice of the

Peace for any county, but it is unlawful for him or for any partner of his to practise directly or indirectly before the Justices for that county or for any borough within that county.

All chairmen of county councils, and of urban and rural district councils, are also *ex-officio* county magistrates. But if a woman happens to be elected to any of these offices, she does not thereby become a Justice.

Borough Justices were first appointed in the reign of Charles I. By the Municipal Corporations Act of 1835 (5 & 6 Wm. IV, c. 76) they were to consist of the Mayor, the Recorder and such other persons as the Crown might appoint by commission.

In all municipal boroughs, even where there is no separate commission of the peace, there are at least two *ex-officio* Justices, viz. the Mayor, for the time being, and the ex-Mayor, for one year. In such a case the Mayor, ex-Mayor, and county Justices have co-ordinate jurisdiction within the borough, but the Mayor takes precedence when acting in relation to the business of the borough, except when the business is "ear-marked" as county business. (See the observations of Farwell, J., in *Lawson* v. *Reynolds* (1904), 1 Ch. 718, hereon.) "The authority of the *county* Justices *includes*, and that of the *borough* Justices is *limited to*, offences committed within the borough," says Mr C. M. Atkinson (*The Magistrate's General Practice*, p. 6).

By section 156 of the Municipal Corporations Act, 1882, the Crown may, on the petition of any borough, grant it a separate commission of the peace on the recommendation of the Home Secretary. But the persons thereby appointed Justices are not authorised to act at the county Quarter Sessions; and if the borough has its own Quarter Sessions, the Recorder is the judge. So that the jurisdiction of borough Justices is strictly limited to the borough and to Petty Sessions. When a municipal borough has a separate commission of the peace, the Mayor takes precedence over all the other borough Justices, and is entitled to take the chair at their meetings. When a municipal borough has a separate court of Quarter Sessions, the Recorder (*q.v. infra*) is *virtute officii* a Justice of the borough, having precedence next after the Mayor.

Borough Justices (other than the Mayor, who is chosen by

the corporation) are appointed by the Crown on the advice of the Lord Chancellor. The Lord Chancellor sometimes adopts the recommendation of the town council, or other bodies; but frequently he acts quite independently of them, or even contrary to their wishes. Borough Justices need not be burgesses, but they must, while acting, reside in or within seven miles of the borough, or have an occupation qualification within the borough.

As regards the mode of their appointment, Justices of the Peace fall into several classes:

1. Those appointed by being named in the schedule to the special commission of the peace for the county, riding, division, borough or liberty for which they act. This is the ordinary mode of appointment.

2. Those who *virtute officii* are always included in such commission, viz. the Lord Chancellor, the Lord President and all the members of the Privy Council, all the Judges of the Supreme Court, and the Attorney- and the Solicitor-General. These are national Justices of the Peace; and their jurisdiction extends to the whole country, as opposed to the first class, whose jurisdiction is local, and is confined to the county, borough, etc., for which they are appointed.

3. Those who acquire the status or position of Justices of the Peace by various statutes, viz. county court Judges, Recorders of boroughs and stipendiary and metropolitan magistrates.

4. Those who become Justices by reason of holding or having held certain municipal or local government offices, viz. all Mayors of municipal or metropolitan boroughs, all ex-Mayors of municipal boroughs, for one year following their year of office, and all chairmen of county councils and urban and rural district councils. But if a woman happens to be elected to any of these offices (as she may now be) she does not thereby become a Justice of the Peace.

5. Justices by charter, *e.g.* the Lord Mayor and Aldermen of the City of London.

A few words as to what Prof. Maitland has described as "That most thoroughly English of institutions, the commission of the peace" (*Justice and Police*, p. 79) may not be out of place. From what has been said above it will have been gathered that each county in England, and every borough which has a bench of magistrates of its own, has a separate commission of the peace. This is a formal document, issued under the Great Seal, which has varied but little in form from the time when it was first instituted, in the fourteenth century. In fact, it was settled in 1590. Its original form in Latin is given in Lambard's *Eirenarcha* (Bk I. chap. VIII). It is delivered into the keeping of the Lord Lieutenant of the county, who is primarily a military officer and as such head of the royal forces in the shire, as the sheriff is the chief executive officer of the shire in legal matters. As such custodian of the commission of the peace, the Lord Lieutenant is *Custos Rotulorum* of the county, and head of the unpaid, county magistracy. Certain older and more experienced justices are signalled out for the honour of being appointed Deputy Lieutenants. As showing their originally military character, they wear on official occasions a military uniform, consisting of a scarlet coat, etc. Whenever the commission is required for the purpose of adding new names to it, it is returned to the Lord Chancellor by the Lord Lieutenant.

In boroughs which have a separate bench the commission is usually entrusted to the Town Clerk. Whenever it is required for the addition of new names it is transmitted to the Lord Chancellor by him.

All Justices of the Peace, both for counties and for boroughs, before acting, must take certain oaths, under penalty of vacating the office or becoming disqualified to enter upon it. These are the oath of allegiance and the judicial oath, the forms of which are settled by the Promissory Oaths Act, 1868, and are as follows:

The Oath of Allegiance

"I, *A.B.*, do swear [by Almighty God] that I will be faithful and bear true allegiance to His Majesty King George the Fifth, His heirs and successors according to law [So help me God]."

The Judicial Oath

"I, *A.B.*, do swear [by Almighty God] that I will well and truly serve our Sovereign Lord, King George the Fifth, in the office of Justice of the Peace, and I will do right to all manner of people after the laws and usages of this realm, without fear or favour, affection or ill will [So help me God]."

The terms of these oaths ought always to be present to the minds of Justices when they are discharging the duties of their office[1].

These oaths may be taken in open court at Quarter Sessions or in any division of the High Court. Chairmen of urban and of rural district councils may take them before two Justices of the Peace at Petty Sessions, and, if re-elected, they may continue to act without again taking the oaths. Borough Justices may take these oaths before the Mayor, and they must also, in addition, make the declaration required by the Municipal Corporations Act, 1882.

This declaration reads as follows:

Declaration by Borough Justices

"I, *A.B.*, hereby declare that I will faithfully and impartially execute the office of Justice of the Peace for the Borough of ———— according to the best of my judgment and ability."

This declaration may be made before the Mayor or two other members of the council of the borough.

The Mayor of a borough, in order to qualify as a Justice of the Peace, may take the necessary oaths before any two Justices of the borough of which he is Mayor; or if there be no such Justices, then before any two councillors of such borough.

If a borough has not a separate commission of the peace, it is regarded as part of the county in which it is situate, and speaking generally, the county Justices can exercise their powers even in and for boroughs which have separate commissions of the peace. "The borough is but a part of the county which has some additional Justices of its own" (Maitland, *Justice and Police*, p. 96). If, however, a borough is a county in itself, the Justices of the county in which it is situate have no jurisdiction within the borough. In the same way their jurisdiction is excluded if the charter of the borough contains a "non-intromittant clause"; but this applies only to Quarter Sessions boroughs.

---

[1] N.B. Wherever an oath is required by law an affirmation may now be made in lieu thereof: see 51 & 52 Vict. c. 16.

Although the necessity of qualification by estate or occupation is now abolished, and although the fact of being a solicitor is now no longer a bar, there are still certain disqualifications which prevent persons from being or acting as Justices of the Peace, *e.g.* no person may act as Justice for a county of which he is sheriff; if a Justice of the Peace become a bankrupt he is disqualified in all parts of the United Kingdom unless and until his bankruptcy is annulled, or he obtains his discharge with a certificate to the effect that his bankruptcy was caused by misfortune without any misconduct on his part; but such disqualification extends only for five years from the date of the discharge, though no such certificate be granted. Moreover, a Justice of the Peace who is reported as having been guilty of a corrupt practice in reference to an election may be removed from the commission.

As regards *ex-officio* Justices, what will disqualify them from holding the office of Mayor or chairman of a district council will also disqualify them as Justices. Finally, the Lord Chancellor has power to remove the name of any Justice from the commission; but it is almost unnecessary to add that such power is exercised only for good cause, in grave cases, and its exercise is justly regarded as a disgrace.

In particular cases Justices may be disqualified from acting by reason of bias or individual interest, *e.g.* where they are shareholders in a company appearing before them. Wherever there is the slightest suspicion of this, it is much better that they should not only not act, but should also retire from the bench. *Nemo debet esse judex in propriâ causâ* is a maxim of the Common Law as well as a rule of common sense.

It is to be hoped that the case of *Mitchell and others, apps.* v. *Croydon Justices, resps.*, reported in *W.N.* May 16th, 1914[1], is unique. In that case certain Justices were sitting as a Borough Licensing Committee (which is not, however, a court of law) and after three cases had been heard by them, one of the sitting Justices came down from the bench and gave evidence, and the licence which was the subject of the case was refused. A case was stated for the opinion of the King's Bench Division as to

[1] See also L.T. Rep. vol. III, p. 632 (Dec. 12, 1914).

whether in these circumstances the Justices were legally entitled
to refuse the licence. The court held that even without the
evidence of the Justice referred to there was evidence upon which
the Justices might act, and consequently that they were entitled
to refuse the licence. But the case is important because of the
principles enunciated by the judges.

Mr Justice Avory said: "I am not sorry to come to this
conclusion, because the course taken at this hearing is not one
to be followed in future. If a member of a judicial body, or of
an administrative body exercising judicial functions, wishes to
be a witness in a case, he ought to make up his mind to do so
before the commencement of the proceedings, and ought not to
fluctuate between the position of a judge and that of a witness.
I should be glad to find authority that evidence so given is not
good legal evidence." Mr Justice Rowlatt said: "The course followed in this case was most unfortunate. It ought not to enter
the mind of a person coming before a body of this kind that one
of its members could combine the functions of adjudicating and
also of giving evidence. *When a man goes on to the bench he
proclaims to all the world that he separates himself from either party
to the case. If that is not kept in view there will be an end of all
confidence in the pure administration of justice.* What must a
litigant think if at any moment the judge who is trying his
case may come down from the bench and give evidence against
him? The two positions are incompatible, and a man must
decide definitely beforehand which character he intends to
assume. It is due to the Justices to say that what took place
was done without any concealment. That shows that they did
not appreciate what was due either to the public or to themselves."
Mr Justice Shearman, the other member of the Divisional Court,
concurred in hoping that what had taken place at the hearing
in question would not be taken as a precedent. The words
quoted above, and italicised by the writer, ought to be inscribed
in letters of gold over the portals of every court of justice.
Justices ought not only to be strictly impartial but they ought
also carefully to avoid even the appearance of evil.

As regards the local limits of their jurisdiction, Justices can
as a rule, execute "judicial acts" only within their own county

or borough; but as regards "ministerial acts" the general opinion is that they may perform them outside such limits. A county Justice may exercise the full powers of his office at any place within the boundaries of his county. Thus he may act in any Petty Sessional division of the county; but in practice he generally confines himself to that division in which he resides; and in certain cases, *e.g.* under the Bastardy Acts and in the grant of licences under the Licensing Acts, his jurisdiction is limited to his division.

Amongst Justices themselves, except in the case of the Mayor of a municipal borough, they take precedence according to seniority, *i.e.* according to the date of their appointment. The whole country, outside those boroughs which have separate commissions of the peace, is mapped out into Petty Sessional divisions[1], and the Justices who usually act in and for such a division, and sit at a certain place, constitute the bench. Such Justices elect one of themselves as chairman, on the ground of some special qualification, *e.g.* his seniority and experience, or the fact that he has had a legal training. The chairman acts as the mouthpiece of the bench and pronounces its decisions; but he has no greater authority than any other Justice, and has no casting vote in case of equality. If several Justices sit, the majority decide. If the votes be equal there is a deadlock, and the matter must drop or be re-heard before a different bench. Sometimes, to get out of the difficulty, a junior magistrate will withdraw his vote.

In counties the necessary court-houses and offices are provided by the county councils. In boroughs which have a separate commission of the peace, *i.e.* their own bench of borough magistrates, such accommodation must be provided by the borough council, and is usually a court in the town hall. No room in a house licensed for the sale of intoxicating liquors may now be used for this purpose.

Ordinary Justices of the Peace are unpaid, a fact which has given rise to their playful appellation of "The Great Unpaid." But it is open to the council of a municipal borough (under

---

[1] There are in all about 1010 separate Petty Sessional and Borough Courts, being an average of about 20 magistrates to a court.

the Municipal Corporations Act, 1882, s. 161) who desire the appointment of a paid or stipendiary magistrate, to present a petition to the Home Secretary to that effect, and thereupon the Crown may appoint to that office a barrister of seven years' standing, who holds office during His Majesty's pleasure, and is by virtue of his office a Justice for the borough. He is paid such a yearly salary as the Crown from time to time directs, not exceeding, without the consent of the council, the sum mentioned in the petition as that which they are willing to pay, since it comes out of the borough funds. He cannot be appointed Recorder of the borough, as in that case he might have to preside at the trials of those prisoners whom he himself had committed for trial. On a vacancy no new appointment can be made until the council again makes application as before the first appointment. More than one stipendiary magistrate may be appointed for a borough.

The Stipendiary Magistrates Act, 1863, also enables cities, towns and boroughs of 25,000 inhabitants (referred to in the preamble of the Act as "populous places") to obtain the appointment of stipendiary magistrates.

The appointment of a stipendiary magistrate does not in any way prevent the other Justices for a borough from holding Petty Sessions. In the provinces, if a stipendiary magistrate sits with other Justices, he has only a single vote like them; but in London he is the sole judge, even though there are other Justices sitting on the bench with him.

The chief objects to be attained in appointing stipendiary magistrates are: (1) the obtaining of the services of a trained lawyer; (2) the securing of the regular attendance at the courthouse of at least one magistrate, since two others are not always available. Moreover, there is this great advantage in the appointment,—a stipendiary magistrate can act alone in all matters (of which there are many) where two other Justices are required (21 & 22 Vict. c. 73). He can also act as one of the Justices for granting or confirming licences under the Licensing Acts, within his jurisdiction. In case of illness or absence he may appoint a deputy, and if he is incapable of doing so, the Home Secretary may now appoint one and assign him suitable remuneration out of the stipendiary magistrate's salary (6 Edward VII, c. 46, s. 1). In case of his death the Home Secretary may make a temporary appointment of a duly qualified deputy for a period not exceeding six months.

In the metropolis all the police magistrates are stipendiaries. There are twenty-seven of them, and they sit at fourteen police-courts, including West Ham. It is worthy of note that the Lord Mayor of London, or any alderman of the City, sitting at the Mansion House or the Guildhall, has all the powers of a stipendiary magistrate. There are about twenty other stipendiary magistrates in the large towns and certain populous districts. (See the Law List.)

As most Justices are laymen, and are not supposed to have any legal knowledge, the Justices for every Petty Sessional division of a county must appoint at least one fit person to act as their clerk, at a salary. The appointment is during their pleasure. The same person must act as clerk of Petty and Special Sessions, and clerk to the Justices, and he is to some extent under the control of the standing joint committee and the county council. The Justices for a borough having a separate commission of the peace must also appoint a fit person to be their salaried clerk, removable at their pleasure. When a borough has not a separate commission of the peace the Mayor and ex-Mayor cannot appoint a Justices' clerk, but a second clerk may, it would seem, be appointed for borough business. The appointment of chief and other clerks to the metropolitan police-courts is made by the Home Secretary; but the clerks to stipendiary magistrates in boroughs are as a rule appointed by the magistrates of the borough, and they are removable at the magistrates' pleasure. In some cases they are appointed by the stipendiaries. It depends on the special Act.

The person appointed a Justices' clerk for a borough or a county must be:

　　1.　A barrister of not less than fourteen years standing;

　　2.　A solicitor of the Supreme Court; or

　　3.　A person who has served not less than seven years as a clerk to a police, stipendiary or metropolitan magistrate.

But any person who has served as, or as assistant to, a clerk

to Justices for not less than fourteen years may be appointed in
any case in which, in the opinion of the Justices empowered to
make the appointment, there are special circumstances rendering
such appointment desirable.

Here a striking anomaly presents itself. As we have seen
above, a barrister of seven years' standing is qualified to become
a stipendiary magistrate, but he cannot become a Justices'
clerk until he is of fourteen years' standing. And to make confusion worse confounded, a barrister of five years' standing may
be a Recorder. But, a solicitor only just passed and admitted
is apparently considered as equal in experience to a barrister of
fourteen years' standing! Of course it is not suggested that any
bench *would* appoint a raw, unfledged solicitor as its clerk; but
he is eligible and they *might* do so. The explanation of this
appears to be that the qualifications of stipendiary magistrates,
Recorders, and Justices' clerks have been fixed by different
Acts of Parliament, and no attempt was made to compare and
harmonise them when the later Acts were passed. It is a remarkable example of the piecemeal character of our legislation.

The offices of Justices' clerk and Justice of the Peace are
incompatible, and therefore a Justices' clerk who becomes a
Mayor of a borough or chairman of a district council *ipso facto*
vacates his office of clerk.

Justices' clerks in boroughs, and clerks to stipendiary
magistrates, are forbidden, under penalties, to be concerned
either directly or indirectly, by themselves or their partners or
otherwise, in the prosecution of any offender committed for
trial at Quarter Sessions or Assizes by the borough Justices
or stipendiary; but no such disqualification exists in regard to
Justices' clerks in counties, and it is a common custom for them,
if solicitors, to instruct counsel in cases committed for trial by
a county bench. This practice has frequently met with judicial
disapproval[1], and it cannot be regarded as satisfactory; it
ought not to be permitted except in those districts where there is
no other solicitor of good standing available. The Justices' clerk
of a Petty Sessional division and of a borough acts as clerk to the
Justices acting as the licensing authority. If he is a solicitor,

[1] See *J. P.* Aug. 2, 1913, at p. 370.

he is forbidden, under penalty, either by himself, his partner, clerk or agent, to conduct or act in any application in respect of any licence or any other proceeding whatever under the Licensing Acts at any Licensing or Petty Sessions held for the district of which he is clerk; but this prohibition does not prevent him from preparing mere notices and forms. The object of this prohibition is clear, and needs no comment.

The duties of a Justices' clerk are: to assist the Justices, when required, with advice upon all matters of law and practice that come before them; to take the depositions in cases of indictable offences; to take minutes of all proceedings before the courts of summary jurisdiction which he attends; to transmit and account for all fines, penalties and other moneys received by him as clerk; to keep a register of the minutes, or memoranda of the convictions and orders of the court, and make returns and accounts in the forms prescribed by the Summary Jurisdiction Rules, 1886. In cases of indictable offences committed for trial, it is his duty to transmit to the court of trial the depositions, the statements made by the accused, and the recognizances (what all these are will be explained later on), and he is subject to penalties if he neglects to do so. When the Director of Public Prosecutions takes up a case, all these documents must be sent to him; and if a prosecution is withdrawn or not proceeded with, he must also inform the same official. In addition, it is the duty of the clerk to prepare all informations, summonses, warrants, forms of commitment and other necessary documents requiring the signature of the Justices.

Since 1877 magistrates' clerks have been in all cases paid fixed salaries. Before that date they were remunerated by fees. S. 34 of the C.J.A. Act, 1914, contains further provisions as to the appointment and remuneration of Justices' clerks, and the mode of accounting for fees, etc., by them.

From what has been said, it will be seen that the office of Justices' clerk is an onerous and responsible one, and that the clerk plays a not inconsiderable part in the work of a police-court and the administration of justice to poor people in small cases. Since the bench may be composed entirely of laymen, the duty of keeping them right in matters of law rests solely upon him, and it is he who, by his continuous attendance at the court, and by his knowledge of its practice in all matters, contributes an element of permanence and stability to its proceedings. It is, therefore, obvious that if the bench is weak and the clerk strong, the clerk may virtually control the bench, and the decisions given may be in effect not those of the bench but those of the clerk. The character of a bench, indeed, depends to a large extent upon the character of its clerk. Great care should therefore be taken in his selection. Generally, however, there is at least one trained lawyer on the bench, and there may be more; and happily there is now a right of appeal in all cases, if there is any substantial departure from law or justice, as well as the check of publicity and criticism. The vast majority of magistrates' clerks perform their duties in an admirable manner.

The late Mr W. Knox-Wigram, himself a magistrate, in the preface to the first edition of his *Justices' Note-Book*, thus describes the lack of legal training of the average Justice of the Peace on his appointment: "In every other profession and business under the sun, a man must serve an apprenticeship of some kind before he takes his turn at the honours and duties of a master craftsman. The exception is that of the Justice of the Peace. His appointment upon the commission implies no acquaintance with the Statutes at large. He need never have heard a case tried. His sole credentials are the instincts and education of an English gentleman. Yet, both in volume and variety, the amount of work which in these days may be instantly forced upon his attention is enormous. He is called upon to encounter it at once. He must do justice, both to himself and others, with no further training in the matter than such as he can accomplish by the way." Hence the greater necessity for a well-qualified, conscientious clerk as his adviser and guide.

It remains only to add that if the position of Justice of the Peace has its honours on the social side, it has also its risks on the legal, and especially for those who have had no legal training. Accordingly the legislature has protected Justices to a certain extent. Against actions in respect of all acts done "within their jurisdiction," provided they were not done "maliciously and without reasonable and probable cause," they are protected

by the Justices' Protection Act, 1848; and they can also claim
the benefit of the provisions of the Public Authorities' Protection
Act, 1893.

The duties of Justices of the Peace, *i.e.* the acts to be performed by them, fall into two classes, viz. those of a merely
ministerial or executive character, and those of a judicial character. It is not always easy, even for lawyers, to draw the
distinction. Examples of the first class are the backing or
endorsement of a warrant on necessary proof being given of its
due issue, the taking of bail, the allowance of a poor rate, the
issuing of distress warrants for non-payment of rates, the transfer
of licences, the attestation of recruits and making of declarations,
etc. These acts may be, and frequently are, performed out of
court. In most well-regulated courts also applications for
summonses and warrants are not permitted to be made in open
court, but must be made before or after the public sitting of the
court. The reason for this practice is that when Justices are
not trying a case, and have not both of the parties before them,
all preliminary matters ought to take place in private.

Besides the work which a Justice of the Peace does in court,
he is frequently called upon to perform ministerial acts outside,
even in his own house (see an article on "The Justice at Home" in
the *Justice of the Peace* for January 1, 1910), *e.g.* backing warrants,
taking statutory declarations, and attesting documents. Following up the subject (on p. 68 of the same journal), a Justice of
the Peace, in a letter, gives a very interesting account of his
labours in this domestic forum. He says: "I was often applied
to for advice by the very poor, chiefly those who were in trouble
with their landlords. I always made it a rule to give them a
patient hearing, and although I had almost always to tell them
that they were in the wrong, I found that the fact of having been
listened to with attention was a satisfaction to them. I was
also sometimes asked to intervene in disputes—a matter which
required much discretion—and some applicants were told that
they had better consult a solicitor. These two latter classes of
cases might have been referred to the court, if it had been more
accessible, but it was kinder to save the poor people a useless
journey, if possible. It is clear that a man who undertakes the

duties of a justice, should not do so for his own gratification, and he ought to be prepared to sacrifice such time as is necessary to help his poorer neighbours when possible, as well as to have possible minute damage done to his carpets, etc."

Some stipendiaries, both in the metropolis and the provinces, make a point of giving free advice to the poor in simple cases, acting in this matter as a "Poor Man's Lawyer." Those who do so usually set apart an hour in which to see the parties in their private rooms, either before the court sits or after it rises.

In giving evidence before the Royal Commission on the Selection of Justices of the Peace on April 13, 1910, the late Sir Charles Dilke, M.P., said: "There was nobody so precious as a magistrate who could always be found at home in a rural village."

Turning to those acts or duties which are of a judicial character, we find that these again fall into two classes, viz. (1) the preliminary examination of prisoners charged with indictable offences, and (2) adjudication in those cases which come within the summary jurisdiction. All offences known to English law are either indictable or non-indictable[1]. An indictable offence is one which at Common Law or by some statute must be tried before a petty jury, upon an indictment, after a true bill has been found by a grand jury. This is the ordinary and regular mode of prosecution at Common Law. Indictable crimes may be treasons, felonies or misdemeanours. The distinctions between these three classes of offences are now largely historical and not of great importance. They formerly represented different degrees of gravity. A non-indictable offence is a petty misdemeanour, which one or more Justices is or are empowered by some Act of Parliament to deal with at Petty Sessions without committing for trial.

But before proceeding to discuss more fully the nature and character of their judicial acts, let us see by what process an offender is brought before Justices. The first step towards this, both in ordinary and summary procedure, is for some one who knows the facts, not necessarily the person aggrieved (unless required by statute, *e.g.* in the case of common assault), to lay

[1] See Appendix A.

an "information" or "complaint." This is the egg out of which all subsequent proceedings are hatched. It is not as a rule necessary that an information should be upon oath, or even in writing; but in indictable offences, unless both these formalities are observed, the Justice can issue only a summons, not a warrant. Except in grave cases a summons only is issued in the first instance; but if the defendant fails to appear, a warrant may then be issued (Indict. Offences Act, 1848, s. 8).

A *summons* is a printed notice warning the defendant (upon whom it is served personally or left at his last or most usual place of abode) to attend at a certain time and place to answer a charge made against him. If he fails to obey it, he runs the risk not only of being arrested under a warrant but also of having the case determined in his absence. The reason for this is that cases begun by way of summons are usually of a less serious nature.

If the complainant or informant, having had notice of the hearing, does not appear by himself, his counsel or attorney, the Justice or Justices may dismiss the complaint or information and may order the complainant to pay costs to the defendant, unless for good reason he or they think proper to adjourn the hearing to some future day upon such terms as he or they may think fit. "If the defendant alone fail to appear, the Court should call for proof of service of the summons. If there is not valid service, the court may issue a second summons, or issue a warrant upon information, as in the first instance. If there has been sufficient service of the summons, there are three courses open: to adjourn the summons with notice to the defendant to attend, to issue a warrant for his apprehension, or to hear the case in his absence" (Mead's *Office of Magistrate*, 4th ed. p. 27).

If both parties appear, either personally or by counsel or attorney, then the Justice or Justices proceed to hear and determine the complaint or information.

A *warrant* is a document of a much more formal and stringent character than a summons. It is issued under the hand and seal of a Justice and authorises a constable or other person to whom it is directed to apprehend the offender and bring him before the said Justice or Justices to answer a charge, usually of a serious nature. A warrant must state shortly the offence, and must name or otherwise describe the offender. It is not returnable at any particular time, but it remains in force until it is executed or withdrawn. When a warrant is issued by an ordinary Justice of the Peace it can be executed only within the district to which his jurisdiction extends; it cannot be executed in any other county or district until it has been "backed," *i.e.* endorsed, by a justice who has jurisdiction there. Warrants may also be issued by the judges of the King's Bench Division in any criminal case, or by a Secretary of State or Privy Councillor in cases of political crimes, *e.g.* treason or sedition. Such warrants can, of course, be executed anywhere in England. So also can certain warrants issued by Bow Street magistrates.

The cases last mentioned are of an exceptional character. Warrants are ordinarily issued by Justices of the Peace out of Sessions. The law on the subject was consolidated by the Indictable Offences Act, 1848. But this statute does not affect the Metropolitan Police or the London Police Acts.

In every case before a warrant is issued or granted an information in writing, upon oath, must be laid before the Justice to whom application is made for the warrant. This is a condition precedent to its issue. But when once it is issued, it may be executed on Sunday and at any time of the day or night and in any place, subject to what is said above as to "backing." The person to be arrested must be specifically named in the warrant. "General Warrants," as they were called, *i.e.* warrants to apprehend all persons suspected of a crime, are void. This result was arrived at only after a grave constitutional struggle about the year 1765. See the cases of *Wilkes* v. *Wood; Leach* v. *Money;* and *Entick* v. *Carrington.*

Justices are however empowered both at Common Law and under many special statutes to issue Search Warrants, *i.e.* warrants authorising the search of premises in which it is suspected that stolen property may be concealed.

A Bench Warrant is one that is issued by a Court of Record, before which an indictment has been found against a certain person, for the arrest of that person and for bringing him immediately before the court. If it is issued at the Assizes, it is signed by the judge; if issued at the Sessions, it is signed by two Justices of the Peace. The issue of a bench warrant is a course that is not usually adopted, but only in urgent cases.

Besides apprehending an offender under a warrant, a police officer may also arrest any person whom he sees actually committing a felony or even, it seems, a mere breach of the peace, but not after the affray is over, except to prevent a repetition of it. He may also arrest any one whom he reasonably suspects of treason, felony or dangerous wounding, although no such crime has been actually perpetrated. He cannot, without a warrant, arrest on a charge of misdemeanour, unless express power to do so be given to him by Act of Parliament. A private individual may arrest, without warrant, any person who in his presence commits a treason, felony, or dangerous wounding, and the better opinion is that he *must* do his best to arrest such a criminal. He may also arrest a person whom he reasonably suspects of having committed such an offence, provided in this case such an offence has been actually committed; but if it has not, he runs the risk of having an action for false imprisonment brought against him and having to pay damages. It has been decided very recently that a private person cannot in an action for false imprisonment justify the arrest of another on suspicion of having committed a felony unless he proves that the particular felony in respect of which he arrested such person was in fact committed; and it is not sufficient for him to prove that other felonies of a similar kind had previously been committed and that he had reasonable and proper cause for suspecting that the person whom he has arrested had committed those felonies (*Walters* v. *W. H. Smith & Sons, Ltd.*, L.T. Rep. vol. 110, p. 345). A private person, therefore, runs considerable risk if he takes upon himself the arrest of an offender; and in all cases where it is possible to procure the services of a police officer, he would be much better advised to do so. Both police officers and private individuals are authorised to effect arrests by various statutes and in various cases too numerous to mention here. The above are their Common Law powers. The powers of a police officer to arrest are considerably wider than those of a private person, and to kill him in resisting arrest constitutes murder. In practice arrests are mostly made by police officers.

When a police officer makes an arrest either under a warrant or without a warrant, and "charges" the accused person, *i.e.* either reads the warrant over to him or states to him the offence of which he is accused and for which he has been arrested, it is the duty of the policeman to inform him also that he need not say anything in answer to the charge, but whatever he may say will be taken down in writing and may be used against him at his trial. This is known as the "usual caution" upon arrest, and the duty arises from the peculiar jealousy with which the law of England regards anything in the nature of a confession or admission, and the safeguards it throws round a prisoner. No confession or admission can be received in evidence unless it has been made quite voluntarily, *i.e.* without any threat, promise or inducement held out to a prisoner by a person in authority; nor can any prisoner be interrogated, and no prisoner is bound to incriminate himself: Cockburn, L.C.J., on one occasion told a police superintendent that "the law did not allow a man under suspicion, and about to be apprehended, to be interrogated at all; a judge, magistrate or jury could not do it." But there are limits to this extreme doctrine; and in a recent case it was held that a statement made by a person to a constable, in answer to an enquiry by a constable, is admissible in evidence on subsequent criminal proceedings against such person, although no caution was given by the constable, provided that the person was not at the time in custody on the charge, that the constable on making the enquiry had not formed the intention of instituting proceedings, whatever the answer might be, and that no inducement was held out or threat made to induce such person to make the statement (*Lewis* v. *Harris*, L.T. Rep. vol. 110, p. 337).

In order to effect an arrest for felony on a warrant a constable may break open doors, but he ought first to signify to those in the house the cause of his coming and request them to give him admittance; and such a request is always necessary when the warrant is only for a misdemeanour; as "an Englishman's house is his castle." Both a constable and a private individual may enter a private house in order to prevent murder, upon a sufficient cry for assistance. If a prisoner escapes from lawful arrest and takes shelter in a house, the constable may break into it and retake him, whatever may have been the cause of the arrest, provided he does so immediately.   But if it be not on a fresh or hot pursuit, the constable should procure a magistrates' warrant.

It has been held that a constable has no right to handcuff a person whom he had apprehended on mere suspicion of felony, unless the prisoner has attempted to escape or it is necessary to do so in order to prevent him from escaping.

Every able-bodied citizen is liable to be called upon to assist the police in the execution of their duty, in effecting the arrest of a violent or escaping prisoner, or in suppressing an affray or a riot; and failure to respond to this duty renders the citizen liable to the penalty of a misdemeanour (fine or imprisonment or both) unless he has some good and lawful reason for refusing. And everyone who obstructs the police in the execution of their duty commits an offence and renders himself liable to a penalty.

By s. 22 of the C.J.A. Act, 1914, the following section is substituted for s. 38 of the S.J. Act, 1879.

"On a person being taken into custody for an offence *without* a warrant, a superintendent or inspector of police, or other officer of police of equal or superior rank, or in charge of any police station, may in any case, and shall, if it will not be practicable to bring such person before a court of summary jurisdiction within twenty-four hours after he was so taken into custody, enquire into the case, and, unless the offence appears to such superintendent, inspector, or officer, to be of a serious nature, discharge the person upon his entering into a recognizance, with or without sureties, for a reasonable amount, to appear before some court of summary jurisdiction at the time and place named in the recognizance; but where such person is retained in custody he shall be brought before a court of summary jurisdiction as soon as practicable."

This is a very important and useful provision, and gives the police a considerably wider power and discretion than they had before, though a similar power was contained not only in the S.J. Act, 1879, but also in the Town Police Clauses Act, 1847, and was applicable in towns where that Act was in operation.

In the metropolitan police district constables in charge of a police station *at night*, and, in the City of London or in any municipal borough, *at any time* when a Justice is not sitting, may admit to bail persons arrested without warrant for petty offences, to appear within two days.

When once an offender is brought before a magistrate or the court, and is in custody, either upon a summons or a warrant, or by arrest, any charge can be preferred against him. The summons or warrant is merely a means of securing his appearance. But if the summons is inadequate or inaccurate the defendant is entitled to have the hearing adjourned, to enable him to meet the new case set up against him.

THE PRELIMINARY EXAMINATION, BEFORE MAGISTRATES, OF
PERSONS ACCUSED OF INDICTABLE OFFENCES (GRAVE CRIMES)

There are certain offences as to which it is known from the first that the magistrate cannot deal with them summarily. Either because of the gravity of the offence with which the accused is charged, or because Justices of the Peace have no jurisdiction to try the case, the prisoner must be committed for trial. In such a case the object of the proceedings is that the Justice shall make but a preliminary examination of the case, to collect the evidence, so to say, and formulate the charge. The powers and duties of Justices of the Peace with respect to persons charged with such offences, known as "indictable offences," are regulated and defined by the Indictable Offences Act, 1848, and an amending Act of 1867. These Acts prescribe the entire course of the proceedings from the information, summons or warrant, to the commitment for trial or discharge of the accused. It would be impossible for us, within the limits of our space, to give even a brief analysis of these Acts. It is sufficient to say that the Justices have full powers to compel the attendance not only of the accused, as above described, but also of all witnesses for the prosecution within their jurisdiction, who will not attend to give evidence without being compelled to do so; to remand the accused for further examination from time to time, for a period not exceeding eight clear days; to admit the accused person to bail (except in case of treason) and to fix the bail.

The object of this preliminary examination is to discover whether there is such evidence against the accused as raises "a strong or probable presumption" of his guilt. It is a relic of the time when, as previously pointed out, the position of justices of the peace was little more than that of superior police officials, when they were merely executive and not judicial officers; but the examination has gradually assumed a judicial form, and is now in effect a preliminary trial. In the words of Sir F. Pollock: "The secret inquisitorial proceeding has become open and judicial; there is no longer an examination (interrogation) of the prisoner, but a preliminary trial in court" (*Exp. Com. Law*, p. 31). Notwithstanding this statement, which is undoubtedly true so far as it represents the change which has taken place in practice, it still remains true in law that the room or place where the examination is held is *not* technically "an open court," and the public can be excluded if the Magistrate thinks that the ends of justice will be better served thereby. (See s. 19 Indict. Off. Act, 1848; and *Reg.* v. *Katz* [1900] 64 J.P. 807.) That such exclusion is very unusual only emphasises the change which has taken place, and points to the growing influence of publicity in our legal proceedings.

Moreover, such examination does not require the presence of more than one Justice; but in practice, as a rule, more are present. If two or more are present, however, they do not constitute a Petty Sessional Court. Again, at Common Law the accused has no right at this preliminary enquiry to the assistance of an advocate. It is needless to say that such assistance would never now be denied to him if he were able to pay for it. And s. 17 of the Indictable Offences Act, 1848, seems to recognise the right of the accused to be represented by "counsel or attorney," at all events so far as the taking of depositions is concerned.

The mode in which the preliminary examination is held is as follows. The prosecutor "opens the case," stating shortly the facts upon which the charge is based, and giving any necessary explanation. ·A solicitor is frequently employed to prosecute, and sometimes, in important cases, a barrister. More frequently a police officer (inspector or superintendent) prosecutes, but in this case he has no right to address the bench (not being an advocate) unless he himself has laid the information, and, therefore, is the prosecutor. Unfortunately there is a growing tendency on the part of the police to attempt to act as advocates, which is strongly, and properly, objected to by the legal profession. The witnesses for the prosecution are then called, sworn and examined in chief, cross-examined and re-examined. Their evidence is taken down in writing as they give it, at the time, by the clerk to the Justices; it is afterwards read over to them and signed by them as correct. These written statements, sworn to by the witnesses, constitute the "depositions," which are made the basis of the charge in the court to which the accused is sent for trial, if committed.

In the case of *The King* v. *Bros; ex parte Hardy* [1910] 1 K.B. 159, it was decided that it is the duty of a Justice of the Peace before whom a person appears, charged with any indictable offence, to take, in the presence of the accused, the depositions of all those who know the facts and circumstances of the case, wherever such a course is practicable. This duty obliges the Justice of the Peace, where it is practicable, to go to the residence of a witness who is dangerously ill and there take his depositions. Whether it is or is not practicable in any particular case to take the deposition of a witness at the residence of the witness is a question for the Justice of the Peace to decide in the exercise of his judicial discretion, and in deciding that question he may take into account the fact that the taking of a deposition will, in the particular case, interfere with the business of his court. Most people would be disposed to agree that the taking of a deposition in such circumstances should have preference over the work of the court.

After all the evidence for the prosecution then available has been taken in this way, it is read over to the accused either by the magistrate or the clerk. The magistrate then says to the accused: "*The charge against you is*" [here he reads the charge]. He then proceeds: "*Having heard the evidence, do you wish to say anything in answer to the charge? You are not obliged to say anything unless you desire to do so; but whatever you say will be taken down in writing, and may be given in evidence against you upon your trial. And you are also clearly to understand that you have nothing to hope from any promise of favour, and nothing to fear from any threat which may have been held out to you to induce you to make any admission or confession of your guilt ; but that whatever you shall now say may be given in evidence against you upon your trial notwithstanding such promise or threat"*—or words to the like effect.

This is the "statutory caution" generally mentioned in newspaper reports. It must be administered to every person accused of an indictable offence before he is committed for trial (Indictable Offences Act, 1848, s. 18), except in those cases to which section 13 of the S.J. Act, 1879, applies.

It has been suggested, by practitioners of considerable experience, that in view of the Poor Prisoners Defence Act, 1903, and with the object of inducing a prisoner who has a good defence to disclose it as soon as possible, in his own interest, it would be well if some such words as these were added to the statutory caution: *Whatever you may now say will be given in evidence upon your trial, both against you and in your favour, to assist the jury in deciding whether you are guilty or innocent.* As the form stands it rather leads a prisoner to think that he must be very careful lest he says anything which may be construed *against* him, and therefore he thinks it better to say nothing at all. Whereas it ought to be brought home to his mind that now is the time to say anything that may be said in his favour, anything that may be of service to him in his trial, and so get it put upon the depositions.

Whatever the prisoner says in answer thereto is taken down in writing and read over to him, and is signed by the Justice, and kept with the depositions of the witnesses and is transmitted with them to the court of trial; and on the trial such statement may be given in evidence against the accused, unless it appears that the Justice has omitted to sign it. But the prosecutor is not prevented from giving in evidence any admission, confession or statement of the accused which by law is admissible as evidence. Instead of making a statement himself, the accused may leave it to his advocate to do so; sometimes he hands in a written statement prepared by his advocate. In many cases, he simply says: "I have nothing to say." Or he may, on the advice of his advocate, reserve his defence. Such a course is not, however, now looked upon with favour, as it raises a suspicion that he has no defence to reserve.

After hearing the prisoner's statement, which is also taken down in writing and read over to him as above, the magistrate says: "*Do you desire to call any witnesses ?*" If he desires to do so, the prisoner's witnesses are then called, sworn, examined, cross-examined and re-examined; and their evidence is taken down in the same way as that of the witnesses for the prosecution, and forms part of the depositions. If the accused tenders himself as a witness (as he may now do) his deposition on oath must also be taken. In this case he gives his evidence immediately after the delivery of the statutory caution. Whether the accused calls witnesses or not, his advocate, if he has one, makes no further speech.

After all the evidence has been heard, the Justice, or if more than one be sitting, a majority of them, must determine whether they will send the case for trial or not. It is this determination which invests the proceedings with a judicial character. If he is, or they are, of opinion that the evidence is not sufficient to put the accused upon his trial, that is to say, that the case against him is so weak that no jury would be likely to convict, he, or they, may order the accused to be discharged. Such discharge, however, is no bar to a further prosecution if additional, stronger evidence can be subsequently obtained, as the accused has not been in "jeopardy.'

But if the Justices are of opinion that the evidence is sufficient to put the accused upon his trial, that is to say, if it "raises a strong or probable presumption" of his guilt, they then, by warrant (*mittimus*), commit him to gaol to await his trial; or they may admit him to bail.

All the witnesses, both for the prosecution and for the defence, are then "bound over" in a certain sum to appear and give evidence at the trial, and some one is bound over to prosecute. Their names are put on the back of the indictment, and if they appear and give their evidence, their expenses are paid and a reasonable sum, according to their position in life, is allowed them for their attendance. If they fail to appear, their recognizances are estreated, *i.e.* the bond into which they have entered for their appearance is enforced.

Costs are now regulated by the Costs in Criminal Cases Act, 1908, and the Rules made thereunder. Under this Act, the court of trial (whether a court of summary jurisdiction or a higher court) has power to direct payment of the costs of a prosecution or defence out of "local funds," *i.e.* funds of a county or county borough. The court has also power, under this Act, to order payment of costs of the prosecution by a defendant, or of the defence by the prosecutor.

It is said above that someone is bound over to prosecute. This is usually the superintendent of police in a county, or a head constable in a borough, if the case is taken up by the police (when it becomes a police prosecution), or it may be the injured party himself (when it is called a private prosecution). In either case (except in those comparatively few instances which are taken up by the Public Prosecutor, when it becomes a public prosecution properly so called), although the costs are defrayed out of local funds, the control of the prosecution remains in the prosecutor's hands and he selects his own solicitor and counsel. Hence, although the Crown is the nominal prosecutor in every case, the real prosecutor is the person bound over to prosecute, and the proceedings are headed or entitled *Rex (in the prosecution of A. B.)* v. *J. S.*; and the proceedings at the trial in every respect are more like private litigation than the criminal prosecution of other countries. The result is that our system of criminal proceedings has been called the "litigious" system, as opposed to the "inquisitorial" system which prevails in France. (See Stephen's *General View of the Criminal Law.*)

The court of trial may be the county, or borough, Quarter Sessions, the Assizes or, in the metropolis, the Central Criminal Court. To which of these courts the prisoner is sent depends upon a number of considerations; the gravity of the offence with which he is charged, the competency of the court to deal with the offence, and the time when the next court will be held. It is very desirable in the interests of justice that accused persons should be kept waiting their trials as short a time as possible.

Before the Assizes Relief Act, 1889, was passed the Judges of Assize, when they came round on circuit, used to clear the gaols of all prisoners waiting trial, under their Commission of General Gaol Delivery. Amongst such prisoners there were many whose offences were of so trivial a nature that they ought properly to have been tried at Quarter Sessions and not at Assizes, and it was no doubt a waste of judicial time and strength to try them at Assizes, as well as a great expense to the county, the scale of costs allowed at Assizes being at that time a much more liberal one than that allowed at Quarter Sessions. Accordingly this Act provided that Justices of the Peace should commit such prisoners to "the next practicable Court of Quarter Sessions" having jurisdiction to try them, "unless such Justice or Justices for special reasons think fit otherwise to direct," and such prisoners are to be tried at Quarter Sessions, and the Judges of Assize are not to be required to deliver such prisoners from gaol unless the High Court of Justice so directs. It will be seen that the Act gives committing magistrates a discretion; but unfortunately it contains no definition of "special reason" or other guide as to what is to be considered as a "special reason." In December, 1896, the Home Office issued a circular which said that when the interval before the next Sessions is considerable, the magistrates might properly send such cases to the Assizes. But on this thorny question the views of the Judges themselves have differed considerably. Thus at Manchester Assizes on November 18th, 1913, Mr Justice Avory made an order that costs on the Sessions scale only should be allowed in certain cases which he said ought properly to have been dealt with at Sessions instead of Assizes; and on December 1st, 1913, in reply to an application (which he refused) to allow such costs on the ground of the hardship to solicitors and others, who were in no respect responsible for the cases having been sent to Assizes, he said that he had repeatedly pointed out that the mere fact of the Assizes coming first was *not* to be held as a "special reason" within the meaning of the Act. (See *The Justice of the Peace*, vol. 77, p. 580.) Yet in charging the grand jury at Lancaster Assizes on June 6th, 1914, Mr Justice Shearman said "he entirely agreed with a decision of the local magistrates in sending a Sessions case for trial at the Assizes, because the Assizes were held first. He held that two principles should govern the administration of criminal justice—that accused persons should be tried as speedily as possible, and that they should be tried in the district in which the cases arose, so that the witnesses (who were discharging a public duty) should be inconvenienced as little as possible." (See *The Justice of the Peace*, vol. 78, p. 294.) In view of these conflicting opinions, what are magistrates to do? It is very difficult to draw the dividing line between the two competing evils, viz.: the keeping of prisoners in gaol waiting trial for long periods, and the wasting of the High Court Judge's time, and consequent expense. The matter therefore still remains one for the discretion of the committing Justices, who must take into consideration all the circumstances affecting the case and arrive at a decision as best they can. In the West Riding of Yorkshire the magistrates have endeavoured to meet the difficulty by holding Special Quarter Sessions shortly before the Assizes so as to deal with the less important cases. However, the matter has now to some extent been settled. The Home Office on December 29th, 1913, with the approval of the Lord Chief Justice, issued another circular on the subject (superseding its previous circular of December, 1896) which is full of excellent advice to magistrates and should be carefully considered by them. It sets out what may be considered special reasons for committing to Assizes prisoners who might be tried at Quarter Sessions, and suggests that in such cases a brief memorandum should be attached to the depositions stating such reasons.

Lambard long ago quaintly pointed out the evil which arises from keeping prisoners in gaol awaiting trial: "For it is daily too well proved that manie (being sent thither for correction) do suck nothing but corruption there; so as they be worse when they come forth, then they were when they were first committed; which evill hapneth by long abode there in wicked companie; whereas, if they had more speedy trial, both they should be ammended, and the countrie lesse charged by it" (*Eirenarcha*, Bk iv. cap. 20).

This evil of keeping prisoners awaiting trial for long periods can also be to a large extent avoided by admitting them to bail; and it is the duty of the magistrates to do this, whenever they can safely do so. By the Bill of Rights, 1688, it was provided that "excessive bail" ought not to be required. Of course there are some cases of such a serious character, *e.g.* murder, that the prisoner ought not to be bailed. It is in every case a matter for the discretion of the Justices, with the advice of their clerk. The number of persons let out on bail who fail to appear and take their trial is surprisingly small (though no accurate statistics on this point are at present available) a fact which may be considered as a strong proof of the confidence which is felt in the administration of justice in this country. It must be remembered, however, that if a person committed for trial fails to appear at the proper time, and his bail is estreated, *i.e.* his sureties are compelled to pay the amount of their bond, he is not thereby absolved, but he may be arrested and put upon his trial at any future time should he come within the jurisdiction. Nor is the standing of bail for an accused person a thing lightly to be undertaken, as the surety may find to his cost. It has recently been decided that any agreement by the prisoner or his friends to indemnify the surety, however innocent, amounts to a conspiracy to defeat the ends of justice, and renders the surety liable to indictment.

If the bail (or surety) fears the prisoner intends to run away and not stand his trial, and desires to protect himself, he may at any time re-arrest the prisoner and hand him back into the custody of the court by which he was bailed, and he may even break into the prisoner's house for the purpose of arresting him. The bail is then discharged from liability. The chief object to be kept in view in granting bail and fixing the amount is to secure that the accused will appear and take his trial.

But besides the possible evil of corruption there is the gross injustice to the accused himself, if he is not admitted to bail and is kept long in prison awaiting trial. The Bail Act, 1898, recites: "Whereas accused persons are sometimes kept in prison for a long time on account of their inability to find sureties, although there is no risk of their absconding or other reason why they should not be bailed," and enacts: "Whereas a justice has power, under s. 23 of the Indictable Offences Act, 1848, to admit to bail for appearance, he may dispense with sureties, if, in his opinion, the so dispensing will not tend to defeat the ends of justice." Commenting on the number of persons let out on

bail in 1908 (ten years after the passing of this Act), the *Law
Times* of April 9th, 1910, observes: "It will be seen that the
effect of the Bail Act, 1908, is rapidly dying away"; and the
latest statistics seem to show the truth of this remark. In 1912,
bail was allowed to 3176 persons out of 13,384 committed for trial,
or 23·73 per cent. Of these 13,384 persons 1659 were acquitted
upon trial, and were therefore presumably innocent; yet we
find that 575 of those acquitted had been kept in prison awaiting
trial less than four weeks; 154 from four to eight weeks; 77
from eight to 12 weeks; 40 from 12 to 16 weeks; and nine for
upwards of 16 weeks. This means that more than half of those
acquitted (855 as against 804) ought never to have been sent to
prison at all, and therefore have suffered grave injustice at the
hands of the State in consequence of mere suspicion. In Scan-
dinavia such persons are compensated by the State. Wherever
possible, therefore, magistrates should admit to bail.

In cases of treason bail can be granted only by a Secretary of
State or a judge of the King's Bench Division. It is not usual
to grant it in cases of murder. The Coroner has a statutory
power to grant it when an inquest has resulted in a verdict of
manslaughter, but not in a case of murder.

The Prison Rules provide that a person who is in prison in
default of bail may see friends at any reasonable hour for the
purpose of finding bail.

S. 19 of the C.J.A. Act, 1914, provides for "continuous bail"
—conditioned for the appearance of the person remanded "at
any time and place to which during the course of the proceedings
the hearing may be from time to time adjourned." S. 20 gives
a court of summary jurisdiction powers of remand "for such
time as may be deemed reasonable"; and provides that in
indictable cases, if the accused and the prosecutor consent, the
period of remand on bail may exceed eight days. S. 21 provides that Justices on issuing warrants of arrest may endorse
thereon conditions as to release on bail, and the officer in charge
of any police station must discharge the person arrested "in
accordance with this endorsement." S. 22 provides for the release on bail of a person arrested without warrant by a superintendent or inspector of police, "if it will not be practicable to

bring such person before a court of summary jurisdiction within twenty-four hours after he was so taken into custody." S. 23 provides that "where a court of summary jurisdiction commits a person charged with any *misdemeanour* for trial, and does not admit to bail, the court shall inform the person accused of his right to apply for bail to a judge of the High Court of Justice."

Should additional evidence be procured between the time when a prisoner is committed for trial and the trial, it may be given at the trial, provided a copy of what the new witness intends to say has been served upon the prisoner.

When a prisoner has a good defence to a charge, it is much better, both in his own interest and that of the public, that he should raise it as fully as possible at the earliest opportunity. The prosecution can then test it, and if they find it to be true, its truth will in all probability be admitted at the trial. On the contrary, a defence which is reserved and kept back to the last moment, *e.g.* an *alibi*, lies under the suspicion of being got up in the interval between the commitment and the trial, and reserved only for the purpose of preventing the prosecution enquiring into its truth.

At the Exeter Autumn Assizes, 1903, in the case of *Rex* v. *Humphries* (67 J.P. 396), Mr Justice Wills laid it down that when a person who is charged with an indictable offence is about to be committed for trial and intends to rely upon evidence for his defence, he should not only call any witnesses he may have, but should also himself give evidence before the committing Justices, and that Justices should impress this upon all prisoners, as otherwise the value of the evidence for the defence will be very much lessened. Other judges have endorsed this dictum, and it seems highly desirable in the interests of the accused that the Statutory Caution given above should be amended so as to bring this clearly to their notice and impress it upon them.

This subject of the disclosure of the defence has been rendered still more important by the provisions of the Poor Prisoners' Defence Act, 1903[1]. Before this Act was passed, every person

---

[1] See Home Office Circular, 31st Aug. 1904; the Rules made under the Act by the Secretary of State (Home Secretary) and the Rules made under the Act by the Attorney-General.

charged with an indictable offence had to bear the cost of any legal assistance he enjoyed, although, if he called witnesses on his behalf before the committing magistrates, and they were bound over to appear at the trial, their expenses were paid in the same way as those of the witnesses for the prosecution. This was considered a great hardship in many cases where the prisoner was too poor to employ legal assistance and too illiterate to conduct his own defence properly. In some cases it was obvious that the case for the prosecution was a weak one, and that if he had been properly defended it was very probable that the prisoner would not have been convicted. Accordingly the above-named Act was passed in 1903. It provides, that where it appears from the nature of the defence set up by any poor prisoner, as disclosed in the evidence given or the statements made by him before the committing Justices, that it is desirable in the interests of justice, that he should have legal aid in the preparation and conduct of his defence, and that his means are insufficient to enable him to obtain such aid, the committing Justices, upon committing the prisoner for trial, or the Judge of a Court of Assize or the Chairman of a Court of Quarter Sessions, at any time after reading the depositions, may certify that the prisoner ought to have such legal aid, and thereupon the prisoner shall be entitled to have solicitor and counsel assigned to him, subject to the provisions of the Act. Briefly, the provisions of the Act are that the expenses of the defence, including the cost of a copy of the depositions, the fees of solicitor and counsel, and the expenses of witnesses shall be paid and allowed in the same manner as the expenses of the prosecution. The Act is carried into effect by means of Rules regulating all these matters. The term "poor prisoner" is a relative one, and does not mean that he must necessarily be a pauper. Regard must be had to all the circumstances of the case, such as the actual means of the prisoner, the nature of the defence, whether it is of a complicated nature or not, the number of witnesses, etc. The committing Justices must grant their certificate upon committing the prisoner for trial; they cannot grant it subsequently. But the prisoner may still apply to the Chairman of Quarter Sessions or Judge of Assize. The grounds upon which legal aid is to be granted are laid down in the following report, which appeared in *The Times* of 26th July, 1904, and was corrected by the Lord Chief Justice himself:

"At Warwick, on Saturday, Lord Alverstone in charging the Grand Jury, referred to the working of the Poor Prisoners' Defence Act. He said that during the six months since the Act had come into force there had been some difference of practice among magistrates as to its scope and the principle upon which it should be applied, and the Home Office had received many communications on the subject. This made it desirable that he should explain the guiding principles of the Act. The Act was not intended to give a prisoner legal assistance in order to find out if he had got a defence. He was not to have solicitor or counsel assigned to him for such a purpose. The governing principle of the Act was that people who had a defence should have every inducement to tell the truth about it at the earliest opportunity. Assistance under the Act could only be given where (1) the nature of the defence as disclosed was such that in the interests of justice the prisoner should have legal aid to make his defence clear; and (2) where also his means were insufficient for that end. Magistrates would have little difficulty in deciding the second point, upon which they could inform themselves by the ordinary means of information. As regards the first point, they should bear in mind that by a defence disclosed was meant not only a defence stated by the prisoner at the end of the hearing, but a defence disclosed on cross-examination or by questions the prisoner might ask or by remarks he interposed, or even in some cases such as might appear on the face of the evidence called for the prosecution. All they had to be sure of was that a defence requiring legal consideration was disclosed at the time by a prisoner devoid of pecuniary means. The Act was passed in the interest of innocent persons; and such would be advised in future not to 'reserve their defence,' but to disclose it at once, so that it could be investigated. The prisoner would thus prevent the suggestion that he had kept back his defence so as to give the prosecution no opportunity of investigating it."

The grounds upon which legal aid may be refused are set out in the following report. On October 16th, 1913, at the Central Criminal Court, the Recorder in refusing a prisoner's application

for legal aid said that "he did so because it seemed to him that
her friends were quite capable of instructing solicitors and counsel
on her behalf. People seemed to think now-a-days that all they
had to do was to apply to the court at the trial and legal aid
would be assigned to them. He did not assign legal aid and let
the taxpayers of this country pay for the defence of people who
were perfectly capable of defending themselves. It had become
a common practice for accused persons to spend a good deal of
money at the police courts quite unnecessarily, and then, when
they were committed for trial to ask for counsel, or solicitors and
counsel, to be assigned to them" (*The Justice of the Peace*,
October 25th, 1913, p. 510).

In many cases the assistance of a solicitor, to put his case
into proper form and to-see to the calling of necessary witnesses,
is even of more value to the prisoner than the employment, at
the last moment, of the most capable and eloquent counsel,
without the requisite instructions and evidence.

As to what is called the *venue*, *i.e.* the place where a person
who commits an offence is to be tried, the rule is that an offence
can be tried only by the court within whose jurisdiction the
offence, or some part of it, was committed; but in larceny the
venue may be laid in any county in which the prisoner has had
the goods in his possession. If the offence is committed within
500 yards of the boundaries of two counties, or is begun in one
county and completed in another, the person charged may be
dealt with in either county (Crim. Law Act, 1826). Where a
river forms the boundary of a county, the 500 yards are to be
measured from the river. The venue, however, embraces not only
the bodies of counties but also land-locked waters (*inter fauces
terrae*) and territorial waters, *i.e.* within a three mile limit of the
shore [see *R.* v. *Keyn* (1876) and the Territorial Waters Jurisdiction Act, 1878].

"As a general rule offences are only triable in the county in
which they are committed, but to that rule there are four exceptions, of which bigamy is one, the others being post-office offences
and offences under the Explosives Act, and until recently, forgery[1].
In such cases the committing magistrates have the option of

---

[1] But see now s. 14 of the Forgery Act, 1914.

sending the case for trial in the county where the offence was committed or retaining it for trial in their own county." (Argument of Mr A. H. Bodkin in *Rex* v. *London County Council* [1914] 3 K.B. 311.)

Section 39 of the Prison Act, 1877, gives a Secretary of State power to make special rules as to the treatment of unconvicted prisoners, *i.e.* prisoners awaiting trial. After reciting that "it is expedient that a clear difference shall be made between the treatment of *persons unconvicted of crime and in law presumably innocent* during their detention in prison for safe custody only, and the treatment of prisoners who have been convicted of crime during their detention in prison for the purpose of punishment," and that "in order to secure the observance of such difference" there shall be made special rules "regulating their confinement in such manner as to make it as little as possible oppressive, due regard only being had to their safe custody, to the necessity of preserving order and good government in the place in which they are confined, and to the physical and moral well-being of the prisoners themselves"; the section then provides that the secretary of state shall make and from time to time repeal, alter or add to, special rules with respect to (1) the retention by the prisoner of books, papers, etc., in his possession at the time of his arrest, which may not be required for evidence against him, and are not part of the property improperly acquired by him, or are not for some special reason required to be taken from him for the purpose of justice; (2) communications between the prisoner, his solicitor and friends; and (3) arrangements whereby prisoners may provide themselves with articles of diet, *i.e.* a "sufficient supply of wholesome food," and "may be protected from being called upon to perform any unaccustomed task or office."

Part II of the Prison Rules, 1899, carry these rules out in further detail as to prisoners awaiting trial; and provide (*inter alia*) that such prisoners shall be kept apart from convicted prisoners and certain privileges may be allowed them by the visiting committee, *e.g.* (on payment of a small sum) to occupy a cell specially furnished, to take exercise separately and (also on payment of a small sum) to have the assistance of some person to relieve him from the performance of any unaccustomed task or office.

No doubt the rules so made are properly carried out, but it is obvious that they are applicable only to the well to do. How can a working man, who is dependent upon his liberty for his power to earn his living, afford to buy a "sufficient supply of wholesome food" if he is debarred from the opportunity of earning money to pay for it? It is clear that he must needs accept "prison fare." It may, perhaps, be urged that some of those who are found not guilty are really guilty and escape by chance. This may be so in a few cases; but it is certaintly not so in all cases; and if a man is presumed to be innocent before he is convicted, still more so is he entitled to be regarded as not guilty when he has been tried and acquitted by a jury of his fellow countrymen.

THE SUMMARY JURISDICTION OF JUSTICES OF THE PEACE

It has already been said that Justices of the Peace were originally executive rather than judicial officers. Their first duty was, and still is, as their name implies, *to preserve the peace*, and in 1912 they bound over no less than 15,929 persons to keep the peace or be of good behaviour.

In *Lansbury* v. *Riley* (1913) (109 L.T. 546; 77 J.P. 440) it was held by a Divisional Court that Justices of the Peace have jurisdiction under the statute 34 Edwd. III, St. 1 (1360-1) to bind over a person to be of good behaviour and to find sureties therefor, although no complainant comes forward to testify on oath that he has been threatened or that he is actually under fear of bodily harm from the person sought to be bound over. This does not mean however that they can do so *mero motu* and without any evidence. They must have some evidence before them that such person is guilty of conduct calculated to incite others to commit offences in violation of the law and in disturbance of the peace.

A relic of their executive character is to be found in the duty of a magistrate to make the proclamation at a riotous assembly, popularly called "reading the Riot Act." But very soon after their creation they began to acquire a judicial character. This change has been already noted. It began in their connection with the administration of the Statutes of Labourers, the Poor Laws and the Game Laws; it grew out of their dealings with vagabonds and poachers, and their punishment of petty assaults and larcenies or thefts.

Bit by bit fresh duties of a judicial character were heaped upon them by various Acts of Parliament. The summary jurisdiction of Justices of the Peace is, therefore, entirely the creation of statutes, and is for the most part quite modern. Formerly Justices could deal, out of Quarter Sessions, only with non-indictable cases. Writing in 1885, the late Professor Maitland said: "Only in the present century have we begun to think of the summary jurisdiction as normal, and to regulate by general statutes the mode in which it must be exercised" (*Justice and Police*, p. 89). The first Summary Jurisdiction Act was passed in 1848; since then the jurisdiction of magistrates has been gradually extended to many indictable offences, mostly felonies, but including also some misdemeanours. The chief Act now in force is the Summary Jurisdiction Act, 1879, amended and extended by an Act of 1899, though the Summary Jurisdiction Act of 1848 is still in force.

By summary jurisdiction, therefore, we mean the judicial functions of Justices of the Peace outside their powers in Quarter Sessions—their authority to determine fact and law without a jury, and to inflict punishment or make orders in certain cases of a less serious character. It may be defined shortly as their "authority to hear and determine informations about petty offences and complaints about civil matters without referring them for decision to Courts of Record," *i.e.* for our present purpose, Quarter Sessions or Assizes. The expression "summary jurisdiction" itself suggests a short and speedy remedy, "an alternative to the more elaborate process of the Common Law," viz. commitment for trial, indictment, and trial by jury. And a Court of Summary Jurisdiction may be defined shortly (as it was in 1889) as a court consisting of "any Justice or Justices of the Peace or other magistrate, by whatever name called, to whom jurisdiction is given by, or who is authorised to act under, the Summary Jurisdiction Acts...and whether acting under the

Summary Jurisdiction Acts or any other Act or by virtue of his
commission, or under the Common Law" (Interpretation Act,
1889, s. 13 (11)).   This definition is a very wide one, and it was
thought that it covered all, or nearly all, the sittings of Justices
at which evidence was taken.   But in the case of *Boulter* v.
Kent JJ., in 1898, it was held that Justices acting as a
licensing authority under the Licensing Acts, *i.e.* in regard to the
grant, renewal or transfer of licences to sell alcoholic liquors, are
not a court of summary jurisdiction; but in sitting to deal with
offences under those Acts they are such a court.   Again it has
been held that Justices sitting to revise jury lists do not form a
Court of Summary Jurisdiction.   Before 1892 it was considered
that Justices who granted distress warrants to enforce payment
of rates were *not* a Court of Summary Jurisdiction; since that date
it has been held that they are such a court.   When they do not
form such a court they are regarded as acting merely ministerially,
in an executive capacity and not judicially.   These decisions
are the result of piecemeal legislation, discovered by the ingenuity
of a number of learned gentlemen, and their effect has been to
produce diversity of procedure as to appeals and costs, where
uniformity was much to be desired.

In *Huish* v. *Liverpool JJ.* [1914] 1 K.B. 109, it was held that
Justices (to whom all the powers under the Cinematograph Act,
1909, had been delegated) sitting to hear applications under that
Act, were not sitting as a Court of Summary Jurisdiction, and
therefore had no power to state a case.

In *Attwood* v. *Chapman* [1914] 3 K.B. 275, it was held by
Avory, J., that licensing Justices do not constitute a court of law,
but are only an administrative body acting judicially.

This summary jurisdiction is not exclusively criminal; it
extends also to some civil cases, and its exercise is subject to certain
stringent conditions as to place, manner and time.

In the first place, every case so dealt with must be *heard,
tried, determined or adjudged* "in open court," that is to say, at
the accustomed place of meeting of the Justices acting in and for
the district.   The court must consist of *two* or more Justices,
except when the statute creating the offence authorises one
Justice to convict.   Such a court forms a Petty Sessions or

Petty Sessional Court; and the place of meeting is a Petty Sessional Court-house. Indictable offences dealt with summarily can be tried only by a Petty Sessional Court sitting on some day appointed for that purpose (of which public notice has been given in such manner as to the Justices seems expedient) or at some adjournment thereof (S.J. Act, 1879, s. 20 (8)). Such notice is usually affixed on the building itself, and specifies the day and hour.

It is usual, however, where the area of the Petty Sessional division is a wide one, to provide one or more subsidiary places of meeting, for use in cases of emergency. Such places are called Occasional Court-houses. When sitting in such a court-house a bench of Justices can inflict no greater penalty than a single Justice can, though they may deal with a greater variety of cases.

The importance of publicity in our legal proceedings has already been referred to. In no class of cases is it more important than in these petty offences, which are tried by unpaid and mostly untrained magistrates, who decide, with the assistance of their clerk, both the law and the facts, and from whose decisions in some cases there is no appeal[1]. Accordingly, in 1848, it was enacted: "The room or place where such Justice or Justices shall sit to hear and try any such complaint or information, shall be deemed *an open and public court*, to which the public have access, so far as it can conveniently contain them" (S.J. Act, 1848, s. 12, and *R.* v. *Justices of Hampshire*, 39 J.P. 101). This provision, however, according to an opinion given by L.C.J., Lord Alverstone (when Attorney-General) and Mr Hugh Frazer, does not prevent Justices of the Peace pursuing the same course as that sometimes adopted by Judges of Assize, viz. the exclusion of women and children from the court when cases of a certain class are being tried and decency requires such a step.

The case of *Scott* v. *Scott*, referred to in the Introduction, on p. 3, appears, however, to render the legality of this course very doubtful. In that case Lord Loreburn, ex-L.C., declared: "The inveterate rule is that justice shall be administered with open doors." And Lord Haldane, L.C., in the same case said: "A mere desire to consider the feelings of delicacy or to exclude

[1] But see now s. 37, C.J.A. Act, 1914.

from publicity details which it would be desirable not to publish is not, I repeat, enough as the law now stands." In the same case, when it was in the Court of Appeal, Phillimore, L.J., had said: "The courts are the guardians of the liberties of the public and should be bulwarks against encroachments upon those liberties from whatsoever side they may come. It is their duty to be vigilant, but they must be doubly vigilant against encroachments by the courts themselves." And in the House of Lords Lord Loreburn spoke of this passage as admirably expressing the duty of the courts.

As to the limitation of time, when no time is mentioned in the statute creating the offence the complaint must be made or the information laid within six calendar months from the time when the matter of it arose; otherwise the jurisdiction of the magistrates is ousted. But this limitation of time does not apply in indictable offences tried by courts of summary jurisdiction; the maxim *Nullum tempus regi occurrit* being applicable thereto (see Art. 70, J.P. 374).

Another important restriction upon the exercise of summary jurisdiction by Justices is that they cannot deal with any question which involves the decision of a *bonâ fide* and reasonable claim to real property. In such case also their jurisdiction is ousted. This arises from the difficulties of the English law relating to land. But the jurisdiction of the Justices is not ousted by a mere fictitious pretence of title, and they must determine, upon the evidence before them, whether or not a *bonâ fide* question of title is raised. Nor is their jurisdiction ousted even by a *bonâ fide* claim of a right which cannot exist in law.

Speaking generally, and subject to the above-mentioned conditions and limitations, the Justices, in exercising their summary jurisdiction, have similar powers of compelling the attendance of the defendant, or accused person, and witnesses, of adjournment, remand and bail (except that the limit of eight days does not apply) as in the case of indictable offences.

"The summary jurisdiction in criminal cases," says Professor Kenny, "covers some hundreds of offences, *e.g.* many petty forms of dishonesty or of malicious damage, acts of cruelty to animals, transgressions against the bye-laws that secure order in streets and highways, and trivial violations of the laws relating to game, intoxicating liquors, adulteration of food, public health and education" (*Outlines of Crim. Law*, p. 431). It is, however, unfortunately the case that the most severe penalties inflicted by Justices are those inflicted by some country benches in respect of "petty forms of dishonesty" and "trivial violations of the laws relating to game." "The matters with respect to which Justices have power to make summary convictions or orders," says another authority, "are of enormous variety, depending on many statutes, and an untold variety of regulations made by many departments of state, and of bye-laws made by local authorities (in either case under statutory powers), for which reference must be made to the collections of statutory rules and to the authorities for the districts to which the regulations apply" (*Encyclop. Laws of Eng.*, *sub* "Summary Jurisdiction"). Offences against these matters constitute what the French call *contraventions de police*. A glance at Stone's *Justice's Manual*, Okes' *Magisterial Synopsis*, or the *Magistrate's General Practice* (ed. Atkinson) will at once prove the truth of these statements.

In particular, the Summary Jurisdiction Acts have authorised magistrates to deal summarily with indictable offences committed by (1) children, (2) young persons, and, in certain cases, (3) adults; (a) where the value of the property does not exceed £20 and the accused consents, (b) where the property exceeds £20 but the prisoner pleads guilty.

First, as to Children; where a "child," *i.e.* above *seven* and under *fourteen* years of age, is charged before a Court of Summary Jurisdiction *with any indictable offence* (*other than homicide*) the court, if they think it expedient so to do, and if the parent or guardian of the child so charged, when informed by the court of his right to have the child tried by a jury, *does not object* to the child being dealt with summarily, may deal summarily with the offender, and inflict the same punishment as might have been inflicted had the case been tried on indictment: provided where detention (in lieu of imprisonment) is ordered, the term shall not exceed one month, and when a fine is imposed, the amount shall not in any case exceed forty shillings[1]. A "child" cannot now

---

[1] See s. 15 (3) C.J.A. Act, 1914. This applies only to charges of felony.

be sent to prison (Children Act, 1908, s. 106). When a child is a male the court may, either in addition to or instead of any other punishment, adjudge him to be privately whipped, with not more than *six* strokes of a birch rod by a constable, in the presence of an inspector of police or other officer of higher rank than a constable, and also in the presence of the parent or guardian of the child if he desires to be present.

For the purpose of proceeding in this manner the court at any time during the hearing of the case, if they become satisfied by the evidence that it is expedient to deal with the case summarily, shall cause the charge to be reduced into writing and read over to the parent or guardian of the child, and then address a question to such parent or guardian, to the following effect: *"Do you desire the child to be tried by a jury, and object to the child being dealt with summarily?"*—together with a statement, if the court thinks such statement desirable for the information of such parent or guardian, of the meaning of the case being dealt with summarily, and of the Sessions or Assizes (as the case may be) at which the child will be tried, if tried by a jury.

Where the parent or guardian is not present when the child is charged the court may remand the child for the purpose of securing his attendance.

This provision does not render punishable for any offence a child who is not, in the opinion of the court before whom he is charged, *above* the age of seven years *and* of sufficient capacity to commit a crime. This is in accordance with the general principle of English law that a child under the age of seven years is absolutely incapable of committing any criminal offence.

If the parent or guardian does not object to summary trial, after such explanation, the case may be dealt with summarily— otherwise it must be sent for trial.

Secondly, as to Young Persons, viz. those above fourteen and under sixteen years of age; where a "young person" is charged before a Court of Summary Jurisdiction *with any indictable offence (other than homicide)* the court, if they think it expedient to do so, having regard to the character and antecedents of the person charged, the nature of the offence and all the circumstances of the case, and if the young person charged with the offence, when

informed by the court of his right to be tried by a jury, consents
to be dealt with summarily, may deal summarily with the offence.
Here, again, the limit of punishment is now one month's custody
in a place of detention (Children Act, 1908, s. 106), or a fine
not exceeding £10, unless the young person is "unruly" or
"depraved," in which case he can still be sent to prison, and
apparently for three months. And apparently a "young person"
may still receive twelve strokes for an offence against section 4
of the Criminal Law Amendment Act, 1885.

For the purpose of proceeding summarily in such cases the
charge must be reduced into writing and read over to the young
person charged, and then a question must be addressed to him
to the following effect: *"Do you desire to be tried by a jury, or
do you consent to the case being dealt with summarily?"* This
question must be accompanied by a statement, if the court
think such statement desirable for the information of the young
person to whom the question is addressed, of the meaning of the
case being dealt with summarily, and of the Sessions or Assizes
(as the case may be) at which he will be tried, if tried by a jury.

Under ss. 57 to 72 of the Children Act, 1908, a Petty Sessional
Court has large powers of sending offenders between twelve
and sixteen, and children under fourteen, to reformatory and
industrial schools, and the Act contains provisions for their
treatment therein.

Where the charge is one of false pretences, owing to its
extremely technical character, the court must explain to the
parent, guardian or "young person" that the false pretences
means (shortly) a false representation of a present or past fact,
not a future one; "and may add any such explanation as the
court may deem suitable to the circumstances." If the accused
consents, after such explanation, the case is dealt with summarily
—if not, he is sent for trial in the ordinary way. It was not
until 1899 that a Court of Summary Jurisdiction was enabled
to deal with the offence of false pretences.

After it has been decided that the case is to be dealt with
summarily, and not sent for trial before a jury, the procedure
both in the case of a child and of a young person is as follows:
the Chairman, or one of the Justices (always remembering that

a stipendiary magistrate can exercise the powers of two Justices),
says to the accused: *"You have heard the charge against you read;
are you Guilty or Not Guilty?"*

If he pleads "Not Guilty," the Justice then asks him: *"What
have you to say in defence to the charge,"* or *"What is your defence
to the charge?"*

The court then proceeds to hear the defence, and having done
so, considers *as a jury* whether the offence is proved, and if they
find that it is, they inform him that they have decided to find
him "Guilty," and address to him this question: *"Have you any
cause to show why judgment should not be passed upon you?"*
And after hearing anything further he may have to say, they
proceed to pass upon him the appropriate sentence, according to
their discretion within the limits now permitted by the Children
Act, 1908.

If, on the contrary, the accused plead "Guilty," the last-
mentioned question is put to him at once, and sentence passed.

Thirdly, as to Adults; (a) Trial with Consent. When an
adult is charged before a Court of Summary Jurisdiction with
certain indictable offences (and in those cases only) the court, if
they think it expedient so to do, having regard to the character
and antecedents of the person so charged, the nature of the
offence, and all the circumstances of the case, *and if the person
charged with the offence, when informed by the court of his right to
be tried by a jury, consents to be dealt with summarily, may* deal
summarily with the offence, and adjudge such person, if found
guilty, to be imprisoned, with or without hard labour, for any
term not exceeding *three* months or to pay a fine not exceeding
£20 (S.J. Act, 1879, s. 12: S.J. Act, 1899, s. 1).

A list of the offences which may be so dealt with is given in
Appendix B.

If the value of the property which was the subject of the
offence, in the opinion of the court before which the charge is
brought, exceeds 40s., such person, if found guilty, may now be
imprisoned with or without hard labour, for any term not
exceeding *six* months, or be ordered to pay a fine not exceeding
£50 (C.J.A. Act, 1914, s. 15 (1)).

In the case of *Rex* v. *Hertfordshire Justices* [1911] 1 K.B.

612, it was held that the power of a Court of Summary Jurisdiction, under s. 12 of the S.J. Act, 1879, to commit a person for trial may be exercised at any stage of the proceedings up to adjudication, notwithstanding that at an earlier stage the defendant has consented to the case being dealt with summarily, and the hearing has proceeded on that basis to the close of the evidence for the defence. The words of the Act are: "*may* deal summarily" with the offence, not "must"; and the prisoner has no right to be so dealt with if the Justices are of opinion that it is not expedient to do so.

For the purpose of dealing with any offence in this manner, if at any time during the hearing of a case the court becomes satisfied by the evidence that it is expedient to deal with the case summarily, the Justices cause the charge to be reduced into writing and read to the person charged, and then address a question to him to the following effect: "*Do you desire to be tried by a jury, or do you consent to the case being dealt with summarily ?*" This question must be accompanied with the usual explanation as to the meaning of the case being dealt with summarily and of the Assizes or Sessions (as the case may be) at which he will be tried, if tried by a jury (S.J. Act, 1879, s. 12). The explanation as to the meaning of false pretences mentioned above must also be given if the charge is of that nature (*ib.*). If he consents, the case is then dealt with summarily. If he does not, but insists on his right to be tried by a jury, he is committed for trial in the usual way. A large number of prisoners, however, consent to be dealt with summarily rather than incur the delay of waiting for trial, with the probability of conviction in the long run; and the country is thereby saved great expense.

(*b*) *Plea of Guilty.* Where an adult is charged before a Court of Summary Jurisdiction with any of the offences mentioned in Appendix B, even though the value of the property in question exceeds £20, if the court at any time during the hearing of the case becomes satisfied that the evidence is sufficient to put the person upon his trial for the offence, and further is satisfied (either after remand, for not more than eight days at a time or otherwise) that the case is one which, having regard to the character and antecedents of the person charged, the nature of

the offence, and all the circumstances of the case, may properly
be dealt with summarily, and may be adequately punished by
virtue of their powers, then the court shall cause the charge to
be reduced into writing, and read it to the person charged, and
shall then ask him whether he is guilty of the charge, or not;
and if such person admits that he is guilty the court shall thereupon cause a plea of guilty to be entered, and adjudge him to
be imprisoned with or without hard labour for not more than
six months, without the option of a fine (S.J. Act, 1879, s. 13).
The prisoner, in such a case, cannot be discharged without some
punishment, and there is no right of appeal in these circumstances.
But apparently the Probation of Offenders Act, 1907, now applies.

The procedure in such a case is as follows: after the charge
has been read to the prisoner (accompanied in this case also, if
necessary, with an explanation of the meaning of false pretences)
the magistrate proceeds:

"*Before asking you whether you are Guilty or not of the charge,
I have to explain to you that you are not obliged to plead or answer,
but that if you plead Guilty you will be dealt with summarily. If
you do not plead or answer, or plead Not Guilty, you will be dealt
with in the usual course. The meaning of being dealt with summarily is, that we shall at once adjudge you to be imprisoned for a
term not exceeding six months. The meaning of being dealt with
in the usual course is, that you will be committed for trial by a
Jury at the next Assizes (or Quarter Sessions) for this County (or
Borough).*" "*I must further state that you are not obliged to say
anything,*" etc. [Here follows the "statutory caution."]

If the accused plead guilty, the magistrate then says to him:
"*Have you any cause to show why judgment should not be passed
upon you?*" And after hearing anything he may have to say
in extenuation, sentence is passed.

If the accused plead *Not* Guilty, whatever he says must be
taken down in writing and read over to him, and signed by the
Justice, and may, if necessary, be given in evidence against him
at his trial without further proof.

By s. 14 of the S.J. Act, 1879, where an *adult* was charged
before a Court of Summary Jurisdiction with any of the indictable
offences mentioned in Appendix C, and it appeared to the court

that the offence was one which, *owing to a previous conviction on indictment* of the person so charged, was punishable by law with penal servitude, the court could *not* deal with the case summarily, but was bound to commit him for trial. But this section is now repealed by s. 15 (2) of the C.J.A. Act, 1914, and the restriction thereby imposed on the power to deal summarily with adults charged with such offences is therefore removed.

Offences may, therefore, be classified as follows:

1. Those with which Justices of the Peace *cannot* deal, viz. grave, *indictable* offences, which must be committed for trial, *e.g.* murder; and those non-indictable offences where the accused elects to be tried by a jury.

2. Those with which they *may* deal, viz. those indictable offences with which they are empowered to deal in the exercise of their summary jurisdiction.

3. Those with which they *must* deal, viz. petty, non-indictable offences created by various statutes (see Appendix A).

While the tendency of modern legislation has been to enable Justices of the Peace to deal summarily with a much larger class of cases than formerly, with a view of avoiding any appearance of injustice, the Summary Jurisdiction Act, 1879, makes a "converse innovation." This Act renders it possible for the graver non-indictable offences to be dealt with, not summarily, but by indictment, by providing (s. 17) that in the case of any offence (*except assault*) for which an offender is liable on summary conviction to be imprisoned for a term exceeding three months, he may, *on appearing before the court, and before the charge is gone into, but not afterwards, claim to be tried by a jury,* and thereupon the court shall deal with the case in all respects as if the accused were charged with an indictable offence. Accordingly, when a person appears before Justices charged with such an offence, *they must, before taking any evidence, inform him of his right to be tried by a jury.*

The manner of so doing is as follows. After the charge has been read, and before it is gone into, one of the Justices says to the accused:

"*You are charged with an offence in respect of the commission of which you are entitled, if you desire it, instead of being dealt with summarily, to be tried by a jury. Do you desire to be tried by a jury? Being dealt with summarily means that you will now be tried by this court. If you desire to be tried by a jury, you can be so tried at the next Assizes (or Quarter Sessions) for this County (or Borough)."*

Apparently (since the Children Act, 1908) this provision does not now apply to a child, as that Act abolishes the imprisonment of children, and limits custody in a place of detention to *one* month.

There is also a right of trial by jury under many other Acts. A fairly complete list of these is believed to be given in Appendix C.

The offences under the Conspiracy and Protection of Property Act, 1875, relate to trades unions; and it is desirable that the accused should have such a right, as many Justices of the Peace are large employers of labour, and might not, therefore, in such cases, form a perfectly impartial tribunal, which it is the object of the legislature to provide.

In all these cases the accused *must* be informed of his right to be tried by a jury.

Until a Court of Summary Jurisdiction assumes the power to deal with an offence summarily, the procedure is the same in all respects as if the offence were an indictable one, but as soon as the court assumes this power, from and after that period, the procedure is the same as if the offence were one punishable on summary conviction, and not on indictment. Thus the evidence of any witness already taken, before the court assumed this power, need not be taken again, but such a witness may be recalled for the purpose of cross-examination, if the defendant desires it.

On the other hand, it sometimes happens that when a case which is being tried summarily has been part heard, it is discovered that the prisoner had a right to be tried by a jury and that he ought to have been informed of this right *at the outset*, so as to give him, or his advocate, the opportunity of electing whether he will be tried by a jury or not; but by an oversight this has not been done. In such a case the better course is to begin the proceedings *de novo*, as "depositions" must be taken if he elects to be tried by a jury, but not otherwise. Moreover,

if the accused is not informed of his right to be tried by a jury
at the outset, any summary conviction which may follow is bad.
It follows from what is said above that the magistrates cannot
proceed in such a case unless the accused is present, or is represented by "counsel or attorney" to make the necessary election
on his behalf. And in all cases the Justices ought to be cautious
how they proceed in the absence of a defendant.

The mode of hearing cases tried summarily is also much the
same as in the case of the preliminary examination of persons
accused of grave crimes. The defendant is "charged," that is
to say, the nature of the charge against him is explained. If
he admits it and pleads guilty, a fine, with the alternative of
imprisonment, is usually imposed. The term of imprisonment
is regulated by a scale, and varies according to the amount of
the fine. It may be with or without hard labour. If he denies
it and pleads not guilty, the case proceeds. The prosecutor or
complainant, or his advocate, "opens the case," and calls his
witnesses, who are sworn, examined in chief, cross-examined,
and re-examined. The defendant or his advocate then opens
his case, calls his witnesses and they are heard in the same way.
If necessary, the other party may then call rebutting evidence;
but no second speech is allowed, except upon a point of law.

In the exercise of their summary jurisdiction Justices have
full power to enforce the attendance of witnesses, either within
their jurisdiction or out of their jurisdiction, by means of summons, or, if necessary, by means of warrant; and if, on the appearance of such person, he shall refuse to take the oath or to be
examined upon oath or affirmation, "concerning the premises,"
i.e. the matter in dispute, or shall refuse to answer such questions
as shall then be put to him without offering any just excuse for
such refusal, any Justice present may commit him to gaol or
house of correction for not more than seven days, "unless he
shall in the meantime consent to be examined and to answer
concerning the premises."

But it appears that Justices have no power to commit an
unwilling witness who has not been brought before the court by
summons or warrant. If he appears as a witness voluntarily,
and refuses to answer, there is no power to commit him, the

court not being a court of record and having no power to commit for contempt. Such cases however are exceedingly rare. Most witnesses do appear voluntarily and are only too anxious to give evidence, being, in fact, friends, if not partisans, of the parties, and it is the task of the Justices to disentangle the truth from the conflicting statements and arrive at a decision.

Every witness must be examined upon oath or affirmation, and the Justices have full power to administer the usual oath or affirmation, and to compel production of documents.

The Justices, after consideration and consultation with their clerk, give their decision. If it is against the defendant, they have power, both in civil and criminal cases, in addition to the penalty or sentence, to order him to pay such costs as they think fit, within certain limits. On the contrary, if they dismiss the case, they may order the prosecutor to pay the costs. No depositions are taken, but a minute of the conviction or order is made by the magistrates' clerk.

By s. 12 of the S.J. Act, 1848 (11 & 12 Vict. c. 43), every party charged with an offence triable summarily "shall be admitted to make his full answer and defence, and to have the witnesses examined and cross-examined by counsel or attorney; and every such complainant and informant shall be at liberty to conduct such complaint or information respectively, and to have the witnesses examined and cross-examined by counsel or attorney."

As to the punishments which may be inflicted by Justices of the Peace in the exercise of their summary jurisdiction, the most severe sentence which they may pass is one of nine months' imprisonment with hard labour, in the case of a second conviction within two years for an assault on a police constable in the execution of his duty. With this exception, the maximum sentence they may pass is six months' imprisonment. In some cases they may inflict very heavy pecuniary penalties, *e.g.* £100 for keeping a betting house; £500 (and not less than £200) on a railway company which provides special facilities for the conveyance of passengers to a prize fight. But by s. 18 of the C.J.A. Act, 1914, Justices may now impose consecutive sentences of imprisonment amounting in the aggregate to twelve months.

The penalties which are imposed on summary convictions are, as a rule, recoverable by distress, and in default, imprisonment, *without* hard labour, unless the statute by which the offence is created expressly authorises the imposition of hard labour. The extent of the alternative imprisonment is proportionate to the amount of pecuniary penalty, and is fixed by scale, viz.:

Where the amount adjudged to be paid	*The imprisonment must not exceed*
Does not exceed 10s.	7 days
Exceeds 10s. but does not exceed £1 . . .	14 „
„ £1 „ „ £5 . . .	1 cal. month
„ £5 „ „ £20 . . .	2 cal. months
„ £20 „ „ £50 . . .	6 „

The court has power to allow payment of fines by instalments (see Home Office Circular of June 14, 1905) and to remit costs (see Home Office Circular of March 23, 1891, and s. 8 of the S.J. Act, 1879): and also, within certain limits, to direct that terms of imprisonment shall be consecutive (see sect. 18, C.J.A. Act, 1914).

It may be observed here that a system of graduated punishments, according to the number of previous convictions, pervades our Criminal Law, a second conviction being punished more severely than a first, and a third than a second. Hard labour may follow simple imprisonment, and penal servitude hard labour; but a Court of Summary Jurisdiction cannot impose penal servitude. That is the sentence of a higher court.

By s. 1 of the Criminal Justice Administration Act, 1914, an obligation to allow time for payment of fines is imposed, subject to the exceptions therein mentioned, and the time allowed shall be not less than seven clear days. Where the person so allowed time for payment is not less than 16, nor more than 21 years of age, he may be placed under supervision until the sum adjudged to be paid is paid. In all cases where no time is allowed for payment, the reasons of the court for the immediate committal must be stated in the warrant of commitment. By s. 2 even when the time fixed for payment has expired further time may be allowed by the court, and it may direct payment by instalments. The object of these provisions is to prevent, as far as possible, the necessity of a man going to prison, where his labour is lost to the community and he incurs the stigma of a gaol bird. S. 3 provides for a reduction of the term of imprisonment on part payment of a sum adjudged to be paid. S. 4 contains provisions for the enforcement of payment of fines or sums due under orders, *e.g.* in bastardy proceedings or arrears of maintenance of a wife, by ordering the prisoner to be searched and applying any money found on him towards payment, provided the money belongs to him. Where a warrant of distress is issued, money as well as goods may be taken. By s. 5 (1) "a Court of Summary Jurisdiction in fixing the amount of any fine to be imposed on an offender shall take into consideration, amongst other things, the means of the offender so far as they appear or are known to the court; and where a fine is imposed the payment of the court fees and police fees payable in the case up to and including conviction shall not be taken into consideration in fixing the amount of the fine or be imposed in addition to the fine"; the section also makes provision for the allocation of fines and fees. The expression "police fees" here used means "all duly authorised fees payable to any constable in the execution of his duty." The effect of this section is that in the future court and police fees, which often amounted to much more than the fine imposed, are not to be paid in addition to the fine and are not to be included in the costs. This is a great revolution in practice and is perhaps the greatest change introduced by the Act. S. 6 provides for a uniform scale of court fees as respects all Courts of Summary Jurisdiction. The words of the Act should be consulted for the exact effect of these provisions, since they necessarily suffer in the process of condensation. Only their bare effect is given here.

Ss. 12 and 13 of the C.J.A. Act, 1914, confer on Courts of Summary Jurisdiction new powers of dealing with offenders. S. 12 provides that where the court has power to pass a sentence of imprisonment, it may, in lieu of so doing, order the offender to be detained within the precincts of the court for one day— till such hour, not later than 8 p.m. of the day on which he is convicted, as the court may direct—regard being had to the distance of the place of detention from the offender's abode, so as to allow him a reasonable opportunity of returning home the same day. S. 13 substitutes "police custody" for imprisonment in case of short sentences, and provides that no person should be sentenced to "imprisonment" for a period of less than five days. If the sentence does not exceed four days, the offender is to be detained in a "suitable place" certified as such by the Secretary of State: and "no place so certified shall be used for the detention of females unless provision is made for their supervision by female officers."

S. 16 (1) of the C.J.A. Act, 1914, provides that where imprisonment is imposed by any court in respect of the non-payment of any sum of money adjudged to be paid the imprisonment shall be *without* hard labour; and further, that where a person convicted by or before any court is sentenced to *imprisonment without the option of a fine*, the imprisonment may, *in the discretion of the court*, be either *with* or *without* hard labour, whether the offence is one at common law or by statute, and if by statute whether the statute does not authorise the imposition, or requires the imposition, of hard labour. The net result of this general provision is to give the Justices or Judge a free hand in every such case in deciding whether to impose hard labour as part of the sentence or not, notwithstanding the provisions of the particular statute dealing with the offence. It places the matter entirely in their discretion, having regard to the circumstances of each case.

In *Rex* v. *Martin* [1911] 2 K.B. 480, it was held that not more than two consecutive terms of imprisonment could be imposed by Justices. S. 18 of the C.J.A. Act, 1914, provides that a Court of Summary Jurisdiction may impose consecutive sentences of imprisonment, "so however that where *two or more* sentences passed by a court of summary jurisdiction are ordered to run consecutively, the aggregate term of imprisonment shall not exceed six months, unless such sentences include at least two sentences for indictable offences dealt with summarily by consent or on a plea of guilty, in which case the aggregate term of imprisonment shall not exceed twelve months." The words "*two or more*" sentences apparently override the effect of *Rex* v. *Martin*, but impose restrictions on the aggregate of such sentences.

It may be convenient to state here the extent of the jurisdiction which can now be exercised by two or more Justices when
sitting in an Occasional court-house and *not* in a Petty Sessional
court-house. In such circumstances they may deal with substantially the same class of cases as two or more Justices sitting
in a Petty Sessional court-house, but their power to sentence is
limited; they cannot impose by their conviction or order any
period of imprisonment exceeding 14 days or adjudge any sum
to be paid exceeding 20*s*. (S.J. Act, 1879, s. 20 (7)). The
apparent reason for this distinction is that when sitting in an
Occasional court-house they are not subject to the same amount
of public observation and criticism as when sitting in a Petty
Sessional court-house, to which the public habitually resort.

The jurisdiction which can be exercised by *one* Justice (not
being a stipendiary magistrate) is still more limited. He may,
of course, (1) receive information or complaints and issue summonses and warrants thereon. (2) He may take the preliminary
examination of persons accused of indictable offences and commit
them for trial. (3) When sitting "in open court" (either in a
Petty Sessional court-house or in an Occasional court-house)
he can try only those cases where the power to deal with them
summarily is specifically given by statute to *one* Justice (see
Appendix D), and he can impose no greater term of imprisonment
or fine than above mentioned. (4) But he may always adjourn
to the next practicable sitting of a Petty Sessional court cases
on which he cannot adjudicate alone or on which he does not
think it proper to adjudicate alone.

In some cases two Justices are required by statute, *e.g.* dog-
stealing. By s. 38 of the C.J.A. Act, 1914, *one* Justice is now
declared to be competent to exercise the powers of a Court of
Summary Jurisdiction when hearing, trying, adjudging and
determining charges of drunkenness. Since the Licensing (Consolidation) Act, 1910, *two* Justices have been required.

It is always open to Justices to dismiss the charge in any
case in which, *sitting as a jury*, in the exercise of their summary
jurisdiction, they come to a conclusion on the facts proved (or
not proved) before them that it ought to be dismissed. When
the court have assumed power to deal with a case summarily,

and they decide to dismiss the charge, upon its merits, the Justices
will, if required, deliver to the person charged a certificate under
their hands of such order of dismissal, and such dismissal has
the same effect as an acquittal after a trial on indictment for the
offence. This power of dismissal is exercised in about five per
cent. of the cases which come before them.

Under s. 16 of the S.J. Act, 1879, the Justices were entrusted
with what Prof. Kenny styles "a remarkable statutory power
of showing mercy" (*Outlines of Crim. Law*, p. 424). But this
section has now been repealed, and re-enacted in wider terms,
by the Probation of Offenders Act, 1907, which will be considered
more fully hereafter. The Act also contains a provision as to
payment of damages, which ought to be more frequently acted
upon by Justices, especially in cases of mischievous damage by
children and youths.

Charges of assault and drunkenness form a very large part
of the work of police-courts.

Assaults are of various kinds, common, aggravated, etc.
A common assault is an indictable misdemeanour punishable
(on conviction by a jury) by imprisonment, with hard labour,
for one year, or by a fine. Any assault must be dealt with by
indictment if it involves the title to land or if it is accompanied
by an attempt to commit a felony. But in all other cases of
assault the offence *may* be tried summarily by two Justices of
the Peace; and s. 17 (1) of the S.J. Act, 1879, which gives a
right of trial by jury when the imprisonment may exceed three
months, does *not* apply to assaults. A common assault may also
be tried summarily if the information has been laid by the person
assaulted himself (or in the case of a child on its behalf) and not
by the police. The adoption of this summary procedure however
takes away the right of civil action for damages. The maximum
penalty for a common assault tried summarily is two months'
imprisonment, with hard labour, or a fine of £5; and in this
case there is no right of appeal unless the offender is sentenced
to imprisonment without the option of a fine The only case of
assault tried summarily in which there is a right of appeal is
that of an assault on a borough constable. Why there should
be a right of appeal in the case of a borough constable, and not

in the case of a county constable, it is difficult to see   This is simply another result of our system of piecemeal legislation [1].

In 1912, Courts of Summary Jurisdiction tried 33,331 persons for common assault; 8729 for assaults on constables; and 807 for aggravated assault. In cases of the first class the charge was withdrawn or dismissed as against 14,887 persons; the same result followed as against 524 persons of the second class; and as against 64 of the third class. But 15,219 of the first class, 7914 of the second, and 722 of the third class, making a total of 23,854, were convicted. Of those convicted of aggravated assaults viz. assaults on women or children, which deserve more severe punishment, 533 were sent to prison for various terms ranging from under 14 days to over 6 months, and 182 were fined. Of those convicted of assaults on the police 2980 were sent to prison, and 4923 were fined. Of those convicted of common assault 2752 were sent to prison, and 11,983 were fined. The others were dealt with in various ways, 488 being ordered to enter into recognizances, *i.e.* bound over to keep the peace and be of good behaviour and to come up for judgment if called upon. It is satisfactory to find that cases of assault are steadily declining. The Report on Criminal Statistics for 1909, commenting on the fact that crimes of violence were decreasing, says it is "eloquent of an increasing orderliness and self control among the masses." Happily the decrease still continues.

In 1912, 140,340 persons were proceeded against for drunkenness with various aggravations, of whom 129,225 were convicted; and of these 6278 were sent to prison for various terms ranging from under 14 days to three months; and 121,199 were fined. In the same year 57,596 persons were proceeded against for simple drunkenness; of whom 48,161 were convicted, 177 sent to prison (in no case for more than one month), 47,601 were fined, and 377 were dealt with by way of recognizance.

These figures show the appalling amount of drinking and fighting that still go on in this so-called civilised and Christian country in the twentieth century, after more than forty years of compulsory elementary education, and indicate the amount and kind of work that police-courts have to deal with. Every

[1] But see now s. 37 of the C.J.A. Act, 1914.

magistrate and every lawyer know that over-indulgence in alcoholic liquor is the direct cause of more than half of the crime and poverty, and consequent misery and squalor, that exist in the country.

Besides their criminal jurisdiction Justices of the Peace have jurisdiction in certain civil matters, which is less important and less frequently exercised than their jurisdiction in criminal matters, but is by no means inconsiderable. In these cases the proceedings are commenced by a "complaint" (not an information) and terminate with an "order" (not a conviction). The Court of Summary Jurisdiction is to be deemed in those cases a court of civil jurisdiction, and the proceedings are not to be deemed criminal. The sums recovered are deemed to be "civil debts" and the Debtors Act, 1869, applies to their enforcement. A typical instance of this jurisdiction is to be found in the Employers and Workmen Act, 1875. But we are not here concerned with this strictly civil jurisdiction.

There are however two matters as to which it is extremely difficult to say whether they are criminal or civil, and the point has never yet been definitely decided. They may therefore be regarded as quasi-civil or quasi-criminal. These are Affiliation Orders and Separation Orders. The mode of enforcing payments in these two cases is the same. One calendar month after the date of the order, the mother of the child (or the wife) may apply to a magistrate for the place in which she may then be residing, and if it be declared on oath that the sums ordered to be paid have not been paid, he may by warrant cause the defendant to be brought before two Justices; and if it be proved that the order was duly served upon the defendant and he still refuses to make payment of the sums due, the Justices may direct the amount due, and the costs of the warrant, to be recovered by distress, and may order the defendant to be detained in custody until a return is made to the warrant of distress, unless he gives or finds security. If no sufficient distress can be levied, or the defendant admits that he has no goods, or if the Justices consider that the levying of a distress would be more injurious to him or his family than imprisonment, they may, if they think fit, commit him to prison, *without* hard labour, for a term not exceeding that fixed by the scale above mentioned on page 55, for non-payment of the arrears, unless the amount and the costs be sooner paid. The warrant must, if necessary, be backed; but the six months' limitation prescribed by the S.J. Áct, 1848, is not applicable to the recovery of such arrears. The better opinion is that the imprisonment wipes out the arrears; and if the putative father dies the mother cannot recover the arrears or any future payments from his estate.

In the case of *R. v. Richardson, ex-parte Sherry* [1909] 2 K.B. 851, the Judges made some valuable observations as to the duties of Justices when enforcing payment of arrears due upon orders made under the S.J. (Married Women) Act, 1895, which apply equally to Bastardy Orders. They suggested that the Justices should be careful not to exercise their powers of imprisonment oppressively, especially if they regarded the application as one made for the purpose of blackmail. Lord Alverstone, L.C.J., said: "Imprisonment must only be ordered in circumstances in which the Justices think that the defendant ought to be punished for non-obedience of the original order."

The Affiliation Orders Act, 1914, s. 1, provides that a "collecting officer" shall be appointed by every bench of magistrates, and that every future Affiliation Order shall contain a provision for the payments due under it to be made through that officer unless, upon representations expressly made in that behalf by the applicant for the Affiliation Order, the Justices are satisfied that it is undesirable so to do. This Act came into operation on July 31st, 1914, and is designed to facilitate the collection of such moneys. But judging from the amount of opposition to it in the professional papers it is not likely to be a great success, the scale of remuneration allowed to the collecting officer being quite inadequate for the amount of work involved.

S. 30 of the C.J.A. Act, 1914, makes provision for the payment of sums ordered by a Court of Summary Jurisdiction to be paid periodically "through an officer of the court or any other person or officer specified in the order." In view of this section it is difficult to see the necessity for the Affiliation Orders Act, 1914, yet there is a saving clause (5) in respect of that Act. The effect of s. 30 is, however, much wider than that of the

Affiliation Orders Act. It apparently applies to *all* sums so ordered to be paid periodically and not only to affiliation orders.

The defendant while in prison is now treated as a debtor, but the imprisonment, if undergone, operates to satisfy the demand, thus showing that the demand is not a civil debt and that the imprisonment is to some extent regarded as a punishment.

In 1912, 6811 Bastardy Orders were made, as the result of 8568 applications, and 1616 of these orders were enforced by imprisonment.

Separation and Maintenance Orders, between husband and wife, are made by Justices of the Peace under the Summary Jurisdiction (Married Women) Act, 1895, where a husband has been convicted upon indictment of an assault upon his wife and sentenced to pay a fine of more than £5, or to a term of imprisonment exceeding two months; or where a husband has deserted his wife, or has been guilty of persistent cruelty to her, or has wilfully neglected to provide reasonable maintenance for her or her infant children whom he is legally liable to maintain, and has by such cruelty or neglect caused her to leave him and live separately and apart from him; or where a husband (or wife) is a habitual drunkard (Licensing Act, 1902, s. 5 (1) and (2)). The court has power in such cases to make an order that the applicant be no longer bound to cohabit with the husband (or wife), and this order while in force has all the effects of a decree for judicial separation on the ground of cruelty; to provide for the legal custody of any children of the marriage; to order that the husband shall pay to the wife personally or to an officer of the court or third person on her behalf a sum not exceeding £2 per week, and the costs. This Act was no doubt a well-meant Act, intended by its framers to provide relief in many cases of great hardship and suffering. Unfortunately it has not answered the anticipations that were formed with regard to it. Whether it is that the rough-and-tumble methods of a police-court, with its vitiated atmosphere of sordid crime, are unsuited to the arrangement of disturbed domestic affairs (always a delicate matter), or whether it is the unsatisfactory status of the parties after such an order has been made, being neither properly married nor single, or whatever the cause may be, the general opinion is that the Act has not been a success; and although large numbers of orders have been made under it (7484 in 1912), it has, on the whole, conduced more to immorality than to justice. At present it is the chief blot on the system. It has all the disadvantages and none of the advantages of a cheap divorce, both as regards the parties themselves and their children, and there is no doubt that a considerable number of persons have abused the Act. The fault does not lie with its administration but is due to the nature of the subject and external causes. Many benches of Justices and Stipendiaries have exercised their powers under this Act with great care and caution, frequently adjourning cases in the hope that the parties might re-consider their position and peace and happiness might be restored between them. The whole question of the relation of the sexes has recently been the subject of an enquiry by a Royal Commission, whose report was published in November, 1912. (See the Report of the Royal Commission on Divorce and Matrimonial Causes.) Unfortunately the Commissioners were not able to come to a unanimous decision, and there was a Minority, as well as a Majority, Report. Amongst the recommendations of the Majority was a proposal to transfer the jurisdiction in these cases from Justices of the Peace to certain County Court Judges, apparently on the ground that such matters can be better dealt with by trained lawyers than by unpaid and untrained magistrates, a result which does not always follow unless the lawyers have had experience in this class of work. But so far nothing has been done in this direction.

The right of appeal from decisions of Justices is purely statutory. S. 37 of the C.J.A. Act, 1914, now contains a very important and sweeping enactment of a general character. It provides that "*any person* aggrieved by *any conviction* of a court of summary jurisdiction in respect of *any offence,* who did not plead guilty or admit the truth of the information, *may appeal* from the conviction in manner provided by the Summary Jurisdiction Acts to a court of Quarter Sessions." A similar right of appeal is given by the same section "from any order made by a court of summary jurisdiction under the enactments relating to bastardy," or from the refusal to make such an order, or from the revocation, revival or variation of such an order. Before this enactment, the right to appeal from decisions of Justices was by no means universal. It did not exist in every case. In some cases it depended on the amount of the fine imposed, or on the conviction being by one Justice only, or on a variety of other circumstances. But there was always a right of appeal where a person was sentenced to a term of imprisonment, however short, without the option of a fine.

In *London* only there is a right of appeal when there is an order to pay a sum of more then £3, whether as a penalty or not, exclusive of costs, or the sentence is one of more than one month's imprisonment (2 & 3 Vict. c. 71, s. 50).

The procedure preliminary to an appeal to Quarter Sessions is now, in most cases, governed and regulated by the S.J. Act, 1879, s. 31, and the Schedule to the Act of 1884. The conditions are, that a notice *in writing* of intention to appeal must be served on the other party and on the clerk of the Court of Summary Jurisdiction, usually within seven days after the conviction, and such notice must state the general grounds of the appeal. The appellant must then, within three days after giving the notice, attend before a Court of Summary Jurisdiction, and enter into a recognizance or bond either with or without sureties for the due prosecution of the appeal. The court fixes the amount of the recognizance, having regard to the probable amount of costs the appellant may have to pay in the event of the appeal proving unsuccessful. It is seldom, if ever, less than £20. If the appellant wishes (and can) instead of giving security, he may deposit the required sum with the clerk of the Court of Summary Jurisdiction. If the appellant is in custody, the court before which he appears to enter into a recognizance, may, if it think fit, release him from custody, pending the appeal.

In most cases it is a convicted defendant who appeals, but in some few cases the prosecutor also may appeal against a dismissal of the charge. When the case is heard at Quarter Sessions it is tried by the Justices there assembled, without a jury, and the majority decide. It is a re-hearing of the whole case, both on the facts and the law, and new witnesses may be heard, who were not called at Petty Sessions.

In his *Outlines of Criminal Law* (5th ed., 1914), Prof. Kenny says: "It may safely be estimated that there is only one appeal (from Justices in Petty Sessions) to Quarter Sessions for every three thousand of those convictions in which there is a power so to appeal. Doubtless considerations of expense have much to do with this; yet, even after allowing for them, these statistics, coupled with the further fact that only a quarter of the appeals to Sessions are entirely successful, afford noteworthy evidence of the satisfactory working of our courts of summary jurisdiction" (p. 438 n.). An impartial observer, who is not a lawyer, but who has spent a large part of his life in our police courts, doing very good and valuable work amongst all classes of prisoners, says: "To hold the balance of justice evenly day after day in all sorts of charges is not an easy task, but it is done; and the fact that very few of their decisions or sentences are annulled or revoked shows that the manner in which justice is administered in our police courts is beyond question" (*The London Police Courts* by Mr Thomas Holmes). We regret that we cannot entirely agree with these optimistic conclusions, much as we should wish to do so.

Hitherto it has been difficult to say exactly in what proportion of the cases tried by Justices of the Peace it was possible to appeal, since, until recently, it was not possible to appeal in all cases; but probably one case in 3000 was a fair estimate. In 1912, there were 118 appeals from decisions of Justices. Of these six were abandoned, and 112 actually heard; 20 were brought in respect of offences against the Intoxicating Liquor Laws, probably by brewers with a view to saving the licences involved; and of these 20, in 8 cases (or 40 per cent.) the convictions were quashed, and in two cases the sentence was modified. Out of the 112 cases, the appeal was entirely successful in 42 cases (or 37·5 per cent.), and the sentence was modified in 19, making a total of 61. In the same year there were 21 appeals against convictions for assault, of which 7 were successful; 14 against convictions in respect of motor-cars, of which 7 were successful; and 10 in respect of cruelty to animals, of which 6 were successful. It remains to be seen how many appeals there will be under the enlarged right of appeal conferred by the C.J.A. Act, 1914.

But when it is remembered that the overwhelming majority of those who are convicted summarily are very poor people, and that the minimum cost of an appeal to Quarter Sessions is £20, it will at once be seen that the expense of such an appeal is practically prohibitive, and we believe that in ninety-nine cases out of a hundred this right of appeal is purely illusory. Those who can possibly pay their fines do so; those who cannot, go to prison. Moreover the appeal is from Justices in Petty Sessions to Justices in Quarter Sessions. It is obvious that no appeal ought to be heard by any of the Justices who sat in the court below or are members of that bench. At the West Riding Sessions there is a rota of Justices who sit to hear appeals.

"So far as summary convictions are concerned, the Crimina. Appeal Act does not apply, and it cannot be said that the existing rights of appeal to Quarter Sessions or (on points of law) to the High Court, both of which require the command of legal assistance and money, are in themselves sufficient" (Art. on the Prerogative of Mercy: *Justice of the Peace*, April 30, 1910, p. 206).

It is arguable that if a Court of Criminal Appeal was necessary in regard to indictable cases, such a court is still more necessary in regard to cases decided summarily, for the most part by untrained magistrates, and without the assistance of juries and counsel; that Quarter Sessions as at present constituted are by no means ideal courts for the purpose of such appeals; and that the conditions of such appeals ought to be much simpler and the hearing of them cheaper and speedier: but the question of an Inferior Court of Criminal Appeal is too large to discuss at length here. Nothing rankles in the mind of a man and tends to make him a bad citizen, so much as the idea that he has been the victim of injustice; and this applies to small offences as well as to great.

In addition to the right of appeal to Quarter Sessions above mentioned (see p. 64) there is always a right of appeal on points of law, generally to the King's Bench Division of the High Court. But under the S.J. (Married Women) Act, 1895, the appeal is to the Probate Division of the High Court. The

King's Bench Division exercises a general control over the proceedings of Justices. This it does in two ways: *First*, by way
of *certiorari*, a writ issued to an inferior court to compel it to
bring up any of its proceedings for review. Thus the higher court
will, if necessary, quash a conviction for some defect of law
apparent on the face of the proceedings, *e.g.* a conviction based
on an information that was not laid within six months would be
quashed. By rule 21 of the Crown Office Rules, 1906, the writ
of *certiorari* shall not be issued to remove any order of Justices
of the Peace unless the writ be applied for within six months
after the making of the order. In *Rex* v. *Amendt* (J.P. Rep.
vol. 78, p. 388) it was held that this rule applies to writs of
certiorari issued on the fiat of the Attorney-General. *Secondly*,
by "Case Stated"; that is to say, the Justices will as a rule
"state a case" on a point of law which arises in the proceedings,
on the application of either party, for the decision of the High
Court. By a "Case Stated" is meant a written statement
setting forth all the facts of the matter, as found by the Justices
together with the point of law that has been determined by them
and the way in which it was so determined; and the superior
court is asked to say whether such determination was right in
point of law or not. The application to state a case must be
made within seven days after the decision is given; the clerk of
the court draws and settles the case, unless the parties can agree
in its terms; the case must be stated within three months and
the appellant must, within three days after receiving the "case,"
transmit it to the court named in his application, which is a
Divisional Court of the King's Bench (or Probate) Division,
consisting of two judges. Security for costs must be given (by
way of recognizance) before the case is stated, and notice in
writing of its transmission must be given to the other party to
the proceeding, who is called the respondent. A good example
of the necessity for a case to be stated is where the defendant
objects that the evidence against him is not legally sufficient to
support a conviction, but the Justices overrule his objection and
convict[1]. On an appeal from Justices of the Peace to the Divisional Court, the appellant will not be allowed to raise any point

[1] See the case of *Lansbury* v. *Riley, supra*, p. 40.

which was not taken before the Justices, unless it is a point of law which arises upon the facts stated and which no evidence could alter. (*Kates* v. *Jeffery* [1914] 3 K.B. 160.) It is, therefore, very important to raise in the court below every point which it is intended to raise in the court above and get the Justices to make a note of it.

Should the Justices be of opinion that no doubtful point of law is involved, and that the application is "frivolous," they may refuse to "state a case," unless the application is made by the Attorney-General, or under his direction.

If the Justices improperly refuse to state a case, when requested to do so, they may be compelled by means of a *Mandamus*. This is a writ by which Justices can be compelled to perform all or any of the duties which devolve on them, *e.g.* to issue a summons, or to hear and determine a charge according to law—when they have declined to do so upon a mistaken view of the facts or the law applicable. But the writ is of too technical a character for the subject to be pursued further here.

The Justice of the Peace has been styled "the state's man of all work" (Maitland, *Justice and Police*, p. 92). "Long ago," says the same learned authority, "lawyers abandoned all hope of describing the duties of a Justice in any methodic fashion, and the alphabet has become the one possible connecting thread" (*ibid.* p. 84). Thus he may be called upon to deal with Apprentices; Assaults; Bakehouses; Bicycles; Birds (Wild); Byelaws; Canal boats; Children; Chimney-sweeps; Clubs; Dogs; Education; Food and Drugs; Friendly Societies; Game Laws; Hawkers; Highways; Intoxicating Liquor Laws; Labour Laws; Larcenies; Lobsters; Locomotives; Lunatics; Markets and Fairs; Midwives; Motor Cars; Nuisances; Pawnbrokers; Pedlars; Poor Laws; Poor Rates; Public Health; Railways; Salmon; Solicitors; Territorials; Theatres; Trade Marks; Vaccination; Vagrants; and Weights and Measures. And these, as we are informed in a note prefixed to the Appendix to Stone's *Justice's Manual*, from which they are taken, are only a "selection" of the matters which come before Justices every day of the week.

The total number of Justices of the Peace in England and

Wales is now upwards of 20,000[1]. In the seven years 1902 to
1908, no less than 7267 were appointed. Of these about two-
thirds are county Justices; and about one-third borough Justices.
It is complained that a large number of them do not act at all.
There are 26 Stipendiary Magistrates in London, and about 20
in other populous places. Magistrates are pretty evenly dis-
tributed over the country, and as a rule it is not difficult to find
one within a reasonable distance.

From time to time the Home Office issues to Justices and
Justices' clerks Circulars and Statutory Rules which contain
instructions or information of a more or less permanent character.
Such circulars are frequently issued when a new Act of Parliment
is about to come into operation, explaining the scope and object
of the Act and the way in which it should be administered, and
circulars which have become obsolete, in consequence of later
legislation or decisions, are omitted or withdrawn. Some of
these circulars deal with the more responsible duties of the
magistracy and call attention to those points of principle or
practice which experience shows are apt to be overlooked.
Other circulars deal with legal points and details of practice,
which should be noted by Justices' clerks and brought to the
attention of the Bench when occasion requires. Many of the
circulars contain information which cannot conveniently be
found elsewhere. A reprint of all these circulars now in force
has recently been issued in the form of a pamphlet (July, 1914)
and may be had on application to H.M.'s Stationery Office,
price 6d. We should strongly advise all those lay Justices who
desire to discharge their duties efficiently to procure a copy of this
pamphlet and read it diligently. They will find it a mine of
valuable information and wise counsel.

Those Justices of the Peace who do recognize the responsi-
bilities of their position are sedulously attentive to their duties,
and sincerely anxious to do justice in all cases that come before
them. It ought not to be forgotten that the unpaid magistrates
of England do an enormous amount of work, of a difficult and

[1] A return issued on July 27, 1912, gives the total number of Justices of
the Peace on May 1, 1911, as 23,039, of which 2171 were on the commission
in Wales.

disagreeable character, gratuitously, and devote much time and ability to the doing of it. They have been well described as "the bed rock of our criminal system" (*Spirit of our Laws*, p. 237) and we gratefully acknowledge their valuable public services.

"Through them," said Lord Brougham (*Speeches*, III. 377), "more than through any other agency (except the tax-gatherer) are the people brought into contact with the Government." The vast majority of our criminal cases, about 730,500 in 1912 (of which over 54,000 were indictable offences dealt with summarily), are disposed of by the Justices at Petty Sessions, and nearly all the rest (about 13,000) are begun and the preliminary stages conducted before them. Considering this, it can hardly be asserted that too much space has been allotted to them. That they do their work on the whole satisfactorily cannot be denied. In the emphatic words of Professor Kenny, "General consent, corroborated by statistical evidence, testifies that in these matters—when, as there is no jury, the questions for the bench to decide are far oftener of fact than of law, and where no punishment of great severity can be imposed—the Justices discharge their duty with conspicuous success" (*Outlines of Crim. Law*, p. 427).

As to the personal qualities desirable in a Justice of the Peace, they appear to be high moral character, a fair degree of education, business knowledge, knowledge of the world, and common sense, together with an admixture of "the milk of human kindness." These are the qualities that win public esteem and confidence in England.

No doubt too often in the past the office of Justice of the Peace has been bestowed on those whose *legal* qualifications (by estate) were greater than their moral; and it has been regarded in many cases as a fitting distinction for those whose social and territorial status demanded it, or whose political services deserved reward at the hands of their party. But those days, we hope, have passed away. A Royal Commission on the selection of Justices of the Peace which had been sitting for some time, issued its Report in July, 1910, which may be obtained at H.M.'s Stationery Office, price 2½d., and forms an exceedingly interesting document. It contains many conclusions and recommendations which are well worth perusal.

Magistrates are only human, and like all human beings are liable at times to make mistakes. Occasionally they pass a harsh and severe sentence which cannot be justified by the circumstances of the case. Fortunately, here come in the advantage of the daily press and the utility of public criticism, which generally result in the intervention of the Home Secretary and the modification or remission of the sentence. In such cases it will frequently be found that the action of the magistrates is due to their having unwisely listened to a private statement made to them by the police. No wonder that in a recent case the local police were "much annoyed at the action of the press." But it is obviously unfair to judge of a whole system by isolated cases of this kind, which are few and far between. Some allowance must be made for the eccentricities and idiosyncrasies of individuals in a body of twenty thousand magistrates. It may be safely asserted that the vast majority of magistrates are not only human but also humane.

It cannot, however, be denied that there is in some quarters considerable dissatisfaction with the present system of unpaid and untrained magistrates, even with the assistance of a trained clerk. The infusion of a democratic element by the putting of chairmen of district councils on the county bench, and the appointment of a certain number of working men magistrates in boroughs, has done something to allay this feeling; but there is still a strong desire for the appointment of a much larger number of Stipendiary Magistrates in populous places. Rightly or wrongly they are believed to occupy a position of greater independence and freedom from external influences. It is thought that they stand between the public and the police to a greater degree, that they are much less in touch with the police than the ordinary magistrate, and that their sentences are much less severe. Against this view, it may be said, that if there is such a desire the public at large is strangely apathetic. In the early part of last century special Acts were passed to provide certain populous districts with Stipendiary Magistrates and Middlesex (now roughly speaking London) obtained power to have a paid Chairman of Quarter Sessions; but this example has not been followed in more recent times. A general Act was passed to establish stipendiaries in any Urban District where the inhabitants desired it. We believe we are correct in saying that there is not now in existence a single magistrate appointed under that Act!

The urban population of the country is constantly and rapidly increasing. New boroughs are created almost every year, about 150 have been created since 1837, yet the number of Stipendiary Magistrates under the Municipal Corporations Act is practically the same as it was thirty or probably fifty years ago. The West Riding County Council has considered the question of the appointment of a number of Stipendiary Magistrates for the Riding two or three times, but nothing has yet been done.

This certainly looks as though the people at large preferred justice to be administered by lay magistrates rather than by lawyers! There are other reasons for such a view besides those of mere economy. It is not easy to secure a sufficient supply of men who are altogether suitable for the post. Under the strain of police court work infirmities of health or temper may be developed; yet the Stipendiary Magistrate, unless he has ample private means, must go on working to earn his living and it is difficult to get rid of him. A poor Bench may be improved by the addition of new members, and the activity of the less efficient and fair-minded magistrates may be restrained by their colleagues. Not so the Stipendiary, he is permanent and indivisible.

Taking the system as a whole, however, it works fairly well, and we believe there are comparatively few cases of substantial injustice under it. That this is so is shown by the admiration of foreign critics, who are in the best position to judge of the system as compared with the systems of their own countries. Thus the Comte de Franqueville, a learned French lawyer, who has made a personal investigation of the English system, says of it: *"Il est difficile d'imaginer une organisation plus simple, plus pratique, plus prompte, ou plus humaine"* (cited by Prof. Kenny, *Outlines*, p. 438). Practical, prompt and humane it may be, and we think it is, but in spite of the learned Frenchman, it is certainly not simple; it requires more than ordinary Gallic lucidity to steer one's way for the first time through the intricacies of summary jurisdiction. But the greatest of all foreign critics of our institutions, Prof. Gneist, of the University of Berlin, said of the office of Justice of the Peace (at a time when it was possible for a German professor to take an impartial view), that it "combines in the honorary office the sense of honour and duty of the higher class, and the same feelings of a professional justice, in one single person, and thus produces the character of the judicial office in its best form" (*den Charakter des Richteramts in seiner besten Gestalt*). Such is our system of summary jurisdiction.

PART II. INDICTABLE OFFENCES, HOW DEALT WITH

II. QUARTER SESSIONS

Technically this is a meeting, or sitting, of two or more Justices of a county, etc. "for the execution of their general authority," to hear and determine felonies and trespasses and inflict punishment therefor, derived from the Commission of the Peace. They are called Quarter Sessions from the fact that they are held quarterly, *i.e.* in each quarter of the year. The distinction between Quarter Sessions and General Sessions is now of little importance. By 1 Wm. IV. c. 70, s. 35, the Quarter Sessions of the Peace for every county, riding or division are required to be held in the first week after the 31st March, the 24th June, the 11th October, and the 28th December in each year.

By the Assizes and Quarter Sessions Act, 1908 (which repeals the Quarter Sessions Act, 1904), a Court of Quarter Sessions for a county or the Justices of the county assembled in a special meeting, which they are thereby authorised to hold, may, at any time when it appears desirable for any purpose, fix or alter the time for holding the next court of Quarter Sessions, so that the Sessions be held not earlier than fourteen days before, nor later than fourteen days after, the week in which they would otherwise be held. As to the provisions of this Act dispensing with the attendance of jurors at Assizes or Quarter Sessions, when there is no business for them to transact, and dispensing with the obligation to hold Assizes and Quarter Sessions in certain cases, see hereafter (p. 83).

There must be at least two Justices present to constitute a Court of Quarter Sessions. As a rule a much larger number are present, from all parts of the county.

Before 1889 the government of English counties was practically in the hands of the Justices of the Peace assembled in Quarter Sessions; and there had grown up a class of country gentlemen who were experts in the work of county administration. On the whole the work was performed with great ability and economy. But it was thought to be out of harmony with the democratic spirit of the age that such large powers of raising money (by means of the county rate) and spending it should be in the hands of unelected and unrepresentative agents. Accordingly, by the Local Government Act of 1888, all the administrative powers of county Justices were transferred to the newly created county councils established by that Act. The control of the county police, however, still remains in the hands of a Standing Joint Committee, so called because it consists of a certain number of Justices and a certain number of members of the County Council. This committee forms, as it were, a link between the judicial body, viz. the Justices, and the executive or administrative body, the County Council. Quarter Sessions still appoint Committees of Justices to visit all prisons and asylums within their jurisdiction.

It is, however, with the judicial, not with the administrative, powers of Quarter Sessions that we are concerned. As a court of law, says Prof. Maitland, "it is a court with high criminal jurisdiction" (*Justice and Police*, p. 85). Its jurisdiction is in fact threefold.

1. As regards its *original* jurisdiction, *i.e.* as a court of first instance, it can try all indictable offences committed to it for trial, *except* the following:

(1) Such felonies, as are punishable on a first conviction by death or penal servitude for life. This of course excludes treason, murder and manslaughter. The jurisdiction of this court was

regulated by the Quarter Sessions Act of 1842 (5 & 6 Vict. c. 38), which took away from it these serious crimes. In a few other cases exclusive jurisdiction has been given to Assizes by later statutes. Burglary, as being punishable by penal servitude for life, was excluded, but by an Act of 1896 (59 & 60 Vict. c. 57), this court was authorised to try cases of burglary which are not of a grave or difficult character, and as a matter of fact more than two-thirds of the charges of burglary, including attempts, are now tried in this court.

(2) Certain crimes which, though less grave than those mentioned above, are likely to involve difficult questions of law, *e.g.* praemunire, forgery, bigamy, concealment of birth, perjury, libel, offences under the Criminal Law Amendment Act, 1885, and misappropriation by bankers, agents and trustees.

All the cases mentioned in these two classes are reserved for trial before a judge of the High Court at Assizes; and excepting these two classes, Courts of Quarter Sessions and Assizes have a concurrent jurisdiction in respect of all indictable crimes. More than twice as many prisoners are tried at Quarter Sessions as at Assizes, including the Central Criminal Court. About two-thirds of these are tried at County Quarter Sessions and one-third at Borough Quarter Sessions. It may be added that in the County of London there are so many cases for trial that the Sessions are held much oftener, viz. twice a month, and at these Sessions nearly a seventh of all the criminal cases in England and Wales are tried. All cases coming under the original jurisdiction are tried by jury.

In *Rex* v. *Hertfordshire Justices* [1911] 1 K.B. 612, there was an omission to administer the necessary "Statutory Caution" and the Court of Quarter Sessions to which the prisoner was committed for trial declined to proceed with the trial of the indictment on account of what had taken place before the committing magistrates; but it was held that the jurisdiction of Quarter Sessions to try the indictment was not ousted by any irregularity in the proceedings before the court below, and that it was the duty of Quarter Sessions to proceed with the trial after the Grand Jury had returned a true bill.

2. As to the *appellate* jurisdiction of Quarter Sessions,

which extends to questions not only of law, but also of fact, it includes:

(1) All appeals from the convictions and orders of Courts of Summary Jurisdiction, already dealt with.

(2) All appeals in rating, licensing, poor law, bastardy and other matters, of a civil or semi-civil character. These cases (with one or two exceptions) are heard without a jury and decided by the majority of Justices present. All licensing appeals, even from boroughs, go to County and not to Borough Quarter Sessions.

3. Closely connected with the last class of matters is a jurisdiction of a ministerial character, in certain miscellaneous cases, conferred by special statutes, *e.g.* the enrolment of certificates relating to the diversion or stopping up of highways (under the Highways Act, 1835) [any objection forms an appeal from the Justices who have made the order for diversion, etc.], the granting of licences to keep private lunatic asylums (under the Lunacy Act, 1891), etc. The indictment of surveyors of highways for non-repair of a highway is of a mixed character. It is criminal in point of form, and the facts are determined by a jury; but it is really civil in its effects, the object of the proceedings generally being to determine the question upon whom the liability to repair rests. But these cases form a small part of the total work of Quarter Sessions.

A curious survival of the connection of Justices of the Peace with the Vagrancy Laws is the power to sentence, at Quarter Sessions, "incorrigible rogues" convicted as such at Petty Sessions.

One advantage of Quarter Sessions is that counsel usually attend, and suitors may have the advantage of their services. "To Quarter Sessions," says Mr Justice Darling, "the barrister of one term's standing goes to make himself acquainted with the 'law of the land' by giving lessons in it to those who administer the one by virtue of owning the other" (*Scintillae Juris*, p. 45). This remark has, to a large extent, lost its sting since the abolition of qualification by estate, but there is still a considerable substratum of truth in it. At the Quarter Sessions of some small boroughs, *e.g.* Doncaster and Pontefract, in the absence of counsel, solicitors are allowed to plead. These are known as "open sessions."

The clerk of the court who keeps its records (for it is a Court of Record) in both counties and boroughs, is styled the Clerk of the Peace. A Court of Record is one whose proceedings are enrolled with great care, so as to be capable of proof, and it usually possesses power to punish those guilty of contempt of court. In counties the jurors are summoned by the Sheriff; but in Quarter Sessions Boroughs they are summoned by the Clerk of the Peace.

If we except a few courts which have salaried chairmen, the presiding Justice or Chairman need not be, and in most cases is not, a professional lawyer. Necessity as well as convenience requires that the Justices assembled at Quarter Sessions should have a president or chairman, though theoretically he has no greater powers than any other Justice present. The decision is that of the court, of the majority of the Justices present, not that of the chairman. Someone, however, must take notes of the evidence and the points of law raised in every case so as to be able to furnish a correct and authentic note, if required, for the purpose of a higher court (see p. 127). Someone also must exercise a controlling power over the procedure and order of business of the court. Nor can all the Justices "sum up" the evidence to the jury. This is perhaps the most important and the most difficult duty which a magistrate has to perform, since on his ruling as to the acceptance or rejection of evidence, and on his direction or mis-direction of the jury, a fellow human being's character and liberty frequently depend. The Justices, therefore, from time to time elect one of themselves as the recognized chairman of the court. He may, or may not, have had a legal training, but he is usually a man of ability and experience, acquainted with the principles of law if not with its details.

It is characteristic of English public life and our method of government that a Chairman of Quarter Sessions, as such, equally with the Prime Minister, had, until very recently, no recognized position in the eye of the law. The only statute, we believe, in which he is mentioned is the Poor Prisoners' Defence Act, 1903, which enacts that "the Judge of a Court of Assize, or *Chairman of a Court of Quarter Sessions,* at any time after reading the depositions," may certify that a prisoner ought to have legal aid (s. 1 (*b*)). But the Criminal Appeal Act, 1907, clearly throws upon the Chairman of Quarter Sessions who presided over the Court before which a prisoner was convicted, the duty of (1) granting a certificate of appeal, and (2) sending a report of the trial; and it is also his duty to sign a special case; for both of which purposes he requires to have taken notes. Thus his position is a somewhat anomalous one. He has important duties to discharge, but his status is undefined. This vagueness, however, has not prevented the formation of a "Society of Chairmen and Deputy Chairmen of Quarter Sessions in England and Wales," for the purpose of the discussion of matters in which they are specially interested and the promotion of uniformity of practice amongst them. Those who wish to pursue the subject further may be referred to an article on "The Powers and Duties of a Chairman of Quarter Sessions" in the *Justice of the Peace* for 5 Mar. 1910.

If the jurisdiction of Quarter Sessions should be exceeded, *i.e.* if an indictment should be found there in a case which Quarter Sessions had no right to try, the proceedings may, on application to a judge of the High Court, "if he shall think fit," be reserved, "so that the same may be dealt with, tried and determined according to law" (say) at the Assizes; and the prisoner may be removed by *habeas corpus*; and all recognizances entered into to appear at Quarter Sessions become obligatory to appear at Assizes.

"The whole proceedings at Quarter Sessions are essentially English, based upon long custom and precedent, varying largely in detail in the different counties—working well in practice owing to the sound social training of our public men, who are content not to insist unnecessarily upon their technical rights so long as justice is adequately dispensed" (*Justice of the Peace*, 5 Mar. 1910, p. 111).

There are Borough as well as County Quarter Sessions. In fact, about 110 boroughs, varying greatly in importance, *e.g.* Liverpool and Pontefract, have separate courts of Quarter Sessions. The judges in these courts are styled Recorders, and are all trained lawyers who receive salaries from £40 upwards, according to the size and importance of the place. They are appointed by the Crown, under the Municipal Corporations Act, 1882, on the advice of the Home Secretary. The Recorders of large towns such as Liverpool, Manchester, Birmingham, Leeds and Sheffield are all distinguished barristers, generally K.C.'s on the highway to promotion, possibly to a judgeship of the High Court. In some places there are also Assistant Recorders, *e.g.* Leeds and Sheffield.

At the Borough Quarter Sessions the Recorder is sole judge, but of course there is a jury in criminal cases. If a borough Justice happens to sit with him and is consulted, that is a mere act of courtesy. The jurisdiction of Borough Sessions is not quite so wide as that of County Sessions, since no appeals relating to licensing matters can be heard there. The Recorder alone determines such appeals as come before him.

More than one court may sit if sufficient Justices are present, and the Sessions possess powers of adjournment. But as the jurisdiction is entirely statutory, the powers of the court cease when the Sessions end, so that woe betide the young solicitor who neglects to tax his costs while the court is sitting, without having got a consent to tax out of Sessions signed by his opponent.

There is a similar right of appeal in civil matters from Quarter Sessions to the High Court by way of Case Stated, to that already explained in regard to Summary Jurisdiction. The Criminal Appeal Act, 1907, also applies to cases tried at Quarter Sessions.

The procedure on the trial of an indictment at Quarter Sessions is the same as at Assizes, allowing for the fact that the latter are presided over by a Judge of the High Court, and the former by a Chairman, who is generally a layman, *i.e.* not a lawyer, except at Borough Quarter Sessions, where the Recorder presides.

It may be asked who sets in motion the machinery for the holding of Quarter Sessions?

In counties the matter is quite simple. The dates between which Quarter Sessions must be held being fixed by statute, the Justices appoint the exact days within these limits a short time beforehand; the Clerk of the Peace issues notices and the Sheriff summonses the jurors, both grand and petty. All depositions are sent to the Clerk of the Peace by the clerks to the committing Justices, so that the Clerk of the Peace knows exactly what prisoners there are for trial. The Governor of the gaol prepares the Calendar. County Justices can also appoint Intermediate Sessions.

In boroughs the matter is not quite so simple. The dates for holding Borough Quarter Sessions are not fixed by statute. The Recorder therefore fixes them to suit his own convenience, having regard to the amount of work to be done, *i.e.* the number of prisoners to be tried and the number of appeals (if any) to be heard, provided he holds a court at least once in every quarter of the year. If it is found necessary for him to hold additional sessions, or to appoint a deputy, or assistant, he can do so only with the consent of the Home Secretary. In boroughs the Clerk of the Peace issues the notices and summonses the jurors.

In the City of London there are no Quarter Sessions for the hearing of criminal cases, but the Central Criminal Court (to be mentioned hereafter, see p. 87) serves at the same time as Quarter Sessions and Assizes. This court sits so frequently that all indictable cases arising in the City are committed for trial to it. Quarter Sessions are, however, held both for the City of London and the Borough of Southwark, on the usual dates, for the transaction of non-criminal business.

The Quarter Sessions for the County of London are at present held at the Sessions House, Clerkenwell, E.C. "for business arising on the north as well as on the south side of the Thames, in the months of January, April, July and October in every year, and the first sessions held in each of these months shall be called General Quarter Sessions." Adjourned Quarter Sessions are held at the same place, and for the same business, "in all the other months of the year at intervals of not less than two weeks or more than three weeks" after the preceding sessions. The result of this arrangement is the Sessions take place twenty-four times a year. Appeals are heard on the fourth day after the General Quarter Sessions, and on subsequent days if necessary.

This is in accordance with a scheme made by the London

County Council in December, 1913, and approved by the Home Secretary, under the provisions of Sect. 42 (7) of the Local Government Act, 1888, and such scheme, by an order dated 22nd Dec. 1914, has been extended "until the 31st day of December, 1916, unless otherwise determined." At these Sessions owing to the large amount of work to be done, including rating and licensing appeals, for the whole of the administrative county of London, there is a paid Chairman and also a paid Deputy Chairman.

The Middlesex Quarter Sessions are held at the Guildhall, Westminster, S.W., within the usual limits fixed by law, in January, April, July, and October in every year; but there are also held, as a rule, seven Intermediate Sessions, one in each of the other months of the year except December. The holding of Intermediate Sessions is "at the pleasure of the Court at the preceding Quarter Sessions."

III. ASSIZES

Until a few years ago no sight was more familiar and impressive in English county towns than the entrance of the judge (or judges) to hold the Assizes; and though time and railways have robbed the scene of much of its pomp and circumstance, the opening of the Assizes is still a ceremony by no means devoid of interest and display. The Commission Day itself is usually occupied by the judges in travelling; the real work of the Assizes begins the next morning when the Commission is opened and read[1] (or taken as read) and the judge delivers an address to the Grand Jury (technically called his "charge"), in which he calls their attention to the state of crime in the county, advises them how to deal with any case that presents unusual difficulty,

---

[1] Formerly the Proclamation against Vice (a long-winded, secular homily) was also read, but it was discontinued some years ago.

The judges when on circuit usually attend in state the Cathedral, or Parish Church, of the assize town the first Sunday after the Commission Day, when the Sheriff's Chaplain preaches. Hence the day is known as Assize Sunday, and the sermon as the Assize Sermon.

and takes the opportunity of making any remarks he thinks proper upon the topics of the day relating to the administration of justice. After this the Grand Jury retire to their duties; and then, and not till then, the members of the Bar come into court It is not etiquette for them to appear in court robed sooner.

If there are two judges, the one who is to take the civil business immediately and quietly settles down to work without any ceremony, as soon as the court is opened. He sits in a black robe; the judge who takes crime, in a red one.

As the Assizes are now held they are in effect a local, temporary branch of the High Court of Justice; but they represent those ancient itinerant tribunals, both criminal and civil, which for more than seven hundred years have been regularly held in every part of England, under royal authority. This is not the place even to sketch their history. There are seven circuits, viz. (1) the Northern, (2) the North-Eastern, (3) Midland, (4) South-Eastern, (5) Oxford, (6) Western, (7) North and South Wales and Chester, but this circuit is split up into two divisions. At the principal towns in the counties comprised within these circuits the Assizes are held twice a year at least, in winter and summer. In autumn an Assize is held for criminal business only, and in some counties there is also an additional Assize in May. The jurisdiction of the Assizes extends to all matters cognizable by the High Court, both criminal and civil, but they have no appellate jurisdiction.

By s. 23 of the Judicature Act, 1875, power is given to the Crown, by Order in Council, to regulate the circuits, including the discontinuance, either temporarily or permanently, wholly or partially, or any existing circuit, and the formation of any new circuit by the union of any counties or parts of counties; the appointment of the place or places at which Assizes are to be holden on any circuit; and the alteration of the day appointed for holding the Assizes at any place on any circuit, where, by reason of the pressure of business or other unforeseen cause, it is expedient to alter the same (as under the Winter Assizes Acts, 1876 and 1877, and the Spring Assizes Act, 1879, see hereafter).

As a matter of history the judges who come on circuit derive their jurisdiction from various commissions; in criminal matters, from the Commissions of (1) *Oyer and Terminer*, and (2) General Gaol Delivery; in civil matters, from the Commission of Assize.

"To this day," says Sir F. Pollock, "the commissions are issued substantially in the old forms" (*Exp. Com. Law*, p. 66); but "since 1884 the names of all the judges of the Supreme Court of Judicature have been placed in the various commissions" (Mr G. J. Turner, *Encycl. Laws of Eng.*, vol. 3, "Circuits and Assizes"), instead of the names of only one or two appointed for a particular circuit. It is usual to include also the names of all the King's Counsel on the circuit, so that they may, if necessary, assist the judges by sitting as Commissioners. Sometimes also a King's Counsel from another circuit is sent as a special Commissioner in place of a judge. This expedient has had to be adopted on several occasions recently, owing to the Bench of the High Court being considerably undermanned. By an Act of Parliament passed in 1910 provision was made for two additional judges in the King's Bench Division (at present it is only the judges of this Division who go on circuit), but owing to deaths the number is now only 16.

Mr Justice Bray, in his address to the Grand Jury at York City Assizes, on July 9th, 1914, referring to the arrears of judicial work, said, "So far as the King's Bench was concerned they were very few, but that would not last, and in his opinion they ought to have the full number of 18 judges." He urged them to press upon their Members of Parliament the necessity for having the full complement of judges, and added that the judges were unanimous in feeling that no assize town should lose the privilege it now had. It was necessary for the best administration of justice that judges should from time to time visit these towns.

It is sometimes said that the circuit system is itself on trial, and that it has broken down. By reason of the shifting of population, and the changed conditions of modern life, some towns at which Assizes have been held from time immemorial in the past, *e.g.* Appleby, have lost their importance, and there is now little or no work, either civil or criminal, to be transacted there. Accordingly, by the Assizes and Quarter Sessions Act, 1908, it is provided that if, not more than five days before the Commission Day, in the case of Assizes, and the day appointed for holding the Quarter Sessions, it appears to the proper officer that there is no business for them to transact, notice may be given to the jurors who have been summoned to attend Assizes or Quarter Sessions dispensing with their attendance; and the obligation to hold Assizes and Quarter Sessions is dispensed with in certain cases. Large places like Birmingham, Liverpool, Manchester and Leeds (where Assizes are already held four times a year) complain that sufficient time is not given to them for the proper hearing of cases, and are agitating for permanent branches of the High Court to be established there. This has already been done to a certain extent in Liverpool and Manchester, where there are practically continuous sittings.

The officials of a circuit, other than the judges, are (1) the Clerk of Assize, who has sometimes a deputy, known as the Clerk of Arraigns, and an assistant, known as the Clerk of Indictments and Taxing Officer; and (2) the Judge's Associate. These receive salaries ranging from £1000 a year down to £150, according to the size and importance of the circuit. The Clerk of Assize is the Clerk of the Crown Court. He calls jurors into the jury box, swears them, arraigns prisoners and takes their pleas, and keeps the record of all proceedings. To him the depositions and exhibits are sent, and he (or his assistant) draws the indictments, or, in the more difficult cases, authorises the prosecuting solicitor to instruct counsel to draw them; marks fees on the briefs of counsel, taxes the costs of solicitors and witnesses, and generally carries on the work of the circuit. The Judge's Associate simply keeps the record of the civil court, and transmits it to the proper quarter. He has nothing to do with the taxation of costs.

The results of the circuit system have been very important in the development of our legal and judicial system. In the beginning there can be no doubt that the practice of the judges going round the country regularly twice a year, into every county, enabled them to ascertain what customs were universal and acceptable, and assisted powerfully in the formation of the Common Law; while in modern times it has produced practical uniformity of procedure throughout England and Wales in all matters relating to the criminal law and its administration, though there are still slight differences on the various circuits.

Both Assizes and Quarter Sessions have these features in common, viz. (1) the Grand Jury, (2) the Petty Jury and (3) the advocates, who must be barristers.

The holding of the Assizes takes place in this way. The judges arrange amongst themselves at a meeting held some time before which of them shall go on circuit, including attendance at the Central Criminal Court, and which of them shall remain in town for the dispatch of civil business. The Clerk of the Crown in Chancery issues the Commissions, and the judges assigned to each circuit then fix the dates of the Commission Days, and issue precepts to the Sheriff of each county on the circuit to summon jurors, etc. All other arrangements are left in the hands of the Sheriffs and Clerks of Assize. The Clerk of Assize is to the whole circuit what the Clerk of the Peace is to a county or borough. If additional Assizes are needed over and above the ordinary Assizes held, if necessary, twice a year in every county, the Home Secretary advises the Crown to that effect and an Order in Council is made under the Winter Assizes Acts, 1876 and 1877, and Spring Assizes Act, 1879, under which Acts there is power to group counties, so as to save time and expense. The Order in Council here referred to is of course an Order made by the Privy Council, which is still "for many purposes the *formal executive* of the country" (Anson), though many of its duties have been transferred to departments and a good deal of its work originates in these departments. It will be observed that the Orders above mentioned are made at the instance of the Home Secretary. Orders in Council are always inserted in the *London Gazette*.

IV. THE CENTRAL CRIMINAL COURT

In London the Central Criminal Court, which sits at the Old (new) Bailey, occupies a unique position. It is a special tribunal, developed out of a very ancient Court of Gaol Delivery for the prison of Newgate by Act of Parliament, in 1834, and serves at once as a Court of Quarter Sessions for the City of London and a Court of Assize for the Metropolitan District, *i.e.* a special district which includes the City of London, the County of Middlesex, and parts of Kent, Surrey, Hertfordshire and Essex, the district so constituted being considered one county. The Commissions of *Oyer and Terminer* and General Gaol Delivery are addressed to the Lord Mayor and Aldermen of the City of London, the Lord Chancellor, the Judges of the King's Bench Division of the High Court of Justice, the Recorder of the City of London (who delivers the charge to the Grand Jury), the Common Sergeant, the two Judges of the City of London Court, "and such others as his Majesty may appoint"—two of whom form a quorum. This tribunal sits twelve times a year, practically every month (except August), and there are usually three, and sometimes four, or even five courts sitting simultaneously, presided over by (1) a Judge of the High Court, (2) the Recorder[1], (3) the Common Sergeant[1], (4) and (5) the two Judges of the City of London Court[1]. Its jurisdiction extends to all indictable offences, treasons, felonies and misdemeanours, committed within its district; and to this tribunal the Act of 1834, by which it was created, appears to have transferred all the criminal jurisdiction of the old Court of Admiralty. Indictments are, however, sometimes removed from this Court for trial in the King's Bench Division (at the Royal Courts of Justice in the Strand), *e.g.* Inspector Syme's case, J.P., 1914, p. 244; and *vice versâ*, for good cause shown.

In July, 1914, the Central Criminal Court (Judge, Counsel, Solicitors, Jurors, and Witnesses) were all kept waiting for a

---

[1] The Recorder of the City of London is elected by the Aldermen: the Common Sergeant and the two Judges of the City of London Court (which ranks as a County Court) are elected by the Common Council.

considerable time by reason of the fact "that no Alderman was present, so that the learned Judge, who could not alone constitute the Court, was unable to proceed with the trial until someone arrived" (*Law Times*, July 11th, 1914, p. 267). This is an anomaly which ought to be and might easily be remedied, without unduly derogating from the dignity of the City. Fortunately it is not often that such a delay takes place. As a rule an Alderman is in attendance every day, to form the necessary quorum, though not necessarily the same person from day to day. A few days before the incident above mentioned took place, the same legal journal which reported it also recorded the following statement: "The Lord Chief Justice of England the other day paid a notable tribute to the zeal, impartiality, efficiency and knowledge of law, displayed by the aldermen of the City of London in the discharge of their judicial duties, for which they received no remuneration" (*Law Times*, June 27th, 1914, p. 220).

It has been said above that the Central Criminal Court is in effect an Assize Court for the home counties. By the Winter Assizes Acts, 1876 and 1877, and the Spring Assizes Act, 1879, power was given to the Crown by Order in Council to unite counties for the purposes of Winter Assizes, and under these Acts the district of this court can be extended into the whole or parts of the adjoining counties. Winter and Spring Assizes may therefore now be held at the Central Criminal Court for an area much larger than its own district, including the whole of the counties of Kent, Surrey, Sussex, Berkshire, Hertfordshire and Essex.

The jurors at the Central Criminal Court are summoned by the Sheriffs of the City of London, and the Sheriffs of the counties of London, Middlesex, Essex, Kent, Surrey, etc., from the parts of those counties which are within its jurisdiction.

The Central Criminal Court has been described as "the first Assize in the kingdom, indeed in the world" (*Justice of the Peace*, October, 21st, 1911, p. 496). Here, at the Old Bailey, have taken place some of the most famous trials in English legal history, and down to the year 1853 it was not unusual for a sum of half a guinea, or a guinea, to be charged for a seat as if for admission to a theatre.

THE HIGH SHERIFF

Closely connected with the Assizes and with the Judges is the High Sheriff. The office of Sheriff is a very ancient, honourable and responsible one; but as the Sheriff exists to-day he may be described as the chief executive officer of a county, in civil as distinct from military matters. He is appointed annually by the Crown (except in the City of London and certain towns) and the office is compulsory and expensive, but we respectfully decline to give any description of the ceremony known as "pricking the Sheriffs," which takes place on November 12th every year[1]. It is described fully in most of the leading newspapers the day after the event.

"As keeper of the King's Peace, he (the Sheriff) is the first man in the county and during his year of office he is superior in rank to any nobleman in the county. He is specially entrusted with the execution of the law and the preservation of the peace in his county, for which purposes he has at his disposal the whole civil force of the county (*posse comitatus*)."

It is the Sheriff's duty to summon jurors, to provide for the proper reception and protection of the King's Judges while on circuit, to be in constant attendance on them, and to make all necessary arrangements for the holding and conduct of Assizes. It is also his duty to arrange for and see carried out all sentences, except sentences of imprisonment or penal servitude, and to enforce fines, whipping (where there is no imprisonment), death and estreat of recognizances. He is usually a country gentleman, a landowner in the county, or otherwise a man of wealth and position and the office carries with it great social distinction. His honorary and less onerous duties are performed by the Sheriff in person, and the sight of the Sheriff, in uniform, sitting by the judges on the bench is a very familiar one to all who attend Assizes. Scarcely less familiar, and frequently more imposing, is the sight of the Sheriff's carriage, accompanied by a number of javelin men and trumpeters, conveying the judges to and from the Assize Court. But the actual, serious work of the office is done by an under, or acting, Sheriff, in contradistinction to whom the Sheriff himself is properly styled the High Sheriff. This official (the under-sheriff)

---

[1] See s. 6 of the Sheriff's Act, 1887.

is appointed annually by the Sheriff, and is remunerated principally by fees; but his experience of the work usually ensures his reappointment from year to year.

The jurors at Assizes and County Quarter Sessions are summoned by the Sheriff (or under-sheriff) and are selected largely at his discretion from the jury lists, which are prepared in every parish by the assistant overseer of the poor.

In the City of London two Sheriffs are elected annually, on Midsummer Day, by the Freemen of the City, but enter upon office at Michaelmas, with the Lord Mayor. They attend at the Central Criminal Court. In those cities and towns which are counties in themselves, *e.g.* York and Hull, the Sheriff is appointed annually by the Town Council on November 9th, immediately after the election of the Mayor. The duties of these Sheriffs are similar to those of the Sheriffs of counties except that they do not summon jurors.

The Sheriff is fallen from his high estate. From being a viceroy he has become a mere figure-head, the real work of the office being done by the under-sheriff, though legally the responsibility for it still rests with the High Sheriff. To quote once more the oft-quoted words of the late Professor Maitland: "Now the whole history of English Justice and Police might be brought under this rubric, *The Decline and Fall of the Sheriff.*" The same writer proceeds: "We know him now as a country gentleman, who, it may be, much against his will, has been endowed for a single year with high rank and burdened with a curious collection of disconnected duties, the scattered fragments of powers that once were vast" (*Justice and Police*, chap. VII.).

The appointment, qualifications, powers, duties and liabilities of Sheriffs are now regulated by the Sheriff's Act, 1887. Every Sheriff is bound to appoint a deputy resident in London, "within one mile from the Inner Temple Hall," for the receipt of writs, warrants, etc.

It is the privilege of the Lord Mayor, commonalty and citizens of the City of London to elect the Sheriff of Middlesex and the Sheriffs of London (see s. 33 (1) of the Sheriff's Act, 1887).

There is only one Sheriff for Cambridge and Huntingdon, as if they were one county (*ib.* s. 32). Every other county has its own Sheriff.

THE GRAND JURY

In criminal matters, both at Quarter Sessions and Assizes, there are two juries, viz. (1) the Grand Jury, the jury "of enquiry or presentment," *i.e.* of accusation; (2) the Petty Jury, the jury "of issue or assessment," *i.e.* of trial. Both these institutions are peculiarly English. Their history is part of that of the English nation.

The Report of the Departmental Committee on the Law and Practice of Juries issued in 1913 comments on the "somewhat vague nature of the qualifications required for grand jurors." Blackstone says they are "usually gentlemen of the best figure in the county." In practice the Grand Jury at Assizes is composed of county magistrates. At Quarter Sessions it is composed of the better class of ordinary jurors, professional men, persons of independent means, merchants, farmers, etc. At both Quarter Sessions and Assizes the Grand Jury must consist of not less than twelve and not more than twenty-three members, and at least twelve must assent to its decisions. They are summoned by the Sheriff of the county, and they deliberate in secret, usually in a room conveniently situated near the court so that the foreman may hand the bills, after they have been "found" to the Clerk of the Peace. But before retiring to the Grand Jury room the Grand Jurors are sworn and "charged" (see p. 83) by the Judge at Assizes, or by the Chairman or Recorder at County or Borough Quarter Sessions. The first duty of the Grand Jurors, after they meet, is to choose one of themselves to act as their foreman, *i.e.* their chairman and mouthpiece. He is as a rule a man of position and experience, and his election is an implied compliment. It is assumed that this has been done before they assemble in court to be sworn and hear the Judge's charge.

The Oath administered first to the Foreman of the Grand Jury

"You, as foreman of this grand inquest for our Sovereign Lord the King for the body of this county of ————, shall diligently inquire and true presentment make of all such manners and things as shall be given you in charge, or shall otherwise come to your knowledge, touching this present service. *The King's counsel, your fellows', and your own, you shall observe and keep secret*; you shall present no one through envy, hatred, or malice; neither shall you have anyone unpresented through fear, favour, or affection, gain, reward, or the hope thereof; but you shall present all things truly and indifferently as they shall come to your knowledge, according to the best of your skill and understanding." [So help you God.]

The other Grand Jurors then take a similar oath.

After being sworn and charged the Grand Jurors retire to their room to begin their duties. They have nothing before them but the indictment, not even the depositions; but they hear the witnesses for the prosecution.

All the Grand Jury has to do is to see that at least a *prima facie* case is made out against the prisoner or defendant, so that, if there is absolutely no case against a man, he ought not to be put to the indignity of standing in the dock, which alone carries with it a stigma. This is their only function. They are not to try the case. Thus they cannot ignore a bill on the ground of the insanity of the prisoner, however patent. If they are of opinion that no case whatever is shown, it is their duty to throw out or *ignore* the bill, by writing across it "No true bill." But if they are satisfied that a *prima facie* case is made out by the witnesses called before them, they find a "true bill" (*vera billa*). This is done by the foreman of the Grand Jury endorsing the bill and delivering it to the presiding Judge in open court. From this moment the "bill" becomes an "indictment." The Grand Jury have "found a true bill." The names of all the witnesses to be called before the Petty Jury are also put on the back of the bill, and this entitles them to have their expenses paid by the county.

In coming to a conclusion as to whether a *prima facie* case is made out or not, the Grand Jury are not bound by any rules of evidence. The evidence necessary is generally got from the witnesses by a few pertinent leading questions put to them by the foreman. It is not necessary to examine all the witnesses for the prosecution, but only a sufficient number to satisfy the

Grand Jury. No witnesses for the defence are heard, but the witnesses examined testify upon oath. The accused is not present, nor any advocates. A bill cannot, however, be ignored unless all the witnesses whose names are on the back of the indictment have been heard.

The Grand Jury through its foreman may also make "presentments" to the Judge as to the state of crime in the county or borough or any other matter of public concern, or matter affecting the administration of justice. As the Judge and the Sheriff represent the Crown, so do the Grand Jury represent the county or borough and its inhabitants.

An ancient statute of 1351-2 (25 Edw. III. stat. 5, c. 3) provides that the members of a Grand Jury shall, if challenged, be debarred from service on the Petty Jury that tries any case presented by them. But it is extremely unlikely now that anyone who is summoned as a Grand Juror would also be summoned as a Petty Juror.

It is sometimes urged that the Grand Jury is useless and ought to be abolished. The arguments for and against its retention are set out in Prof. Kenny's *Outlines of Criminal Law*, 5th ed. pp. 456-7, notes. But it certainly ought not to be abolished unless a preliminary examination before magistrates is made compulsory in every case. It is one of our oldest institutions; it costs very little to keep up, since Grand Jurors pay their own expenses; and it does occasionally perform a useful public service.

The proposal to abolish the Grand Jury has been recently revived by a recommendation to that effect made in the Report of the Royal Commission which sat in 1913 to consider the causes of the delay in the King's Bench Division; but it has not met with unanimous approval. Commenting on this recommendation, in an article which appeared on January 17th, 1914, the *Justice of the Peace* observes: "The result is...to disclose a sharp conflict of expert opinion on the point."

On October 13th, 1911, on the trial at the Central Criminal Court of John James Puckrose, 59, moulder, who pleaded "Guilty" to the manslaughter of his wife, it appeared that the Grand Jury threw out the bill for murder, and also that they threw out

the bills for murder in three other cases, upon which Mr Justice
Scrutton observed: "I can only say that I think such a course
is extremely to be regretted. The prisoner has to come for trial
anyhow, and it is very unfortunate that the Grand Jury, without
any direction in law from the Judge as to the difference between
murder and manslaughter (an obscure subject which even some
of us do not understand) should take upon themselves to settle
what crime a prisoner is to be tried for" (J.P., October 21st,
1911, p. 497).

Upon this, it may be observed (while admitting that it
might have been wiser for the Grand Jury to have returned a
true bill for murder, and let the Judge and Petty Jury between
them decide the question whether the facts amounted to murder
or to manslaughter only), the Grand Jury, as it exists to-day,
was within its rights in so doing, and that if the distinction
between murder and manslaughter is so obscure in point of law
as a Judge of the High Court admits it to be, then the sooner the
Court of Criminal Appeal or Parliament lays it down in clear
terms what is the difference the better for the community.

In 1883 Grand Juries found "no true bill" in 530 cases, and
"true bills" in over 14,000, which went to trial—about 3·65
per cent. In 1912 they found "no true bill' in 208 cases out of
13,286 brought up for trial, and found "true bills" in over 13,000
cases which were actually tried—about 1·6 per cent.

This decrease in the number of bills thrown out seems to
show either that the Justices have become more careful in committing for trial, or that Grand Juries have become more careful
in rejecting bills.

INDICTMENTS

The first thing a prosecuting solicitor has to do, when he
arrives at the Sessions or Assizes, is to get his bill through the
Grand Jury. The police officer in the case usually looks after
the witnesses, and keeps them together ready to go into the
Grand Jury Room when they are required. The depositions
and exhibits thereto have been forwarded to the Clerk of the
Peace or the Clerk of Assize; and from them, either by him or
counsel, the indictment has been drawn, and engrossed on

parchment. So far it is only a "bill"; it will presently become
an "indictment."

An indictment is a formal, written accusation (engrossed on
parchment) made against a person by a Grand Jury. Theoretically, at Common Law, any one can present a bill to a Grand
Jury against any other person; but practically, in the vast
majority of cases, bills are now presented only against those
persons who have been committed for trial after a preliminary
examination before magistrates, and sometimes (in cases of
murder and manslaughter) before a Coroner and Coroner's Jury
as well.

Perhaps the simplest form of indictment is that which is
preferred in the most serious case, viz. murder, and runs as
follows:

"*Central Criminal Court to wit:*—The Jurors for our Lord, the
King, upon their oath present, that J. S., on the   day of
          , in the year of our Lord, one thousand nine hundred
and   , feloniously, wilfully, and of his malice aforethought, did kill and murder one J. N., against the peace of our
Lord the King, his Crown and dignity."

Upon such an indictment the prisoner may be acquitted of
murder and found guilty of manslaughter only. If he is charged
with manslaughter in the first instance, the words "wilfully
and of his malice aforethought" are omitted from the indictment
and the word "slay" is substituted for "murder."

Homicide is a felony at Common Law; but if the offence is
one created by statute, the indictment concludes: "against the
form of the statute in such case made and provided, and against
the peace," etc.

If the facts set out in the depositions disclose another legal
offence than that with which the prisoner is charged it is usual
to make an application to the Judge for leave to send up a second
indictment.

Only one felony is usually charged in one indictment, but
a recent decision says this is a matter of practice only and not
of law. The decision referred to is that of the *King* v. *Lockett
and others* [1914] 2 K.B. 720, in which it was held that there is

no rule of law that separate and distinct felonies cannot be tried together in one indictment. As a matter of practice and procedure the Judge presiding at the trial can in the exercise of his discretion quash the indictment, or call upon the prosecution to elect upon which of the counts for felony they will proceed, in order to safeguard the interests of the prisoner and prevent him being embarrassed by being put upon his trial upon an indictment in which there are several counts for distinct felonies. In exercising his discretion as to putting the prosecution to their election, the material element to which the Judge should direct his attention is whether the overt acts relied on as proving the different offences charged are in substance the same.

If the offences charged are misdemeanours any number can be included in one indictment; in such a case each charge forms the subject of a separate "count" or "averment." The example of indictment given above is very short and simple; but in some cases, where the facts are complicated, *e.g.* false pretences, falsification of accounts, fraud, etc., the indictments are very long and very technical.

All indictments were formerly exceedingly technical, and were vitiated by very slight defects; but the Court now possesses (under 14 & 15 Vict. c. 100) large powers of amendment in case of merely formal defects. Indictments presenting any difficulty are usually drawn by counsel in the instructions of the prosecuting solicitor, otherwise they are drawn by the Clerk of Assize or Clerk of the Peace, or their assistants.

The objects of an indictment are twofold: (1) to let the prisoner or defendant know exactly and definitely what charge he has to meet, so that he may plead to it; (2) to enable the Court to know clearly what sentence can be legally passed on conviction.

Objections to the sufficiency or validity of an indictment are now usually taken by a "motion to quash" the indictment, made by the defendant (or his counsel) on arraignment, and before pleading. The grounds for such a motion are that (1) it discloses no offence known to the law; (2) it is too vague and general, not sufficiently precise and definite; (3) it is preferred before the wrong court; (4) it has been preferred without compliance with the necessary preliminaries under the Vexatious Indictments Act, 1879; (5) it contains counts for more than one distinct felony, or for more than one misdemeanour, which cannot in fairness to the accused be tried together. In such a case the prosecution is put to their election upon which charge they will proceed.

Whether the court will quash an indictment, or not, is a matter entirely within its discretion. But any decision of the court of trial on a legal objection to the indictment, unsuccessfully taken for the defence, if the defendant is convicted, may be the subject of an appeal under the Criminal Appeal Act, 1907.

It has been said above that the Grand Jury is free to consider voluntary indictments, that is to say, indictments preferred by anybody without any previous magisterial enquiry. It is obvious that such a power may be made use of to cause great annoyance and expense, by instituting groundless prosecutions, either from spite or in the hope of extorting money. The only remedy the innocent defendant has is an action for malicious prosecution, which may prove fruitless. Accordingly, by an Act of 1859 (known as the Vexatious Indictments Act), the legislature has imposed restrictions on certain cases which were found to be the most frequent subject of false accusations.

In those cases in which a bill is presented to a Grand Jury without notice to the party accused, if a "true bill" is found, it is usual to adjourn the hearing of the case to the next Sessions or Assizes, to enable the accused to prepare his defence.

THE CORONER AND THE CORONER'S INQUEST

The Coroner is an official of great antiquity. The origin of the office has not yet been fully investigated (see vol. ix., Selden Society's Publications), but it was in existence in the twelfth century. By Magna Charta (A.D. 1215) Coroners were forbidden to hold "pleas of the Crown," i.e. to hear and determine criminal cases. Thus they were deprived of their character of criminal judges and reduced to a position of inferiority as mere enquirers and accusers.

There are three classes of Coroners in England: (1) County Coroners, (2) Borough Coroners, and (3) Franchise Coroners.

Before 1888 County Coroners were elected by the freeholders of
the county; they are now appointed by the County Council.
In county boroughs, and boroughs which in 1881 had a population
of over 50,000 and a Court of Quarter Sessions, Borough Coroners
are appointed by the Borough Council. Franchise Coroners are
those for certain jurisdictions, *e.g.* the Duchy of Lancaster, the
University of Oxford, the City of London, etc., and are appointed
by the persons who have inherited a right conferred some
centuries ago by royal grant. There is one county that is
wholly covered by franchises, and others of which the greater
part is so covered. In smaller boroughs the County Coroner
acts. All the judges of the High Court are *ex-officio* Coroners
for the whole of England, and the Lord Chief Justice is the chief
Coroner of the Kingdom.

The duties of Coroners, which have not materially altered
since Magna Charta, are now regulated by the Coroners' Act,
1887, which consolidated and amended most of the earlier
statutes. By the Coroners' Act, 1892, every Coroner must
appoint a deputy to be approved by the Council. The Coroner
acts as substitute for the Sheriff, when the latter is disqualified
from acting by reason of interest; but his main duty relates to
the holding of inquests in cases of death. In the City of London,
under the City of London Fire Inquests Act, 1888, inquests are
held as to the cause of every fire, fires being in many cases the
result of crime (arson) and the cause of deaths.

The Coroner must hold an inquest on the dead body of every
person found or lying within his jurisdiction, (1) if there is
reasonable ground to suspect that the deceased has died a violent
or unnatural death, or has died suddenly from some unknown
cause; (2) if the deceased has died in prison, or in such place, or
under such circumstances, as render an inquest desirable in the
interests of the public and for the protection of the inmates, *e.g.*
in a lunatic asylum, an inebriates' retreat, or what is known as
a "baby farm."

"The chief object of the Coroner's jury is to determine whether
death is or is not due to a criminal act, and if it is found to be
so by the verdict of the jury, and the suspected person is found,
criminal proceedings follow, the inquisition of the Coroner being

equivalent to an indictment found by a Grand Jury" (*Introd. to the Criminal Statistics* for 1912, p. 12).

The enquiry is held by the Coroner with the aid of a jury of not less than twelve nor more than twenty-three. No qualification appears to be necessary for the members of a Coroner's jury, except that they must be "lawful men" and householders in the district. The officer by whom they are summoned generally gets hold of any respectable male householder he can. They receive about 1*s.* a case. The inquest must take place *super visum corporis*, *i.e.* the jury are bound to view the body. The evidence is taken upon oath. Most witnesses attend voluntarily, but the Coroner has power to summon persons to give evidence, and they are bound to do so, subject to the right of any witness to refuse to answer an incriminating question. The Coroner takes notes of the evidence (depositions) and directs the jury, sums up the evidence and informs them as to the law, and they then return their verdict as to the cause of death, by a majority.

The verdict is recorded under the hands of at least twelve jurors; and if it accuses any person of murder or manslaughter it must be engrossed on parchment and be under the seals of the jurors and the Coroner. It is then returned to the Court of Assize for the district, and, as is stated above, it has the same effect as an indictment found by a Grand Jury. It is the duty of the Coroner to be present in court when any case committed for trial by him is heard.

The Coroner's Court being a Court of Record, he has at Common Law a right to commit for contempt of court; he has also statutory powers to fine witnesses and jurors for disobeying his summons; and he has full power to bind over the witnesses to attend the Assizes, and to commit for trial persons accused by inquisition of murder or manslaughter and to issue warrants for their arrest. He may also order the exhumation of a body.

When a person is committed for trial upon a Coroner's warrant, after arrest the usual practice is to bind over a police officer to prosecute. The case is then placed before the Public Prosecutor, who gives directions in the matter by virtue of the Prosecution of Offences Act, 1908, and the regulations thereunder.

The High Court may quash an inquisition if it is irregular,

and may order a Coroner to hold an inquest, if he refuses to do
so. County Coroners are now paid salaries based upon the
average number of inquests held within their districts during
the preceding five years; but in boroughs they are still usually
dependent upon fees. Franchise Coroners are now paid like
County Coroners.

It will be noted that the criminal function of the Coroner's
inquest, like that of the Grand Jury, *is only to accuse and not to
try.* "The finding of a Coroner's inquest, accusing a person of
murder or manslaughter, is equivalent to an indictment by a
Grand Jury" (Kenny, *Outlines*, p. 426). In practice, however,
there is nearly always, in such cases, also a commitment by
magistrates, and a bill of indictment is presented to the Grand
Jury. If this bill is thrown out, it is not usual to offer any
evidence upon the Coroner's inquisition. If a "true bill" is
found by the Grand Jury, the accused is put upon his trial both
upon the indictment and the inquisition; and if he is found
"Not Guilty" upon the indictment he is usually discharged
upon the Coroner's inquisition; he must, however, be formally
discharged in regard to the latter, as he is "given in charge" to
the jury upon it.

Sometimes, where the Coroner's inquest has been an unusu-
ally full and careful investigation, the magisterial enquiry is
omitted as unnecessary. This was so in the case of *Paine*, in
1880, the Coroner's inquest having lasted five days. In such
circumstances, the case goes directly to the Petty Jury at the
Assizes, without the intervention of the Grand Jury.

There are altogether 330 Coroners in England, viz. 200
County Coroners, 76 Borough Coroners, and 54 Franchise
Coroners. Hitherto no professional qualification has been
required, though as a matter of fact most Coroners are either
barristers, solicitors, or medical men.

The total number of inquests held in 1912 was 37,098, and
the annual average for the five years (1907–1911) was 36,720.
Of the 37,098 cases of death investigated by Coroners' juries in
1912, 14,458 were found to be due to natural causes, 15,118
were found to be accidental, and in 2169 cases open verdicts
were returned. In the same year there were 3605 verdicts of

suicide, 586 of death from excessive drinking, and 231 of death from want, exposure, etc.

The second report of the Departmental Committee appointed to enquire into the law relating to Coroners, Coroners' inquests, and the practice of Coroners' courts, was issued in March, 1910, and contains many valuable suggestions.

The report lays great stress upon the value of publicity. Referring to the right of the Coroner to exclude the public from an inquest, if he thinks fit, it states:

"We do not think any sufficient case has been made out for altering the law and taking away the Coroner's discretion. In certain cases, no doubt, publicity is of the greatest value. For instance, in a recent case, where a lady died at a hairdressing establishment, it was most important to bring to public notice the dangers of tetrachloride of carbon. On the other hand, the gratification of the public curiosity cannot be weighed for a moment against the intense pain caused to the relatives of the deceased by the disclosure of family matters, which may have nothing to do with the cause of death. The presence of the jury is a sufficient guarantee that the proceedings at the inquest are fair and above board."

THE PETTY JURY

The Petty Jury is the Jury of Trial. It is they who (as Sir Thomas Smith says) give the "deadlie stroke," of Guilty, or Not Guilty. It is curious to observe how the relative positions of the Grand and the Petty Jury have altered, how the power of the one has declined as that of the other has increased. As Sir F. Pollock has so well pointed out, in the Middle Ages an accusation by a Grand Jury was almost equivalent to a verdict of Guilty. "A man solemnly accused by the witness of his countrymen is more than half guilty, and our ancestors dealt with him accordingly" (*Exp. of Com. Law*, p. 43). Trial before a Petty Jury seems therefore, at first, to have been somewhat in the nature of an appeal from the decision of a Grand Jury. The accused elected to be tried by his countrymen, his peers, as opposed to the magnates of whom the Grand Jury was composed. *Posuit se super patriam.*

There are two fundamental principles of our system of trial by jury which ought never to be lost sight of, *viz.*: (1) that the Petty Jury must be unanimous in finding their verdict, and (2) that if there is a reasonable doubt in the case the accused is entitled to the benefit of it. This strong presumption of innocence in favour of the prisoner is a marked characteristic of English Law. Every man, however heinous the crime with which he is charged, is entitled by our law to be considered and treated as innocent until he is found guilty by a jury of his fellow countrymen.

It would be unprofitable, even if we had space, to consider the question, at one time very much discussed, whether the jury are judges of law as well as of fact. It is now well settled that the proper function of the Petty Jury is the decision of questions of fact.

As to the qualifications of jurors, every man, subject to certain exceptions, between the age of 21 and 60 years, who has, within the county in which he resides and in which the action is to be tried, freehold or copyhold lands of the clear value of £10 a year; or has within the same county leaseholds of the clear value of £20 a year; or who is a householder rated to the poor, in Middlesex at not less than £30, or in any other county at not less than £20, is liable to serve as a common juror. In the City of London a juror must be a householder or the occupier of premises for the purpose of trade or commerce within the city, "and have lands, tenements, or personal estate of the value of £100" (County Juries Act, 1825, s. 50).

A special juror must be "an esquire, or a person of higher degree, or a banker or merchant" (Juries Act, 1870, s. 6).

The exemptions from jury service are very numerous: Peers, Members of Parliament, Judges, Clergymen, Priests, Ministers, Barristers, Solicitors and their managing clerks, Officers of the Supreme Court, Clerks of the Peace and their deputies, Coroners, Gaolers and their subordinate officers, Physicians, Surgeons, Pharmaceutical Chemists, Officers of the Army, Navy and Territorial Forces, Pilots, Officers of the Post Office, Household Servants of His Majesty, Commissioners of Taxes, Sheriffs' Officers, Magistrates, Police Officers, Justices of

the Peace, Town Clerks, etc.—in fact almost everyone who holds
a public office or whose absence from his usual occupation would
cause serious inconvenience to the public (see the Schedule to
the Juries Act, 1870).

A juror who is duly summoned is liable to a fine if he fails to
attend, or does not answer his name after being called three times,
or after having been called does not appear, though present, or
after appearance wilfully withdraws himself from the Court,
unless he can prove some reasonable excuse, of which the Court
is the judge.

Jurors at Assizes and County Quarter Sessions are summoned
by the Sheriff; at Borough Quarter Sessions, by the Clerk of
the Peace. They are entitled to six days' notice by post, and,
with certain exceptions, are unremunerated.

By the Oaths Act, 1909, jurors are now sworn with the right
hand uplifted, holding therein a copy of the New Testament.
The form of the oath is as follows:

"*I swear by Almighty God that I will well and truly try the
issue joined between our Sovereign Lord the King and the prisoner
at the bar, whom I shall have in charge, and a true verdict give,
according to the evidence.*"

Until 1909, in felonies each juror was sworn separately;
in misdemeanours they were sworn in batches of four. But the
new form of the oath prescribed by the Oaths Act, 1909, requires
that each juror shall be sworn individually. Notwithstanding
this Act, a juror may still affirm, if he objects to swear.

Taking the jury system as a whole it works well, particularly
in criminal cases. There are of course great differences in juries.
Every practising lawyer knows there are acquitting juries and
convicting juries. Sometimes one master mind seems to dominate
and control the rest. But most lawyers would agree that taking
them all round juries do show intelligence, fairness and a high
sense of responsibility, and reflect in a remarkable degree the
average feeling of the community. One satisfactory feature
about the system is that so far, as well as one can judge, this
sense of responsibility has not in any way been impaired by the
establishment of the Court of Criminal Appeal.

The Report of the Departmental Committee on the Law and

Practice of Juries issued at the end of 1913 (pp. 56), contains
a mass of information on the working of the jury system, including
a short history of trial by jury, the jury laws in modern times,
and the existing law and practice relating to juries of all kinds.
The Report states: (p. 28) "we believe that as regards the trial
of all criminal cases a jury is still acknowledged everywhere to
be for many reasons the tribunal most suitable for determining
any question of a prisoner's guilt or innocence." And also:
(p. 31) "It is generally admitted that so far as regards criminal
cases no alteration is possible in the historic practice of allowing
a jury to condemn or acquit." Accordingly the Committee
recommends: (2) "That trial by jury remain as of right in all
criminal cases" (p. 47). A separate Memorandum (p. 50) signed by
Mr Rupert S. Gwynne, M.P. and Mr English Harrison, K.C.,
emphasises "the value of trial by jury in the administration of
justice," in all cases, both civil and criminal, and says: "No one
familiar with our courts can have failed to be struck by the attention paid by juries to the cases they have to try and their anxiety
to arrive at a right conclusion.".. . "The presence of the jury
operates also beneficially on the judge.... The duty of summing
up the case to them compels him to keep his attention unceas-
ingly alive throughout the trial, and the necessity of making a
complete exposition of his views is a security to the suitors
(including prisoners) and the public for impartiality and honesty
on his part."

"Not the least, however, of the advantages of this institution
is, that it familiarises the people with the law, and popularises
the administration of it."

The Petty Jury must consist of twelve, and they must agree
upon their verdict, that is to say, they must be unanimous. The
reason for this appears to be that in the Middle Ages, when the
Jury system was formed, the concurrence of not less than twelve
men was the minimum standard of proof required in all cases
(cf. the Court of the Lord High Steward, the Grand Jury and the
Jury at a Coroner's Inquest). No such verdict as that of Not
Proven, which may be found by juries in Scotland, is possible in
our courts. It must be a verdict of Guilty or Not Guilty outright.
It is for the prosecution to prove the prisoner's guilt, and if they

cannot do so, if there is a reasonable doubt in the case, he is entitled to the benefit of that doubt and an acquittal. If the jury, after long deliberation, find it really impossible and hopeless for them to agree, they may be discharged, and there is no other course to pursue but a fresh trial at the next Sessions or Assizes. Sometimes, in such a case, the Crown enters a *nolle prosequi, i.e.* abandons the prosecution.

THE ORDER OF PROCEEDINGS AT A CRIMINAL TRIAL

Assuming that a "true bill" has been found against a prisoner by the Grand Jury, the first step in his trial is that he is called upon to plead. He is called into the dock and arraigned at the bar. Now is the time for him to take objection to the indictment, and move to quash it, if that course is advisable. The prisoner may also plead one of several technical pleas, *e.g.* a plea to the jurisdiction, a plea in abatement, a pardon from the Crown, autrefois convict, autrefois acquit, etc., it being a maxim of the Common Law, *Nemo debet bis vexari pro unâ et eâdem causâ.* But in the majority of cases he pleads simply the general plea of Guilty or Not Guilty, as the case may be. If the prisoner refuses to plead when called on to do so, a jury must be empanelled to decide (1) whether he is fit to plead, or (2) whether he "stands mute" (*a*) of malice, or (*b*) by the visitation of God. If a prisoner committed for trial is obviously so insane as to be unfit to be arraigned, and is so certified in manner prescribed by the Act while in prison, the Criminal Lunatics Act, 1884, empowers a Secretary of State (Home Secretary) to order his removal from prison to a lunatic asylum and his detention as a criminal lunatic. "If the Secretary of State acts under the statute, the hand of the Court is stayed." This power gets rid of a difficulty experienced in *R. v. Dwerryhouse* (2 Cox, 446). In the first case, if on arraignment a prisoner is found by the jury specially empanelled for that purpose, "unfit to plead or take his trial," and his unfitness arises from a temporary cause, which prevents him giving instructions for his defence, his trial may be adjourned. *R. v. Joseph Harris* [1897] 161 J.P. 792. C.C.C. But if the jury find that the cause of his unfitness to plead is not temporary but permanent and that he is "not of sufficient intellect to comprehend the course of the proceedings at the trial, so as to make a proper defence," they ought to find that he is not of sane mind; and the court may then direct such finding to be *recorded*, and order such person to be kept in custody "until his Majesty's pleasure be known" (Criminal Lunatics Act, 1800, s. 2). It is to be noted that this provision does not apply to Grand Juries, who have nothing to do with the prisoner's sanity or insanity.

The proper time to raise the question of the prisoner's fitness to be tried is before he pleads, and the issue to be tried by the jury so empanelled, is the state of the prisoner's mind at the time of the arraignment, not at any prior date. The defence that the prisoner was insane at the time he committed the offence with which he is charged, will be considered hereafter (see p. 115).

In the second case, if the jury find that he stands "mute of malice" a verdict of Not Guilty is now entered for him, and the trial proceeds. If he is found to be "mute *ex visitatione Dei*," attempts are made to make him understand the nature of the charge and proceedings by means of signs. Formerly a prisoner charged with treason or misdemeanour, who stood mute, was held to confess himself guilty; if charged with a felony he suffered the dreadful punishment of *peine forte et dure*, and some prisoners preferred to do this, so as to prevent the consequences of conviction for felony, before the Forfeiture Act, 1870. Very few prisoners now stand mute.

As a rule at Assizes and Quarter Sessions all the pleas of prisoners are taken first, as soon as the bills come from the Grand Jury, and such prisoners as plead Guilty are dealt with before trials begin. If a prisoner pleads Guilty the jury has no function to perform. The Judge, Recorder or Chairman, usually asks for a short statement of the facts of the case (although he has the depositions before him and is supposed to have read them), makes any enquiries he thinks necessary as to the prisoner's character and antecedents, hears anything the prisoner himself, or his counsel, has to say in mitigation, and then passes sentence (as to which see p. 117).

It is an honourable tradition of the English Bar that the prosecuting counsel in making this statement of facts against a prisoner who has pleaded Guilty should omit nothing which tells in the prisoner's favour.

Those prisoners who plead Not Guilty have meanwhile been ordered to stand back. After all the pleas of Guilty have been disposed of, the trials of those who have pleaded Not Guilty begin[1]. A jury is then empanelled and sworn to try each case.

As the jurors are called and come into the box to be sworn, the prisoner may "challenge" them on various grounds. The Clerk of Assize addresses the prisoner thus:

"*J. S., the jurors who are now about to be sworn are the jury who are to pass between you and our Sovereign Lord the King upon your trial. If therefore you object to them, or any of them, you must do so as they come to the book to be sworn, and you shall be heard.*"

In cases of felony the prisoner may peremptorily challenge twenty jurors, *i.e.* without assigning any reason. The object is to secure an impartial jury. The peremptory challenge of jurors by prisoners, and the corresponding right of the Crown to order jurors to stand by in large numbers in Criminal cases, is an ordinary everyday practice in the Irish Courts, and still more so in America, where the greatest difficulty seems to exist to get a jury together at all. But in this country the difficulty is practically unknown. "In the course of my experience," writes Sir Fitzjames Stephen, "I do not remember more than two occasions on which there were any considerable number of challenges" (see *Law Times*, June 20, 1914, p. 176).

When a man who is let out on bail fails to turn up and take his trial, he is formally "called into court." This is usually done at the end of the session or assize, after all the other prisoners have been tried, and the court is about to close. The crier of the court shouts in a loud voice three times:

"*J. S., come into court, or your recognisances will be estreated.*"

This cry is taken up by the police officers outside the court

---

[1] About three-sixths, or one half, of the prisoners indicted at Quarter Sessions and Assizes plead Guilty. About two-sixths or one-third, are tried and found Guilty; and one-sixth are tried and acquitted.

and repeated through the corridors. If there is no response, after waiting a few minutes, the judge says:

"*Let his recognisances be estreated.*"

The meaning of this is that the recognizances (or bond) of the prisoner himself and his bail, or sureties, into which they have entered, a memorandum of which has been entered upon the record of the court, are extracted (estreated) and sent to the Sheriff to be enforced *viz.* by levying execution upon their goods and chattels, unless of course the money is forthcoming. This process is popularly called "forfeiting his bail."

Assuming that there are no objections, the jurors are sworn, and the trial proceeds.

After the jury have been sworn, in cases of treason and felony, the Clerk of Arraigns says to them:

"*Gentlemen of the Jury, the prisoner stands indicted by the name of J. S., for that he on the   day feloniously did, etc.* [as in the indictment]. *Upon this indictment he has been arraigned, and upon his arraignment he has pleaded that he is Not Guilty ; Your charge therefore is to enquire whether he be Guilty or Not Guilty, and to hearken to the evidence.*"

This is called "Giving the prisoner in charge to the jury"; and after this the jurors were formerly not allowed to separate.

If a number of prisoners are given into the charge of the jury at one time they are said to constitute an "arraignment"; and at the Central Criminal Court, and on some circuits, after an arraignment has been made, the crier of the court makes the following quaint proclamation:

"*If anyone can inform my lords, the King's Justices, the King's Sergeant or the King's Attorney General, ere this Inquest be taken between our Sovereign Lord the King and the prisoners at the bar, of any treasons, murders, felonies or misdemeanours, done or committed by the prisoners at the bar, let them come forth and they shall be heard, for the prisoners now stand at the bar on their deliverance ; and all persons who are bound by recognisances to prosecute or give evidence against the prisoners at the bar, let them come forth, prosecute, and give their evidence, or they shall forfeit their recognisances. God save the King.*"

The presence of a prisoner at his trial is necessary in cases of treason and felony; but if he creates a disturbance, it is said, the trial may go on in his absence, and he may be punished for contempt of court in creating the disturbance. His presence is not necessary in misdemeanours.

It was long ago decided that a prisoner is to be brought to the bar without any irons, shackles or other restraint, unless there is a danger of his escape; and he "ought to be used with all the humanity and gentleness which is consistent with the nature of the thing, and under no other terror or uneasiness than what proceeds from a sense of his guilt or the misfortune of his present circumstances" (2 Hawk P.C. c. 28, s. 1). The very use of such language seems strange to us now.

All prisoners are searched before they enter the dock—and with special care if they have just surrendered to take their trial, after having been out on bail—for obvious reasons.

A prisoner may be brought up out of prison, if his presence is necessary as a witness, (1) by writ of *habeas corpus ad testificandum*; (2) by Judge's order (under s. 9 of the Criminal Procedure Act, 1853); or (3) by an order of a Secretary of State (Home Secretary) under s. 11 of the Prison Act, 1898.

When all these preliminaries have been disposed of counsel for the prosecution "opens the case," that is to say, he states the facts as shortly and concisely as is consistent with clearness, explaining the nature of the charge, and making such observations as his experience suggests. He ought not to state anything he is not prepared to prove. He then calls the witnesses for the prosecution, in such order as he thinks best, and examines them in chief, *i.e.* gets from them their evidence *in the form of answers to questions put to them by him*. This is a great check upon the garrulity of witnesses. Examination-in-chief is perhaps the most difficult task of an advocate in an English Court of Law, because in such examination it is a rule of the Law of Evidence, very strictly enforced, that he must not ask what are known as "leading questions," *i.e.* questions which suggest the answer which he wishes the witness to give. Counsel has before him the "depositions," and knows what the witness said before the magistrates, and that evidence he wishes him to repeat. With an intelligent and truthful witness this is a comparatively easy task; but with an unintelligent, untruthful or unwilling witness, or one with a bad memory, it is sometimes an extremely difficult thing to get him to give his evidence without transgressing the above rule. Sometimes the Judge will render counsel a little assistance, sometimes he will not. A witness manifestly hostile may, with the leave of the Judge, be treated as such, and cross-examined. The witness, when the prosecuting counsel has got from him all he can, is cross-examined by the prisoner or his counsel, if he is defended by counsel, with the object of weakening the witness's testimony by showing that it is unreliable, or extracting facts favourable to the accused. Cross-examination in the hands of an expert advocate is a very powerful means of arriving at the truth, and few persons who are not used to it care to undergo the ordeal of the witness box. Contrary to the generally received opinion, however, it is really very easy to cross-examine, if there is plenty of good material to work upon; but it is of course impossible to shake the credit of a perfectly respectable, truthful witness. The art of cross-examination, it has been well said, does not consist in examining crossly, and anything in the nature of offensive bullying is now discountenanced at the bar. Counsel for the defence is not bound by the rule as to "leading questions." He may make his questions as direct as possible. If necessary, after the cross-examination, the witness is re-examined by the counsel for the prosecution, for the purpose of enabling him to explain any statement he may have made in the course of his cross-examination. When all the witnesses for the prosecution have been called, and have given their evidence, what takes place next depends on the course pursued by the prisoner or his advisers. If he elects to call witnesses (other than himself) they are called, and give their evidence, subject to cross-examination in the same way as the witnesses for the prosecution. If the prisoner is defended by counsel, in important cases, his counsel sometimes opens the case for the defence before calling witnesses; but more frequently he addresses the jury only once, *viz.* after the witnesses for the defence have given their evidence. Counsel for the prosecution then addresses the jury and so gets the last word with them before the Judge sums up. If no witness (other than the prisoner himself) is called for the defence and no documentary evidence put in, his counsel then addresses the jury, and so secures the last word, which is often a matter of considerable importance. In such a case counsel for the prosecution has no right of reply; all he can do is to sum up his case to the jury before the prisoner's counsel addresses them. The Attorney-General however, as representing the Crown, always has a right of reply.

What is said above will perhaps be made clearer by the following tables, which are designed to show the various steps in a trial according to circumstances:

I. *Where the prisoner is not defended by counsel and does not call any witnesses (other than himself) except as to character.*

   1. Counsel for the prosecution opens his case.

   2. Counsel for the prosecution calls his witnesses.

   [2*a*. Prisoner himself gives evidence[1].]

   3. The prisoner addresses the jury and calls his witnesses as to character.

N.B. In this case it will be observed that the counsel for the prosecution has no right of reply. He makes only one speech, and the prisoner gets the last word with the jury before the Judge sums up.

This is the simplest form of a trial. A full trial is where the prisoner is defended by counsel and calls witnesses in his defence (see IV). But between these cases fall two others, *viz.*:

II. *Where the prisoner is not defended by counsel but calls witnesses in his defence.*

   1. Counsel for the prosecution opens his case.

   2. Counsel for the prosecution calls his witnesses.

   3. Prisoner calls his witnesses [himself first].

   4. Prisoner addresses the jury.

   5. Counsel for the prosecution replies.

---

[1] The prisoner's statement (if any) made before the committing Justices, is always read at the close of the case for the prosecution.

III. *Where the prisoner is defended by counsel but does not call witnesses (other than himself) except as to character.*

   1. Counsel for the prosecution opens his case.
   2. Counsel for the prosecution calls his witnesses.
   [2*a*. Prisoner himself gives evidence.]
   3. Counsel for prosecution addresses the jury.
   N.B. This, though sanctioned by law, is a course not often pursued.
   4. Counsel for the defence addresses the jury and calls his witnesses as to character.
   N.B. In this case the counsel for the defence gets the last word with the jury before the Judge sums up.

IV. *Where the prisoner is defended by counsel and also calls witnesses in his defence.*

   1. Counsel for the prosecution opens his case.
   2. Counsel for the prosecution calls his witnesses.
   3. Counsel for the defence opens his case.
   4. Counsel for the defence calls his witnesses [prisoner first].
   5. Counsel for the defence addresses the jury.
   6. Counsel for the prosecution replies.

Even where the prisoner is defended by counsel, he is sometimes permitted to supplement his counsel's speech (though he has not given evidence himself) by a statement made from the dock, his Common Law right to do this not having been taken away by the Criminal Evidence Act, 1898; but he may now give evidence on his own behalf.

Down to 1898 the prisoner's mouth was (except in certain cases) closed—"in mercy to him," as it was said, lest he should convict himself. But what was mercy to the guilty man was cruelty to the innocent one. The very person who necessarily knew most about his own case was excluded from giving evidence. Accordingly, by the Criminal Evidence Act, 1898, it was enacted that prisoners and their wives (or husbands, as the case might be) should be competent, but not compellable, to give evidence for the defence; and their failure to do so must not be made a subject of comment by the prosecution. The presiding Judge, however, may comment on such abstention. A prisoner, like any other witness, giving evidence under the sanction of an oath, is liable to be prosecuted for perjury if he swears anything material to the issue which he knows to be false. But in his charge to the Grand Jury at Flint Assizes in July, 1898, Mr Justice Wills said that a prisoner who had been acquitted of an offence (after giving evidence on oath and denying that he had committed the offence with which he was charged) ought not subsequently to be convicted of perjury on the ground that such denial was false, on the principle, which lies at the root of the administration of justice, that when once a question has been decided in a court of justice it can never again be raised between the same parties (see the *Law Times*, August 6, 1898).

Contrary to the general rule of English Law, which is expressed in the maxim *Nemo se ipsum prodere tenetur*, a prisoner who gives evidence on his own behalf may be asked in cross-examination questions which tend to incriminate him as to the offence charged, but not as to any other offence, or to show that he is of bad character, unless evidence of such other offence is admissible (as it is in some cases, *viz.* in offences involving fraud or dishonesty), or unless he has given evidence of good character or made imputations upon the character of the prosecutor or his witnesses. If the prisoner elects to give evidence on his own behalf, he does so under the sanction of an oath and in the witness-box. He is then called "immediately after the close of the evidence for the prosecution," and the fact that he alone is called does not confer on the prosecution the right of reply. In certain cases mentioned in the schedule to the Act, *e.g.* offences against wives, sexual offences, and cruelty to children, the husband or wife of a person charged with such an offence may be called as a witness for the prosecution or the defence without the consent of the other. This again is contrary to the rule of English Law, which regards husband and wife as one person (except in case of bodily injury to the wife); but in such cases the unity of husband and wife and the sanctity of married life must give way to practical necessity and the demands of justice.

A witness is now sworn in the following way. He holds the New Testament in his right hand, which is uplifted, and says (either reading from a card or repeating after an officer of the Court) these words:

"*I swear by Almighty God, that the evidence which I shall give to the Court and Jury sworn between our Sovereign Lord the King and the prisoner at the bar, shall be the truth, the whole truth, and nothing but the truth.*"

A Jew is sworn on the Pentateuch, and with his head covered.

This form of oath came into force on January 1, 1910, by virtue of the Oaths Act, 1909. It is much more impressive and sanitary than the old form of oath, though it takes longer time to administer. A witness may, however, still affirm, if he wishes; and if the witness is neither a Jew nor a Christian, the oath must be administered in some form binding on his conscience.

The Judge then "sums up," reviewing the evidence given on both sides, pointing out its strong features and its weak ones, and putting the whole case as fairly and impartially as he can before the jury, leaving the decision of all doubtful facts to them. In some few cases, however, all that he can say is, "*Well, gentlemen, if you believe the evidence that has been given, it is your duty to return a verdict for the Crown.*" In most cases a much longer and more elaborate summing-up is necessary. The beneficial effect upon the Judge himself of having to sum up the case to the jury has already been mentioned (p. 104). When the Judge has finished, he, or the Clerk of the Court, says to the jury, "*Gentlemen, consider your verdict.*"

In summing up the Judge directs the jury as to any points of law involved in the case, though strictly the decision of them belongs to him, and advises them as to the bearing and value of the evidence. The jury find the facts, generally giving due weight to the Judge's directions as to the law, though there is nothing to prevent them finding a general verdict of Guilty or Not Guilty, both upon the facts and the law, if they are so minded.

Sir Henry Maine, the great jurist, has pointed out that "we have in England a relic of an ancient popular justice in the functions of the Jury" (*Popular Government*, Essay II); and that in the Judge, "an expert" who "presides over their investigations," we have "the representative of the rival and royal justice." But we have also "a security unknown to antiquity, the summing up of the expert President, who is bound by all the rules of his profession to the sternest impartiality. If he errs, or if they flagrantly err, the proceedings may be quashed by a superior court of experts."

The jurors then turn round in the box and put their heads together. If they can come to a decision quickly, they do not leave the box; but if not, they retire. Formerly, after they had been sworn, jurors were not allowed any fire, light or refreshment until they had found their verdict; but by the Juries Act of 1870 this rule has been relaxed, and in long cases they are now allowed reasonable refreshments, at their own expense, unless the Sheriff thinks fit to provide them. Formerly also in felony cases they were not allowed to separate until they had found their verdict. But by the Juries Detention Act, 1897, "upon the trial of any person for a felony, other than treason felony, the court may, if it think fit, at any time before the jury consider their verdict, permit the jury to separate in the same way as the jury upon the trial of any person for misdemeanour are permitted to separate."

If the jurors wish to retire, a bailiff is sworn to keep them in some safe and convenient room, and not to speak to them himself, or suffer any other so to do, except to ask them if they are agreed upon their verdict.

When the jury have agreed on their verdict, if they have retired, they come back into court, and one of them (who has been chosen as their foreman) delivers the verdict.

The Clerk of the Court says:

"*Gentlemen, have you agreed on your verdict?*"

The foreman then says: "*Yes.*"

The Clerk: "*Do you find the prisoner Guilty or Not Guilty?*"

If the verdict is Not Guilty, the Judge orders the prisoner to be discharged, unless there is another charge pending against him.

In one case, the jury returns a special form of verdict, *viz.* where the defence of insanity is set up and established. The proper verdict in such a case, by the Trial of Lunatics Act, 1883, is "Guilty, but insane at the time of committing the crime charged." This is an illogical but convenient form of verdict, and forms another instance of the manner in which, in English Law, mere logic yields to practical convenience. The order in such a case is that the prisoner be detained "during His Majesty's pleasure," *i.e.* generally for life, and the Home Secretary orders his removal to some asylum, in most cases but not always a Criminal Lunatic Asylum. The consequences of the plea being so serious it is rarely set up except in capital cases.

In *Felstead* v. *Rex* [1914] A.C. 534 the House of Lords decided, on appeal from the Court of Criminal Appeal, that a special verdict given under the Trial of Lunatics Act, 1883, is one and indivisible and is a verdict of acquittal. Therefore an accused person who by the special verdict is found guilty of the act charged, but insane at the time, is not a "convicted person" within s. 3 of the Criminal Appeal Act, 1907, and cannot appeal from that part of the verdict which finds that he was insane at the time of doing the act. This decision sets at rest a point which had been a good deal discussed in two or three previous cases.

The jury have a right to return a general verdict of Guilty or Not Guilty; and that being the case, however legislators and lawyers may define and refine as to the legal distinction between murder and manslaughter, and however well an intelligent jury may appreciate the subtle differences between them, as lucidly explained by a learned judge, it always remains open to the jury so to find the facts as to bring the case under either head. Hence it has been said that murder is a crime for which a jury of twelve of his fellow countrymen unanimously think that a man ought to be hanged, and manslaughter is a crime for which such a jury think he ought not to be hanged, but to receive some lesser degree of punishment. Hence also it is said that manslaughter is "the most elastic crime known to English Law," as it may vary in degree from an act which is almost praiseworthy, the appropriate punishment of which is one day's imprisonment, to an act which comes very near to murder and deserves a sentence of penal servitude for life.

If, however, the verdict is Guilty, the Judge proceeds to pass sentence, making any observations he thinks proper on the case; but before this, the clerk of the court says to the prisoner:

"*J. S., you have been found guilty* [of such and such an offence].

Have you anything to say why the Court should not pass sentence upon you?"

In olden times, this was the prisoner's opportunity to plead "benefit of clergy," and now it is the proper time for him to move in arrest of judgment. But it is more frequently taken advantage of by the prisoner to say anything he may wish to say to the Judge in mitigation of his sentence.

SENTENCE

The sentence may be one of death, penal servitude, imprisonment, with or without hard labour, fine, or whipping, according to the character of the offence. There are now only five cases in which the sentence of death can be passed, and in the last two it is only recorded: *viz.* (1) treason, (2) murder, (3) piracy on the high seas, with violence, (4) setting fire to a royal dockyard or arsenal, (5) setting fire to a ship in the Port of London. At the beginning of the nineteenth century there were upwards of one hundred and fifty offences punishable with death. The minimum term of penal servitude is three years; the maximum term of imprisonment with hard labour is two years. In some few cases the prisoner may be ordered to be whipped, but flogging is now out of fashion. S. 36 of the C.J.A. Act, 1914, provides that "no person shall be sentenced to be whipped more than once for the same offence"; and "no person shall be sentenced to be whipped otherwise than under a statutory enactment."

A sentence of penal servitude for life practically means twenty years' penal servitude or less, since it is the practice to review such sentences after the lapse of seven, ten, fifteen or twenty years.

The maximum penalty is usually fixed by the statute which governs the offence: and within this limit the Judge (or Justices) has (or have) to exercise his (or their) discretion.

Before passing sentence the Judge usually asks for some information as to the prisoner. As a rule this is furnished by a police officer who has made enquiries about him. The form of oath administered to such a person runs: "*You shall true answer make to all such questions as the Court shall demand of you. So help you God.*" But doubts having been expressed as to the legality of this course, Lord Alverstone, L.C.J., in a recent case took an opportunity of expressing the opinions of the Judges.

In delivering the judgment of the Court (Lord Alverstone, L.C.J., Lord Coleridge and Hamilton, JJ.) refusing leave to appeal, he said that "they had been asked to express an opinion on the practice of taking evidence from a police officer, after conviction, as to the results of inquiries which he had made into the antecedents of the prisoner, it being alleged that such evidence was objectionable as being largely mere hearsay. Inasmuch as this matter had been under consideration by the Home Secretary and by the judges, he would take the opportunity of stating what the practice was. It had for years been considered to be the duty of some responsible officer of police to be prepared to give to the Court, after the conviction of a prisoner, all that he had been able to find out about him, whether in his favour or against him. If legal evidence were required as to the details of the prisoner's antecedents and character, considerable expense would be entailed. This practice was well known on some circuits, especially the Northern, though on some other circuits the practice was not always followed. He (the Lord Chief Justice) accordingly gave instructions some time ago that on all circuits a responsible police officer should be prepared to give the Court information, which the officer believed from inquiries he had made to be accurate, as to the antecedents and character of the prisoner, though legal evidence of the statements might not then be available, and this practice had now prevailed generally for some time.". . ."A police officer might, no doubt, say more than he ought, but there was no evidence that in the present case the police officer had said more than it was proper for him to have said before the Court. If a statement was made which the prisoner considered was not accurate, he or his counsel could at once inform the Court that he challenged the accuracy of the statement. If the statements were not challenged the judge might properly take them into consideration. If any of the statements were challenged as being untrue, it was the duty of the judge to inquire into the matter, and if he thought it of any importance he should adjourn the case so as to have legal evidence of the matter in dispute, and allow the prisoner an opportunity of contradicting it; or he might, as was often very properly done, disregard any statement challenged by the prisoner and not take it into consideration at all. They thought it right, as they had been asked to do so, to state what the practice was" (see *Rex* v. *Campbell*, C.C.A. (1911), W.N. 47).

It may, therefore, be taken that this practice is now well settled. The practice set out above is of course quite familiar to the Judges of the High Court and Recorders; but it may not be so familiar to Chairmen of Quarter Sessions and other Justices of the Peace who have to pass sentences at Petty Sessions. The weighty words of the Lord Chief Justice deserve careful consideration, more especially those which recommend that such statements, if challenged by the prisoner, should be entirely disregarded.

Another practice which has sprung up recently is, for the Judge, when there are several other charges pending against a prisoner who is just about to be sentenced (charges in respect of offences committed, it may be, in other jurisdictions, for which he is liable to be arrested on coming out of prison after serving the sentence about to be passed on him), to ask the prisoner if he wishes such charges to be taken into account in the sentence which the Judge is about to pass. The advantage to the prisoner is that he will come out of prison with a clean slate, with no other charge hanging over his head. If he admits the truth of the charges, *i.e.* in effect pleads Guilty to them also, then the Judge passes a heavier sentence than he would otherwise do for the single offence, and a note is made to that effect and communicated to the police concerned in the outstanding charges in order that those charges may be dropped. But it is obvious that this course cannot be pursued without the consent of the prisoner.

Where a prisoner has been found Guilty of one offence, and there is another indictment against him in the same court for another offence, it is not usual to proceed with the second indictment unless there is some special reason for doing so. In such a case counsel for the prosecution, with the leave of the court, "offers no evidence," and the jury return a verdict of Not Guilty or the indictment remains on the file.

To pass an appropriate sentence is by no means an easy task. It is a matter of nice discrimination, and all the circumstances of the case ought to be taken into careful consideration and receive due weight. A good deal depends on the experience and temperament of the Judge, and his knowledge of the prisoner and the prisoner's character. Some Judges are severe on one class of crime; others on another. In *Rex* v. *Green* [1911] 76, J.P. 351, the Court of Criminal Appeal held that severity of sentence may be justified by the prevalence of a particular form of crime in a particular neighbourhood, apparently on the ground that the severity is intended to repress it. As regards the prisoner much depends on what Bentham calls "circumstances influencing sensibility," *e.g.* age, sex, etc. A sentence which would be savage and brutal if passed on a clerk would not be so if passed on a navvy or blacksmith. With very few exceptions the English Judges have always been humane men, considerably in advance of the law which they have had to administer, and they have devised many expedients for mitigating its severity. Since the public press acquired so great influence it has done much to expose and render unpopular any ill-considered sentence; and the fact that the Court of Criminal Appeal has now power to revise not only convictions but also sentences has had its effect towards the standardisation of sentences. The most unequal sentences now are probably those passed by the inferior courts, *viz.* Petty Sessions in country districts. Then again the objects of punishment are various; the protection of the public, the satisfaction of the injured person, the deterrent effects of an exemplary penalty, and finally the possible reformation of the offender, are all objects to be kept in view. In modern times the excessive severity of the old criminal law has been greatly modified and short sentences are now the rule wherever possible with safety to the public. A writer who is now considered out of date, but who was much in advance of his time in this respect, *viz.* the learned Archdeacon Paley, seems to have struck the right note in the following passage.

"The *certainty* of punishment is of more consequence than the severity. Criminals do not so much flatter themselves with the lenity of the sentence, as with the hope of escaping. They are not so apt to compare what they gain by the crime with what they may suffer from the punishment, as to encourage themselves with the chance of concealment or flight. For which reason, a *vigilant magistracy, an accurate police, a proper distribution of force and intelligence, together with due rewards for the discovery and apprehension of malefactors, and an undeviating impartiality in carrying the laws into execution, contribute more to the restraint and suppression of crime than any violent exacerbations of punishment.* And, for the same reason, of all contrivances directed to this end, those perhaps are the most effectual which facilitate the conviction of criminals" (*Moral and Political Philosophy*, Book VI, ch. ix).

Following the same train of thought, in 1810 Sir Samuel Romilly speaking in the House of Commons said: "If it were possible that punishment, as a consequence of guilt, could be reduced to an absolute certainty, a very slight penalty would be sufficient to prevent almost every species of crime, except those which arise from sudden gusts of ungovernable passion."

Speaking generally, an English criminal trial is conducted with dignity, and in capital cases with solemnity, as befits the occasion. There is a sense of responsibility on the part of all concerned, they knowing well that the liberty, or even the life, of a fellow human being is at stake. But in the less serious cases a good joke or repartee, whether it proceeds from the bench, the bar, or a witness, is welcomed as a happy relief from the tension. Experience shows that a little judicial wit goes a long way, particularly with the junior members of the bar. It cannot, however, be denied that crime is an ugly, sordid thing, a social excrescence, and its associations are unpleasant and apt to beget callousness. An eminent judge now dead once expressed the opinion that it is impossible for an average clean-minded citizen to sit for a day in a criminal court and hear the common run of cases without having his moral tone appreciably lowered. It familiarises him with a mass of vice and depravity with the existence of which he was before totally unacquainted. It is a common remark of newly elected Mayors of Boroughs and Chairmen of District Councils that at first they find their magisterial duties very unpleasant and depressing.

V. THE KING'S BENCH DIVISION OF THE HIGH COURT

The "Supreme Court of Judicature" established by the Judicature Acts, 1873–5, consists of an upper and a lower division. The upper, known as "His Majesty's Court of Appeal," has no criminal jurisdiction. Before the establishment of the Court of Criminal Appeal in 1908, the only Court which had appellate jurisdiction in indictable offences was known as the "Court for the consideration of Crown Cases Reserved," but this court was superseded by the Court of Criminal Appeal. The lower division of the Supreme Court is called the "High Court of Justice"; and it is the King's Bench Division of the High Court which takes cognizance (*inter alia*) of criminal matters.

The King's Bench Division is a very august tribunal. At its head is the Lord Chief Justice of England, who receives a salary of £8000 a year; he represents, in his person, the King, and is the King's deputy, doing justice. The Judges of the High Court are appointed by the Crown, on the advice of the Lord High Chancellor, from successful barristers, generally but not always King's Counsel. The office is one of great dignity, honour and responsibility, and they receive salaries of £5000 a year, and a very liberal allowance for travelling expenses.

As a Court of first instance the K.B.D. has original jurisdiction in four classes of cases, though such jurisdiction is now seldom exercised, *viz.*:

1. Any crime committed out of England by a public official in the execution of his office, *e.g.* a governor of a colony.

2. Any misdemeanour, in whatever part of England committed, in respect of which an "information" has been filed by some officer of the Crown, *e.g.* the Attorney-General, as in the recent case of *Rex* v. *Mylius*. The filing of such an information dispenses with the necessity of going before a Grand Jury with an indictment.

3. Any indictable offence (treason, felony or misdemeanour) committed within the county of Middlesex.

4. Any indictable offence, in whatever part of England committed, an indictment for which has been found by a Grand

Jury in some other court, either Assizes or Quarter Sessions, and has been removed into the King's Bench Division, by *certiorari*, for trial there.

In such cases the trial is "at bar," *i.e.* it takes place before at least three of the Judges of the Division (of whom there are at present, including the Lord Chief Justice, sixteen) with a special jury. The last case of importance tried in this way was the trial of Major Lynch for treason in 1903.

If, however, a case of felony is removed from the country (technically called "changing the venue") on the ground that it is impossible, owing to local prejudice, to get a fair trial there, the trial takes place before one Judge and a jury, usually at the Central Criminal Court. Finally it may be said that the King's Bench Division has no power or control over the Crown Court at the Assizes, although under present arrangements this division supplies the Judges who go on circuit. Although they are members of this Division, the Judges of Assize sit under their commissions, and not in virtue of the fact that they are Judges of this Division. Appeals from the Assizes in criminal cases go direct to the Court of Criminal Appeal, just as in civil matters they go to the Court of Appeal.

The *appellate* jurisdiction of the King's Bench Division is much more active than its original. It is exercised by what is known as a Divisional Court, consisting of two (or more) Judges of the Division without a jury. The appeals which come before a Divisional Court are of two kinds:

1. By a writ of *certiorari*, by means of which the proceedings of Quarter Sessions or other inferior courts may be brought up to be reviewed and (if necessary) quashed, on some point of law. But no such course can be taken in regard to the proceedings of Courts of Assize, which are not inferior courts, but courts of co-ordinate jurisdiction.

2. By Case Stated, (*a*) by Justices of the Peace at Petty Sessions, (*b*) by Justices at Quarter Sessions, in appeals to them from Petty Sessions. By this means, at the instance of either prosecutor or defendant, any question of law which has arisen in the court below may be brought up to the King's Bench Division for determination.

The King's Bench Division also intervenes to compel Justices of the Peace to perform their duties, by way of *mandamus*, or rule, *e.g.* requiring them to issue a summons, or hear and determine a charge, if they have improperly refused to do so. Speaking in the House of Commons on 1st June, 1853, Mr Isaac Butt, Q.C., said: "The Law and the constitution had invested the Court of Queen's Bench with the superintendence and control of all inferior criminal jurisdictions."

*   *   *   *   *

In a book referred to above (Paley's *Moral and Political Philosophy*, first published in 1755) which lacks the scientific basis of modern ethics but which, notwithstanding, is full of sound practical wisdom (particularly the chapter which treats *Of the Administration of Justice ;* Book vi, ch. viii), there are laid down four propositions as the guiding principles which should be observed in the administration of justice, *viz.*:

1. "The first maxim of a free state is, that the laws be made by one set of men, and administration by another; in other words, that the legislative and judicial characters be kept separate."

2. "The next security for the impartial administration of justice, especially in decisions to which the government is a party, is the independence of the judges."

3. "A third precaution to be observed in the formation of courts of justice is, that the number of judges be small."

4. "A fourth requisite in the constitution of a court of justice and equivalent to many checks upon the discretion of judges, is, that its proceedings be carried on in public, *apertis foribus*" (p. 311); "Not only before a promiscuous concourse of bystanders, but in the audience of the whole profession of the law. The opinion of the bar concerning what passes, will be impartial, and will commonly guide that of the public."

Tested by each one of these four principles the King's Bench Division, which may be regarded as the chief Criminal Court of the kingdom, the Assizes and Central Criminal Court being offshoots from it, comes out well.

As to the first: it is clear that the Judges, being appointed by the Crown, are independent of Parliament. No Judge can sit in the House of Commons, by Common Law; but it was not till 1875 that the Master of the Rolls was disqualified.

As to the second: the Act of Settlement, 1700–1, provides that the Judges shall hold their offices during good behaviour (*quamdiu se bene gesserint*) and can be dismissed only upon the address of both Houses of Parliament. The effect of this is to render them completely independent of the Crown.

As to the third: the number of Judges of the King's Bench Division is 18 (at present only 16) for a nation of 35,000,000. It is, however, only right to add that there are also about 60 Chairmen of Quarter Sessions and 120 Recorders, before whom indictable offences are tried, and who dispose of the bulk of the criminal work of the country.

As to the fourth: the importance of publicity in legal proceedings has already been insisted on. The influence of the Bar upon English public life and legal proceedings has always been, and still is, considerable. Mr Taswell-Langmead in his *English Constitutional History*, dwells on the learning and ability of lawyers and their services in the cause of freedom.

VI. THE COURT OF CRIMINAL APPEAL

After long agitation a Court of Appeal in Criminal Cases was established in 1908. The immediate cause of its establishment was the remarkable series of official prejudices and mistakes which culminated in the wrongful conviction of Mr Adolf Beck, and brought home to the minds of lawyers and the public at large the necessity for a court for the rectification of such errors. Errors are always possible in every human institution, but the consequences of them are particularly serious in criminal matters.

By the Criminal Appeal Act, 1907, which came into force on April 18, 1908, it was enacted that "There shall be a Court of Criminal Appeal," which now (by an amending Act of 1908) consists of all the Judges of the King's Bench Division. The Court is summoned by direction of the Lord Chief Justice, and must consist of an uneven number of Judges, not less than three. If necessary it may sit in two or more divisions. It sits in London, unless the Lord Chief Justice otherwise directs.

The Lord Chief Justice, if present, is the President of the Court; in his absence the senior Judge present presides. It decides by a majority of the members of the Court who hear the case. Unless the Court directs to the contrary (in cases where the question is one of law and it is convenient that separate judgments should be pronounced), the judgment of the Court is pronounced by the President. If the decision of the Court involves a point of law of exceptional public importance and it is desirable in the public interest that a further appeal should be brought, and if the Attorney-General gives a certificate to that effect, a further appeal, to the House of Lords, is possible; otherwise the decision of this Court is final. The working of the Act is carried on by the Registrar of the Court of Criminal Appeal, assisted by a staff (s. 2).

As to the right of appeal; any person convicted on indictment may appeal to this Court, (a) against his conviction, on any ground of appeal which involves a question of law alone; and (b) *with the leave of this Court, or upon the certificate of the judge who tried him, that it is a fit case for appeal*, against his conviction, on any ground of appeal which involves a question of fact alone, or a question of mixed law and fact, or any other ground which appears to the Court to be a sufficient ground of appeal; and (c) with the leave of the Court of Criminal Appeal, against the sentence passed on his conviction, unless the sentence is one fixed by statute (s. 3).

On any such appeal against a conviction, the Court may allow the appeal, if they think that the verdict of the jury should be set aside on the ground that it is unreasonable or cannot be supported by the evidence, or that the Court before which the appellant was convicted, has wrongly decided any question of law, or if they think that there has been a miscarriage of justice; but in any other case the Court shall dismiss the appeal. Nevertheless, even though the Court are of opinion that the point raised in the appeal might be decided in favour of the appellant, they may dismiss the appeal "if they consider that no substantial miscarriage of justice has actually occurred."

If the appeal against a conviction is allowed, the conviction is quashed and a verdict of acquittal is entered (s. 4).

The Court has on several occasions expressed its strong regret that it has no power to order a new trial. Such a power is very desirable in many cases.

On an appeal against a sentence, if the Court think that a different sentence should have been passed, they may quash the sentence passed at the trial, and pass such other sentence, warranted in law by the verdict (either more or less severe), in substitution therefor as they think ought to have been passed; or they may dismiss the appeal (s. 4 (3)).

If on appeal it appears to the Court that the appellant was guilty of the act or omission charged against him, but he was insane at the time the act was done or the omission was made, so as not to be responsible according to law for his actions, the Court may quash the sentence passed at the trial and order the appellant to be kept in custody as a criminal lunatic under the Trial of Lunatics Act, 1883, as if a special verdict had been found by the jury under that Act (s. 5).

The Court also possesses considerable powers to make orders annulling or varying any order made on a trial as to the revesting and restitution of property on conviction (s. 6).

The person convicted who desires to appeal must give notice of appeal, or notice of his application for leave to appeal, "within ten days of the date of conviction"; but the Court may at any time on application extend the time, except in case of a conviction involving sentence of death. In case of a conviction involving sentence of death or corporal punishment, the sentence shall not be executed until after the prisoner has had an opportunity of appealing.

The judge, or chairman, of any court before whom a person is convicted, in case of an appeal, must furnish to the Registrar his notes of the trial, and also a *report* giving his opinion upon the case or any point arising out of it (s. 8).

A very important provision of the Act is that shorthand notes shall be taken of the proceedings at the trial of any person on indictment, who, if convicted, is entitled or may be authorised to appeal under the Act; and on any appeal, or application for leave to appeal, a transcript of the notes shall be made and furnished to the Registrar for the use of the Court. Under this provision an official shorthand writer has been appointed and attached to each court in which indictable cases are tried.

The Court possesses all necessary and incidental supplementary powers, including the granting of legal assistance to the appellant, who has a right to be present at the hearing of his appeal, if he desires it, except where the appeal is on a question of law only (ss. 9, 10, 11).

As a rule under this Act no costs are allowed on either side, but the expenses of any solicitor or counsel assigned to the appellant, and the expenses of any witnesses attending on the hearing of the appeal, etc., are allowed. The Court may, if it thinks fit, admit an appellant to bail pending the determination of his appeal; but the time during which the appellant is admitted to bail does not count as part of any term of imprisonment or penal servitude which may ultimately be imposed on him.

Finally, nothing in the Act is to affect the prerogative of mercy possessed by the Crown and exercised on the advice of the Home Secretary, who may however refer the whole case to the Court of Criminal Appeal, or seek the assistance of that court, by referring to them for their opinion thereon any point arising out of a petition for the exercise of His Majesty's mercy.

Notwithstanding our vaunted superiority in the administration of justice, the number of cases in which convictions have been quashed or sentences reduced since this Act came into operation has raised a very uncomfortable feeling in the minds of all thinking men as to what took place before the Act was passed. During the nine months of 1908 that the Act was in operation, there were 108 appeals and 326 applications for leave to appeal, of which 79 were granted. "In 18 cases the conviction was quashed, and in 14 the sentence was reduced—a quite sufficient justification for the establishment of this tribunal" (*Law Times*, April 9, 1910, p. 511).

In 1912 there were 615 applications for leave to appeal, and leave was granted in 74 cases. There were also 30 appeals on grounds involving questions of law, five with the certificate of the judge at the trial, and five appeals against sentences of preventive detention, making a total of 114 for hearing. Of these one appeal was abandoned, and in 65 cases the appeal was dismissed; in 19 cases the conviction on sentence was varied, and in 29 the conviction was absolutely quashed.

"Only about six per cent. of the persons convicted on indictment in 1912 sought to have their cases reviewed, and only one in 23 of the persons who invoked the intervention of the Court of Criminal Appeal obtained immediate discharge" (*Introd. to Criminal Statistics for* 1912, p. 10).

"Out of the twenty-five persons sentenced to death (in 1912) seven applied for leave to appeal, and five appealed on grounds involving questions of law. All the appeals were unsuccessful" (*ib.*).

During the four years and nine months this Court has been in existence (down to the end of 1912) the figures show that no less than 2704 persons applied for leave to appeal, and 843 appeals were set down for hearing (of which, however, 17 were abandoned) but in 150 cases the conviction or sentence was varied, and in 141 cases the conviction was quashed. In some of these cases, however, instead of quashing the conviction the Court would have ordered a new trial, had it had the power to do so. It is much to be regretted that this power has not yet been conferred upon it. In some of these cases also there was another indictment on the file on which the prisoner could be tried.

The expenses of the Court of Criminal Appeal for the year which ended March 31, 1914, were £11,213.

Generally speaking, there can be no doubt but that the establishment of the Court of Criminal Appeal has led to a much more careful administration of the law in indictable cases by all concerned. Yet in the face of these figures (141 persons wrongly convicted) it cannot be denied that the establishment of this Court has been abundantly justified.

VII. THE HOUSE OF LORDS AS A CRIMINAL COURT

Notwithstanding the establishment of a Court of Criminal Appeal, and notwithstanding the intentions of the framers of the Judicature Act, 1873, the House of Lords, as the representative of the ancient *Magnum Concilium Regni*, still retains its jurisdiction as the final court of appeal in this kingdom, both in civil and criminal matters. In the latter class of cases, indeed, it is both a court of first instance and a court of appeal. It is not intended here to treat of Impeachment, which is a parliamentary proceeding for the punishment of political crimes, as it is beyond the scope of this book and practically obsolete. The last instance was that of Lord Melville in 1806. Impeachment has been described as "a criminal proceeding in which the Commons are the accusers and all the Lords are the judges, both of fact and of law" (Maitland, *J. and P.* ch. vi). The same learned writer adds: "In the past it has been a powerful engine whereby Parliament has controlled the ministers of the Crown, but there is little likelihood of its being used in the immediate future" (*ib.*). Those who wish to know all about it may consult May's *Law and Usages of Parliament* (10th ed., 1893): Anson, *Law and Custom of the Constitution*, Part I, ch. x. s. 2; and Blackstone, *Comm.* Bk. IV, ch. 19.

The House of Lords is a court of first instance for the trial of peers accused of treason or felony, or the misprision (concealment) of either.

When Parliament is sitting, the trial would take place before a full House. But when Parliament is *not* sitting, the judicial powers of the House of Lords as a court of first instance in criminal matters are delegated to the Court of the Lord High Steward, who summons not less than twenty-three temporal peers, of whom at least twelve must concur in the verdict. (The analogy between this court, though not strictly a jury, and a Grand Jury, and the jury at a Coroner's Inquest, is obvious.) Happily cases of impeachment are now merely historical, and cases of the trial of peers very rare. "Where a grand jury finds a true bill against a peer of the realm, the court must forthwith acquaint the House of Lords. A writ of *certiorari* will then be issued, and the matter removed to the jurisdiction of the House" (*Enc. Laws of Eng.*, vol. 7, sub tit. Jury). The last case of the trial of a peer was the trial of Earl Russell, for bigamy, in 1901, when this course was followed. The indictment was found at the Central Criminal Court; the Recorder of London reported the fact to the House of Lords, and the proceedings were called up into that House by *certiorari*. The Lord Chancellor (Lord Halsbury) was appointed Lord High Steward, and the Judges were required to attend the trial. Eleven of them did so.

As a Court of Appeal in criminal matters, its functions, before the establishment of the Court of Criminal Appeal, were confined to dealing by way of Writ of Error with "errors of law which appeared on the face of the record," a very rare class of cases. The Criminal Appeal Act of 1907 provides that the decisions of the court thereby created "shall be final, and no appeal shall lie from that court to any other court" (s. 1 (6)), except, as we have seen, in cases of exceptional public importance and interest. In such cases there may still be an appeal to the House of Lords, if either the Director of Public Prosecutions, the prosecutor, or the defendant, obtains a certificate to that effect from the Attorney-General. For instances of such appeals see *Rex* v. *Ball* [1911] A.C. 47; *Felstead* v. *Rex* [1914] A.C. 534 and *Rex* v. *Christie* [1914] A.C. 545.

The constitution of the House of Lords when sitting as a Court of Appeal in criminal matters would no doubt be the same as when sitting as a Court of Appeal in civil matters, *viz.* the Lord Chancellor (as President), the four Lords of Appeal in Ordinary, who receive salaries and are life peers (to secure a quorum, three, of properly qualified peers), and such of the Law Lords, *i.e.* peers who hold or have held "high judicial office," as care to attend.

THE POSITION OF THE LORD CHANCELLOR IN REGARD TO CRIMINAL LAW

Although the Lord High Chancellor is the head of our judicature, he has singularly little to do with the administration of the criminal law. Beyond the fact that the judges of the High

Court and Justices of the Peace are appointed by the Crown on his nomination, and that he may sit as a Judge in the House of Lords on the rare occasions when it sits to deal with criminal matters, he has practically nothing to do with crime. The reason for this appears to be twofold, and both reasons are connected with the history of his office. In the first place, before the Judicature Acts, 1873 and 1875, the Lord Chancellor was the chief Judge in Equity. Now criminal law is essentially a matter of Common Law, and the chief Common Law Judge was the Lord Chief Justice of England, the head of the Court of King's Bench, which, as we have seen, was the chief criminal court and exercised supervision over all inferior criminal courts. The Lord Chancellor, as a Judge, was never brought into contact with the criminal law, except in the issue by him of the writ of *habeas corpus*. In the second place it happened that just about the time the Home Secretary rose into prominence as a great executive officer of state, about a hundred years ago, there was a sudden and large increase in the urban population and a corresponding extension of the sphere of local government, and consequently many of the executive duties in regard to the administration of the criminal law, which might otherwise have fallen upon the Lord Chancellor, were imposed on the Home Secretary. The placing of the Metropolitan Police, on its establishment in 1829, under the immediate control of the Home Secretary brought him into direct connection with the administration of justice. The Municipal Corporations Act, 1835, provided that a separate Commission of the Peace might be granted to a borough on the recommendation of the Home Secretary, and the tendency of recent legislation has been to put all duties and powers of a purely administrative or executive character on him, leaving to the Lord Chancellor the control of purely judicial and civil matters. Thus the Lord Chancellor, by statute, appoints the County Court Judges, that being a civil matter. On the other hand the Home Secretary appoints the Metropolitan magistrates and stipendiaries.

The Lord Chancellor, however, and not the Home Secretary, makes Rules for the carrying out of the Summary Jurisdiction Acts (see s. 29, S.J.A., 1879) and this power has recently been extended by s. 40 of the C.J.A. Act, 1814. This is a matter which appertains to the executive rather than to the judicial power; but it is understood that these rules, though signed by the Lord Chancellor so as to give them effect, are really prepared in the Home Office.

VIII. THE JUDICIAL COMMITTEE OF THE PRIVY COUNCIL (AS AN IMPERIAL COURT OF CRIMINAL APPEAL)

Although not quite within the purview of this work, it may not be altogether out of place to state the position of the above-named authority in regard to criminal law, more particularly as the matter has very recently been the subject of an important judicial pronouncement. In *Arnold* v. *The King-Emperor* (L.T. Rep. Vol. III, p. 324; Oct. 24, 1914) it was decided that "although the Crown has authority, by virtue of the prerogative to review the decisions of all colonial courts, whether the proceedings be of a civil or a criminal character, unless such authority has been expressly parted with, the Judicial Committee will not review or interfere with the course of criminal law *unless there has been such an interference with the elementary rights of an accused as has placed him outside the pale of regular law, or unless, within that pale, there has been a violation of the natural principles of justice* so demonstratively manifest as to convince their Lordships that the result arrived at was opposite to the result which they would themselves have reached, and that the same opposite result would have been reached by the local tribunal if the alleged defect or misdirection had been avoided."

The judgment of the Board (*i.e.* the Committee) was delivered by Lord Shaw, who in the course of it said: "The frequency of the applications made to the Board for leave to appeal against the judgment of criminal tribunals in various parts of the Empire, as well as the thoroughness with which the powers and practice of the Judicial Committee were discussed in this case, incline their Lordships to make a deliberate survey of this important topic."

"The question is not truly one of jurisdiction. The power of His Majesty, under his royal authority, to review proceedings of a criminal nature, unless where such power and authority have been parted with by statute, is undoubted. Upon the other hand, there are reasons, both constitutional and administrative, which make it manifest that this power should not be lightly exercised. The overruling consideration upon the topic has reference to Justice itself. If throughout the Empire it were supposed that the course and execution of justice could suffer serious impediment, which in many cases might amount to practical obstruction, by an appeal to the royal prerogative of review on judicial grounds, then it becomes plain that a severe blow would have been dealt to the ordered administration of law within the King's dominions."

He then proceeded to discuss the authorities, *i.e.* the decided cases, and state the practice of the Committee as given above. From these authorities it appears that the Board will not interfere unless they are of opinion that the sentence pronounced against the appellant "formed such an invasion of liberty and such a denial of his just rights as a citizen that their Lordships feel called upon to interfere," on the ground that "justice has gravely and injuriously miscarried."

In other words, the Judicial Committee is not a general Court of Criminal Appeal for the colonies and dependencies of the British Crown, and it will interfere only in extreme cases, "in which it must be established demonstrably that justice itself in its very foundations has been subverted, and that it is therefore a matter of general Imperial concern that by way of appeal to the King it can then be restored to its rightful position in that part of the empire[1]."

The position of the Committee in this respect reminds one very strongly of what Sir F. Pollock has called the "residual jurisdiction" of the Crown, which gave rise to the Court of Star Chamber, that court of "criminal equity," possessing "extraordinary criminal jurisdiction"—"analogous to the equitable jurisdiction of the Chancellor in civil matters"—before it became an instrument of tyranny. The foundation of both jurisdictions is the same, *viz.* the royal prerogative, which "is nothing but the law specially concerning the King." (See *Exp. Com. Law*, ch. III.)

---

[1] *Cf.* the case of *Ibrahim* v. *The King* [1914] A.C. 599; where their Lordships declined to interfere.

The survival of this relic of a power that was once vast and unlimited, and its present application to a purpose that was never contemplated in its inception, when England was a small self-contained kingdom, *viz.* the preservation of justice throughout a great empire, is a striking example of the continuity and vitality of our institutions. It speaks of a time when the King was in deed and in truth the source and fount of justice, as he still is, subject only to the law.

Another manifestation of the royal prerogative is that of mercy, now exercised by the Crown on the advice of the Home Secretary. It is something above and beyond the ordinary law (see p. 146).

THE ATTORNEY-GENERAL, THE SOLICITOR-GENERAL, AND THE DIRECTOR OF PUBLIC PROSECUTIONS

These three officials play a very important part in the administration of the criminal law. It is they who, in very important cases, set the criminal law in motion and (or) afterwards conduct or control the proceedings.

The Attorney-General is the chief law officer of the Crown, and a great officer of State. He is appointed by letters patent, and is *ex officio* head of the Bar so long as he holds the office. The office is now a political one, and the holder goes out of office with the party to which he belongs. But the English law officers (unlike the Scottish and Irish) are not usually privy councillors.

The Attorney-General has the superintendence of all legal proceedings affecting the royal prerogative. He is also the chief legal adviser of all the various departments of Government. It is a matter almost of necessity that he should be a member of the House of Commons, as he takes charge of all legal measures and affairs in that House. He is a member of the Government or Administration in office, but he is not a member of the Cabinet. He prosecutes for the Crown in all important criminal matters and in revenue cases. There are many legal proceedings which cannot be initiated without his sanction (see Appendix E).

He, or during the vacancy of his office, the Solicitor-General, may, in the exercise of their discretion, file informations for misdemeanours in the King's Bench Division, but this right is seldom exercised except in cases of a dangerous and serious nature requiring immediate action on the part of the law officers of the Crown, *e.g.* sedition, libel, etc. No *ex officio* information, we believe, was filed after 1887, until the recent case of *Rex* v. *Mylius.*

As representative of the Crown in criminal matters the Attorney-General has power to enter a *nolle prosequi,* and he may do so *ex mero motu,* without consulting the prosecutor. On the application of the Attorney-General, acting officially, writs of *certiorari* will be granted as a matter of right, to remove any conviction or order of a Court of Summary Jurisdiction into the King's Bench Division without any affidavit and without service of any notice on the Justices.

The Attorney-General is the only legal representative of the Crown in the courts, but the courts exercise over him the same authority as they exercise over every other suitor; and accordingly he is not permitted to proceed with any matter which is merely vexatious and has no legal object.

Although he is an officer of the Crown, he is also, in a sense, an officer of the public, and he may properly take proceedings on behalf of the public, when acts tending to the injury of the public are being done without lawful authority, though no evidence can be produced of actual injury; and when he is suing on behalf of the public, delay or laches (acquiescence) cannot be imputed to him, as it may to a private individual.

The law officers of the Crown were formerly allowed to take private practice, but this privilege has now been abrogated. By a Treasury Minute of 1895 it is prescribed that the Attorney-General and Solicitor-General shall not for the future undertake business of any kind on behalf of private clients, but shall, instead, receive salaries of £7000 and £6000 per annum respectively, and in addition fees, according to the ordinary professional scale, in respect of all contentious business, criminal or civil, in which they represent the Government, either as prosecutor, plaintiff, or defendant.

Both the Attorney-General and the Solicitor-General, when they appear in court in person to prosecute, have a right of reply in all cases, whether evidence is adduced for the defence or not. Other counsel have no such right unless the prisoner submits some evidence.

The Solicitor-General is also one of the law officers of the Crown and is appointed by letters patent. His office, like that of the Attorney-General, is semi-political and depends upon the continuance in power of the party to which he belongs. He is a member of the Government, but not of the Cabinet, and his duties also require that he should be a member of the House of Commons. He is an *ex officio* member of the General Council of the Bar. His duties are substantially the same as those of the Attorney-General, to whom he is subordinate and assistant.

The same regulations as regards private practice, salary and fees, apply to him as to the Attorney-General; and when he appears in court on behalf of the Crown he has the same right of reply.

Before 1879 there was no provision for the systematic prosecution of offences in England such as there was in Scotland and in most countries on the Continent. Except in those cases in which the Attorney-General intervened on the ground that they were of special public importance, the initiation of prosecutions was left to the injured parties, encouraged by the provision made for defraying the costs of the prosecution out of the public funds. By the Prosecution of Offences Acts, 1879 and 1884, more adequate provisions were made for a national and public system of prosecutions. By the Act of 1879 a new department of "Director of Public Prosecutions" was created, to be distinct from the previously existing legal departments of the Crown. By the Act of 1884 this department was merged in that of the Solicitor to the Treasury. But this arrangement was found not to work well, and accordingly, by the Prosecution of Offences Act, 1908, the two departments were again separated and power was given to the Secretary of State to appoint a Director of Public Prosecutions, and such number of assistant directors as the Treasury may sanction. Nothing in the Acts of 1879, 1884 and 1908 precludes any person from instituting or carrying on any criminal proceedings, so that the rights of private prosecutors are preserved; but the Director of Public Prosecutions may, if he thinks fit, at any stage, undertake the conduct of the proceedings.

He is subject in all matters, including the selection and instruction of counsel, to the directions of the Attorney-General.

By the regulations in force the duties of the Director are generally (under the supervision of the Attorney-General)—

1. To institute, undertake or carry on criminal proceedings, at any stage, and in any court;

2. To give advice and assistance to all persons concerned in criminal proceedings, whether officials or not, as to the conduct of the proceedings. The cases in which he is to act thus are prescribed by regulations made under the Act.

The Director *must* institute, undertake or carry on criminal proceedings in the following matters:

a. All offences punishable with death;

b. Offences the prosecution of which, prior to 1886, was undertaken by the Treasury Solicitor, *e.g.* coinage offences;

c. Cases in which he receives an order from the Secretary of State or Attorney-General;

d. Wherever it appears to him that the offence, or the circumstances of its commission, is or are such as to call for prosecution, in the public interest, or is such as, owing to its importance or difficulty, is unlikely to be prosecuted without his intervention;

e. Cases in which prosecutions are ordered by the Boards of Trade or Agriculture.

By s. 2 of the Merchandise Marks Act, 1891 (54 Vict. c. 15), the Board of Trade may, with the concurrence of the Lord Chancellor, make regulations providing that in cases appearing to the Board to affect the general interests of the country, or of a section of the community, or of a trade, the prosecution of offences under this Act shall be undertaken by the Board of Trade, and prescribing the conditions on which such prosecutions are to be undertaken. The expenses of prosecutions so undertaken shall be paid out of monies provided by Parliament, and the regulations so made are to be laid before Parliament as prescribed. The power of any other person to prosecute is not, however, affected.

The Board of Agriculture and Fisheries may also prosecute in cases which appear to the court to relate to agricultural or horticultural produce [Merchandise Marks (Prosecutions) Act, 1894] or to the produce of any fishing industry [Board of Agriculture and Fisheries Act, 1903 (3 Edw. VII, c. 31) s. 18)].

In these cases the Director of Public prosecutions takes up the prosecution by virtue of his office.

He has also important duties with respect to attending the trial of Election Petitions and prosecuting for election offences.

In all these cases he may take such steps as he may deem necessary; and as regards cases in the Court of Criminal Appeal, where no counsel is instructed for the prosecution, he may instruct counsel, if he thinks the case of sufficient importance, or if he is so directed by the Attorney-General.

He *may*, on his own initiative, or on application to him, give advice, in any case of importance or difficulty, to Justices, their clerks, chief officers of police or other persons; and he may assist private prosecutors by authorising them to incur special costs in obtaining scientific evidence, in preparing plans or models, in paying special fees to counsel, or for any special purpose sanctioned by the Attorney-General.

He may even sanction retrospectively the payment of such costs, where they have been properly incurred, on an emergency, without his previous authority. He may employ a solicitor as his agent in a prosecution, and after examining his charges certify them as reasonable and proper to be paid.

He cannot be compelled to disclose the sources of his information in any case in which he undertakes the prosecution. He is not bound over to prosecute, nor required to give security for costs, if he takes up a case. His intervention, however, does not affect the right of any person to obtain restitution of property. Subject to what is said above the costs of public prosecutions are defrayed in the same way as those of private prosecutions.

The chief officers of police of every district are required to give information to the Director of Public Prosecutions with respect to certain indictable offences alleged to have been committed within their districts, *viz.*:

1. All offences punishable with death;
2. Other offences which appear to the officer to be of such importance or difficulty as to render the assistance of the Director desirable.

When the Director has instituted or undertaken or is carrying on criminal proceedings, it is his duty to give notice to the Justice or Coroner; and it is the duty of the person receiving such notice (subject to any special direction by the Attorney-General), within three days of its receipt, to transmit to the Director by registered letter or by railway or messenger, every recognizance, information, certificate, requisition, deposition, document and thing connected with the case, which it would otherwise be his duty by law to deliver to the proper officer of the court of trial. Failure to comply with this application exposes the Justice or Coroner to certain penalties, to be fixed by the court of trial.

On receipt of the documents, etc., the Director is under the same obligation as to giving copies, etc., as the Coroner, Justice or officer of the court of trial; and he must, within a reasonable time before the trial, cause the originals to be delivered to the proper officer of the court of trial.

When a prosecution for any offence, whether indictable or not, instituted before a Court of Summary Jurisdiction, is withdrawn, or not proceeded with within a reasonable time, the clerk of the court must send to the Director a letter stating the circumstances of the case, and enquiring whether he wishes for a copy of the documents, etc. The effect of this provision is to put a check on the improper withdrawal of criminal proceedings.

The Public Prosecutor makes an Annual Report of the work of himself and his department to the Home Secretary, and this Report is laid before Parliament.

In his Annual Report for 1913 the Public Prosecutor sets forth the number, nature, result, and cost of the proceedings instituted by him during that year; from which it appears that he prosecuted in 503 cases (including Mint cases); he appeared in 165 cases under the Criminal Appeal Act, 1907; and granted his consent in 101 cases, and refused it in 47, under the Prevention of Crimes Act, 1908. Applications were made to him in 1229 other matters in respect of criminal or alleged criminal offences, in which he did not institute or adopt prosecutions. These included appeals to Quarter Sessions, extradition and miscellaneous matters.

In 1913 there were 118 charges of murder, against 128 persons (61 men and 67 women); 24 men were convicted of murder, 1 as an accessory after the fact, and 17 of manslaughter; 4 women were convicted of murder, 9 of manslaughter and 19 of concealment of birth or some lesser offence. Of 15 prisoners charged with manslaughter, where the cases were taken up by the Public Prosecutor, 5 were convicted.

In 8 cases the Public Prosecutor considered it to be his duty to take proceedings against solicitors for alleged misappropriation of clients' moneys; in 4 cases there were convictions and sentences of penal servitude.

PART III. THE EXECUTIVE IN RELATION TO CRIME

I. THE HOME SECRETARY AND THE HOME OFFICE

At the back of our legal and judicial system, overshadowing it, and always ready to intervene, if needs be, stands the Home Secretary. This great officer of state, whose proper title is "His Majesty's Principal Secretary of State for Home Affairs," has under his supervision and control the whole internal organisation and economy of the country. We are, however, concerned with him only in his relations to the administration of justice. The office of Home Secretary, like that of the Attorney-General and Solicitor-General, is a political one, the holder of it is always a member of the Cabinet and a Privy Councillor, and comes in and goes out of office with the party to which he belongs. From being a mere personal and confidential servant of the King he has come to be a great executive officer of state in a democratic country; and his position may perhaps be compared most justly with the "Minister of the Interior," or the "Minister of Justice," in France[1]. On his advice, approved by his colleagues in the Cabinet, the Crown acts in all matters relating to the administration of the criminal law and "the safety, honour and welfare of our Sovereign and his Dominions," *i.e.* so far as England and Wales are concerned. The Home Secretary has as his assistant a Parliamentary Under-Secretary, who is also a politician, and whose continuance in office depends on that of his party, but he is not a member of the Cabinet.

There are five Principal Secretaries of State, of whom the Home Secretary is one. Theoretically all the five Principal Secretaries of State have equal and co-ordinate powers. ["Except in so far as statute gives powers to one or other of the five Secretaries of State, each is capable of performing any one of the functions of the various departments" (Anson, *L. & C.C.* vol. II, p. 159).] Custom and usage, however, are gradually crystallising their respective spheres. It is only in comparatively recent times and as a matter of convenience that their functions have become specialised. Consequently Acts of Parliament do not, as a rule, speak of the Home Secretary specifically, but simply say a "Secretary of State" or "one of His Majesty's principal Secretaries of State." If the matter falls within the Home Secretary's department then he is the Secretary of State referred to or intended.

The Home Secretary is at the head of the Home Office, located in Whitehall, S.W. and for the time being influences its policy and activity; but in order to secure permanence and continuity of the work, there is also a Permanent Under-Secretary, three Assistant Under-Secretaries (one who devotes his attention entirely to legal matters) and six Principal Clerks, who are all permanent officials and highly trained Civil Servants, specialists in their own branches; and these, together with a

---

[1] The late Professor Maitland suggested (*Justice and Police*, ch. VI.), that the appropriate title of the Home Secretary would be "The Minister of Criminal Justice and Police"; but he has many other functions to perform of a general and domestic nature in no way connected with the criminal law, *e.g.* the regulation of Factories and Mines.

number of Senior and Junior Clerks and Clerks for special purposes, *e.g.* statistics, constitute the working staff of the Home Office.

The connection of the Home Secretary with prisons and prison administration, because of its importance, is dealt with separately hereafter. The Prison Commission is really a sub-department of the Home Office; as is also the recently established Board of Control (Mental Deficiency). The duties of the Home Secretary in regard to prisons, says Sir Wm. Anson, forms a "long history of prison management and discipline," falling under the two heads of punishment and prevention.

Speaking generally, the first and chief duty of the Home Secretary is the maintenance of law and order and the suppression of crime in England and Wales. He is the medium of communication between the Crown and its subjects, by which the King acquaints his people with his pleasure; and all addresses to the Crown and replies thereto are forwarded through him. He has a general responsibility to Parliament for the administration of criminal justice and the exercise of their duties by magistrates and the police. If anything goes wrong in the administration of justice it is the Home Secretary to whom questions are addressed in the House of Commons, and it is in this way that Parliament exercises over him, and over the executive department of which he is the head, its powers of criticism and censure, and so brings him and it into touch with public opinion, the basis of modern government.

Dealing first with the Home Secretary's indirect powers in regard to the administration of justice, that is to say, his powers as to the maintenance of the peace and the enforcement of public order; he admits to citizenship, at his discretion, by means of letters of naturalisation; he controls part of the secret service money voted by Parliament, and in this way is enabled to keep an eye on undesirable aliens; he may detain and open letters in the Post Office, a power rarely used; he controls the movements of the King's subjects and for this purpose he may obtain, without showing cause, the issue of the writ *ne exeat regno*; he may authorise the appointment of special constables and call out the Reserve Forces of the Crown for the purpose of suppressing or preventing real or anticipated disorder. Although

he is not a Justice of the Peace *ex officio*, he may, in virtue of
the power of the Crown delegated to him, commit to prison
any person charged with treason or an offence against the
State.

As to his direct powers, it has been very well said, by Sir
William Anson, that "as regards the control of courts, his powers
increase as the importance of the court diminishes." Thus he
has practically no control whatever over the Judges of the High
Court, but he has a very real and effectual control over Justices
of the Peace. He advises the Crown as to the frequency of holding
or not holding Assizes, and the best arrangements for the trial
of prisoners. He has little to do with County Quarter Sessions,
except those for the County of London, but much with Borough
Quarter Sessions. It is on his advice that the Crown grants to
a Borough a separate Court of Quarter Sessions; the Recorder
is appointed by the Crown on his recommendation, and any
increase in the Recorder's salary, the holding of Sessions more
than four times a year, and the appointment of a Deputy or
Assistant Recorder, are all in his discretion.

It is on his recommendation that the Crown appoints the
Chairman and Deputy Chairman of the County of London
Sessions, and their salaries, though paid by the London County
Council, are settled in consultation with the Home Office.

The appointment of Police Magistrates in the Metropolis, and
of Stipendiary Magistrates elsewhere, is in his hands, and he
regulates the business of their courts. He settles the salaries of
Clerks of the Peace, in counties and in boroughs, and the fees to
be paid to them are subject to his approval. He has various
functions to perform with regard to Clerks to Justices. He
fixes the table of allowances to be paid to prosecutors and
witnesses in criminal cases, and it may in fact be said that
whenever Parliament has imposed duties in connection with
criminal justice on any Minister of the Crown, that Minister
has almost invariably been the Home Secretary.

Should a bench of magistrates unfortunately make a mistake,
a private admonition from the Home Secretary is usually all
that is made in order to keep them within due bounds and make
them more careful for the future. It is only in very grave cases

(happily very rare) that it is necessary for him to intervene publicly.

Upon all these matters and many others, directly and indirectly affecting the administration of justice, the Home Secretary, through the Home Office, is in constant communication and inter-communication with the other Government Departments, the Lord Chancellor and the Judges, the Law Officers of the Crown, the Sheriffs and Governors of Prisons, Coroners, the heads of Police, the Clerks of Assize, the Clerks of the Peace and Clerks to Magistrates, as well as with the Public Prosecutor,—advising, consulting, assisting, controlling, and in some cases supplying the motive power, by urging them to take action—keeping in working order the vast, far reaching and complicated machinery of the administration of criminal justice in all its parts.

We see here the connection between Constitutional Law and Criminal Law, since the Home Secretary is the connecting link, at the apex of the executive system, between the legislature (Parliament) on the one hand, and the judiciary (including in this term both the Judges of the High Court, Recorders, and Justices of the Peace) on the other hand. In a word he represents the Crown as head of the executive. Yet it is only *before* and *after* trial that the work of the Home Secretary appears. With the conduct of a trial itself he has nothing to do. The Judges (including all those mentioned above) while exercising their judicial functions are absolutely unfettered and free from control by the Home Secretary. Hence they are equally independent of the executive, as we have seen (p. 125) they are of the legislative, branch of our government.

"*Si la justice anglaise—plus redoutée des malfaiteurs qu'aucune autre justice dans le monde entier—est universellement respectée, si personne ne critique ses décisions, si tous les sujets du roi Edouard VII sont fiers d'elle, cela tient à deux raisons principales : la première c'est qu'elle traite les accusés et exige qu'on les traite avec impartialité ; la seconde—d'où tout dépend—c'est qu'elle est complètement indépendante du pouvoir exécutif*" (article by M. Michels on "La Justice Criminelle en Angleterre," *Le Gaulois*, December 20, 1909).

The practice of the Home Office in issuing circulars to Justices of the Peace and their Clerks has been mentioned above (p. 70), yet in so doing there is nothing on the part of the Home Secretary in the nature of "tuning the pulpits." The circulars in question are designed simply to assist Justices of the Peace in the exercise of their duties; many of them are laymen, not lawyers, and are not always able to obtain easily the information they require. There is no attempt made to influence them in what is beyond all question the most important of their duties, *viz.* the exercise of their judicial discretion. They are told only what they *may* do, not what they *must*. It rests entirely with them to say what they *will* do, so long as they do not exceed their jurisdiction.

Of late years a great number of duties and powers of a statutory character have been placed upon the Home Secretary. "The bulk of the present work of the Home Office," says Sir Wm. Anson, "is the creation of modern statutes." But there are a few of the Home Secretary's powers and duties which require special mention, *viz.*: (1) his duty to advise the Crown in regard to the exercise of its prerogative of mercy; (2) his duty in regard to the extradition of criminals; (3) his power to make rules for the carrying out of various Acts of Parliament; and (4) the work of the Home Office in the collection and digesting of statistics.

(1) The first of these powers or duties, *viz.* the prerogative of mercy or the right to pardon, is perhaps the best known of the Home Secretary's functions. Certainly it is the one which looms up most largely in the public eye. "This prerogative is nothing more (nor less) than an exercise of a discretion on the part of the Crown to modify punishments which Common Law or Statute would require to be inflicted" (Anson). It is in fact a survival, in an unobjectionable form, of the old dispensing power of the Crown, and would probably never have assumed the importance it has but for the fact that, before the establishment of the Court of Criminal Appeal, there was no other means of rectifying the mistakes of the Criminal Law, except by Writ of Error, a highly technical and narrow proceeding, and by the Court for the Consideration of Crown Cases Reserved, both now abolished. There are, however, certain limits to its exercise. In the first place it cannot be exercised in cases of a public

THE PREROGATIVE OF MERCY

character. Thus the Crown cannot pardon the creation of a public nuisance until the nuisance is remedied. In the second place it must not affect private rights, *i.e.* civil rights, and thirdly it must not be anticipatory, *e.g.* the Act of Settlement provides that no pardon granted by the Crown can be pleaded by a Minister as a bar to an impeachment by the House of Commons. Fourthly, it cannot be pleaded as a defence to a charge of sending a person out of the kingdom to avoid a writ of *habeas corpus*. Finally, it must not do more than grant an immunity, *e.g.* if an office has been corruptly acquired the Crown may relieve from the penalty but not from the liability to vacate the office.

The form which the exercise of the prerogative of mercy takes is twofold. It may be by reprieve, *i.e.* postponement of execution, or by pardon. No formality is required for the exercise of the former, it consists simply of an official communication from the Home Secretary to the officer responsible for carrying out the sentence, usually the Sheriff. Formerly no pardon was complete unless it were granted under the great seal of the realm; but since 1827 it has been sufficient if it be granted under a sign manual warrant, countersigned by the Home Secretary. A pardon may be absolute, *i.e.* unconditional, or conditional. In the former case it takes effect at once; in the latter case only on performance of the condition. A conditional pardon is in effect a commutation of sentence. A free pardon relieves a man of all the consequences of conviction; while a remission of sentence merely relieves him of part or the whole of the penalty imposed.

Professor Maitland says of the prerogative of mercy, that "a clumsier means could hardly be imagined of practically nullifying an unsatisfactory verdict." Be this as it may, the prerogative of the Crown was preserved by the Act which created the Court of Criminal Appeal; but the Act enabled the Home Secretary to seek the assistance of that Court in the exercise of it (see p. 128).

It is said, however, that the establishment of the Court of Criminal Appeal, so far from having lightened the work of the Home Office in this respect, has considerably increased it.

It will surprise most people to hear that in the year 1912 the prerogative of mercy was exercised in regard to no less than 495 persons, 320 males and 175 females; in 114 cases, however, the remission was simply that of liability to police supervision. In only four cases, less than one per cent. of the whole, were free pardons granted. Out of 25 sentences of death 10 were commuted to penal servitude for life; 57 convicts were released on licence at earlier dates than they would have been in the ordinary course. Remissions of various terms of penal servitude, imprisonment, and other punishments were granted to 305 persons. In 265 cases there was a simple mitigation of sentence; in 172 the remission was on medical grounds, and in only 13 cases on grounds affecting the conviction.

(2) Secondly, most civilised countries have now made arrangements with each other by which criminals who have committed crimes in one country and managed to escape from justice into another country may be handed over to the country in which the crime was committed to be there tried and punished. This arrangement is known as extradition. In England the Extradition Acts, 1870, 1873 and 1895 afford a complete system of extradition law, specifying the crimes for which extradition may be granted, the persons who may be extradited, the conditions of surrender, and the procedure. It will be easily understood that no State makes any attempt to enforce the processes of its own law in the territory of another, the integrity of which is jealously guarded. In other words with one or two exceptions Criminal Law is strictly territorial. The only two offences known to English Law which are extra-territorial are murder and bigamy. If either of these offences is committed by an English subject on land, no matter where, he may be punished for it whenever he comes within the jurisdiction of our courts. In the same way each country may punish an offence committed against its own laws by a subject of another State while resident in the country where the offence is committed. In all other cases the process of extradition is required.

By s. 2 of the Act of 1870 (which is the principal Act) "where an arrangement has been made with any foreign state with respect to the surrender to such state of any fugitive criminals,

His Majesty may, by Order in Council, direct that this Act shall apply in case of such foreign state." Every such order must recite or embody the terms of the arrangement, and must be laid before both Houses of Parliament and published in the London Gazette. The Crown takes good care that the arrangement so made, whether by treaty or convention, is a reciprocal one, and the treaties or conventions are usually terminable at six months notice. Most countries refuse to give up their own subjects.

Such treaties or conventions have now been made with all European countries, except Turkey and Greece, and with most other countries of the world with any pretentions to civilization and importance, but they vary very greatly in their terms.

There are certain restrictions on the surrender of criminals under the Extradition Acts. In the first place, in England it is strictly limited to non-political offences. England is and always has been the traditional home of freedom and the refuge of those who are "rightly struggling to be free," and she will not surrender a person whose offence is or is suspected to be a purely political one, in order that the vengeance of tyranny may be wreaked upon him. His offence must be a *crime*, in the strict sense. This raises the question, What is a political offence, or "offence of a political character"? Sir J. F. Stephen, in his *History of the Criminal Law* (Vol. II, ch. 16), discusses the meaning of the term "offence of a political character," and shows that it is capable of at least three meanings. The conclusion at which he arrives is that the true meaning of the expression is an offence which is "incidental to and forms part of political disturbances," *viz.* the struggle between two recognised parties holding different views in a State. This is the definition adopted in one of the few cases which have come before the High Court for decision (*in re Castigione*), though it is logically defective, since it contains the thing to be defined. Thus the causing of bomb explosions by an anarchist would not be regarded as an offence of a political character but a crime against humanity. The expression is a vague and ambiguous one, but applications for extradition which raise the question are of very rare occurrence. A prisoner committed for extradition

may apply to the High Court for *habeas corpus* on the ground
that the offence charged is of this character.

Further, the alleged criminal is not to be tried in the country
to which he is given up for any other crime than that for which
he is surrendered, unless he has first had an opportunity of
returning to His Majesty's Dominions; if he is accused of some
offence committed within the English jurisdiction, he will not be
surrendered until he has been tried and acquitted, or has undergone sentence, for that offence here; moreover, he is not to be
surrendered until the expiration of fifteen days after he is committed to prison to await surrender.

The procedure by which extradition is effected is as follows.
The first step may be taken in one of two ways. A requisition
for the surrender of a fugitive criminal, who is suspected of being
in the United Kingdom, may be made to the Home Secretary by
a recognised diplomatic representative of the State which demands
his surrender. The Home Secretary may then, by order under
his hand and seal, signify to a "police magistrate" (see p. 152)
that such requisition has been made and require him to issue a
warrant for the apprehension of the alleged criminal. If the
Home Secretary is of opinion that the offence is one "of a political
character," he may refuse to make any such order, and may
also, at any time, order a fugitive criminal accused or convicted
of such an offence to be discharged from custody. On the receipt
of the said order of the Home Secretary, and on such evidence
as would in his opinion justify the issue of a warrant if the crime
had been committed in England, the police magistrate may issue
a warrant for the apprehension of the accused person. This is
the course usually adopted. But a police magistrate, or *any*
justice of the peace in any part of the United Kingdom, on such
information or complaint and such evidence as would in his
opinion justify the issue of a warrant if the crime had been committed in that part of the United Kingdom in which he exercises
jurisdiction, may, *without* the order of the Home Secretary, issue
a warrant for the apprehension of such accused person; in such
circumstances, however, he shall forthwith send a report of the
fact of such issue, together with the evidence and information
or complaint or certified copies thereof, to the Home Secretary,

who may, if he think fit, order the warrant to be cancelled and the person who has been apprehended to be discharged. This is the second mode of apprehension. A fugitive criminal who is apprehended on a warrant issued *without* the order of the Home Secretary must be brought up before a "police magistrate"; and must be discharged by the police magistrate, unless within such reasonable time as the police magistrate may fix, with reference to the circumstances of the case, such magistrate receives from the Home Secretary an order signifying that a requisition for the surrender of such criminals has been made. So that ultimately a requisition for surrender, and the intervention of the Home Secretary, is necessary in every case, however the apprehension may be effected.

When a fugitive criminal is brought before the "police magistrate" he hears the case in the same manner and has the same jurisdiction and powers, as nearly as may be, as if the prisoner were brought before him charged with an indictable offence committed in England, and he receives any evidence to show that the crime of which the prisoner is accused is "an offence of a political character" or is not an "extradition crime." If the police magistrate comes to the conclusion that the foreign warrant is duly authenticated, and that the evidence produced (subject to the provisions of this Act) is such as would justify him in committing the prisoner for trial, if the crime of which he is accused had been committed in England, he commits him to prison; but otherwise, he orders him to be discharged.

The prisoner is to be committed to some prison in Middlesex, there to await the warrant of the Home Secretary for his surrender; and the police magistrate must forthwith send to the Home Secretary a certificate of the committal. He must also inform such criminal that he will not be surrendered until after the expiration of fifteen days and that he has a right to apply for a writ of *habeas corpus*. Unless he is defended by competent legal advisers the magistrate will also probably explain to him what this means (see p. 155). In this case the writ of *habeas corpus* affords a means of appealing from the decision of the Home Secretary and police magistrate to the Judges of the High Court. An innocent prisoner has therefore three chances of escape, *viz.*: (1) he may be released by the Home Secretary; or (2) by the police magistrate; or (3) by a Judge of the High Court, when brought before him on *habeas corpus*.

After the expiration of fifteen days, if no writ of *habeas corpus* is issued, or if such writ is issued, after the decision of the court upon the return to the writ, or after such further period as may be allowed by the Home Secretary, the Home Secretary may by warrant under his hand and seal order the fugitive criminal (if not released by the decision of the court) to be surrendered to a person duly authorised to receive him by the foreign State from which the requisition for his surrender proceeded, and such fugitive criminal is then surrendered accordingly. But if the fugitive criminal is not conveyed out of the kingdom within two months he is to be discharged, upon application made by him to a judge of the High Court, unless sufficient cause is shown to the contrary.

It will thus be seen that the alleged fugitive criminal has every opportunity of showing that the offence of which he is accused is a political one, or that it is not an "extradition crime," *i.e.* one included in the treaty under which his surrender is claimed (in addition to any defence which would be open to him if the alleged crime had been committed in England), and that his interests are protected in every way.

The term "police magistrate" wherever used throughout these Acts, means the chief magistrate of the Metropolitan Police Courts, or one of the other magistrates of the Metropolitan Police Court in Bow Street, London; Bow Street being the chief Metropolitan Police Court and the chief magistrate sitting there. Until the passing of the Extradition Act, 1895, all extradition cases were heard at Bow Street; but that Act authorised the hearing of them elsewhere; and now the Home Secretary may in his discretion direct the case to be heard where the prisoner was apprehended, or for the time being is, if his removal to Bow Street would be dangerous or prejudicial to his health.

As to what are "extradition crimes," they are set out in the schedules to the Acts of 1870 and 1873. They include murder, manslaughter, coinage offences, forgery, embezzlement, larceny, false pretences, frauds, rape, arson, burglary and housebreaking, robbery with violence, piracy, kidnapping and false imprisonment, perjury, etc., in fact all the principal offences known to the criminal law; but in practice it is only the graver instances of these offences for which extradition is sought. Applications for extradition are made to a foreign government through the Home Office and Foreign Office, the form in which they are made varying under different treaties.

During the year 1912, 67 applications for extradition were received by the Home Secretary from foreign governments. These included 24 applications from Germany and 15 from France. In 38 cases the request for extradition was granted and in 7 refused; in 13 cases the fugitive was not found, and 9 cases had other results. The offences included 30 cases of larceny and embezzlement, 25 of fraud or false pretences, and 5 cases of forgery. During the same year the British government made 9 applications for extradition from other countries to the United Kingdom; 4 of these were addressed to France and 3 to the United States.

Somewhat analogous powers and duties are imposed on the Home Secretary by the Fugitive Offenders Act, 1881, in respect of persons who commit offences in one part of the British Empire and are found in another. The procedure for procuring the return of an accused person to the United Kingdom from some other part of His Majesty's dominions involves, first, presumptive proof of the charge before a colonial magistrate; secondly, an opportunity for the accused person to apply to a colonial court of law, which has a discretionary power of discharging him or ordering him to be sent back to England; thirdly, an order by the Colonial Governor, who may again exercise his discretion in the matter. In this way there is reciprocity as to the surrender of accused persons between the different parts of the King's dominions.

In the year 1912 under the Fugitive Offenders Act, ten persons were sent back from this country for trial in various British Colonies; and two fugitives from justice were brought back to be tried in England.

By the Territorial Waters Jurisdiction Act, 1878, the consent of the Home Secretary is required to any proceedings against a foreigner under that Act.

(3) Thirdly, under many modern statutes the duty of framing Rules for the purpose of carrying them into effect is entrusted to the Home Secretary. Such rules when framed are generally required to be law before Parliament and must receive at least the sanction of its silence. The rules made under the Prison Acts are a notable example of this power. Without such rules many of the modern Acts of Parliament would be quite unworkable. The system is in effect a delegation of the powers of legislation as to details to experts.

(4) The fourth matter above mentioned is the collection, preparation, classification and analysis of statistics relating to a variety of matters, judicial, factory, mining, etc. In carrying out this work the Home Office performs a public service of great value both to trade and legislation. The *Judicial Statistics*, 1912, *Part I* (*Criminal*) giving carefully compiled and digested statistics relating to criminal proceedings, the police, coroners, prisons, reformatory and industrial schools and criminal lunatics, with an excellent Introduction written by Mr W. J. Farrant, Superintendent of the Statistical Branch, is a really remarkable production, invaluable to legislators, sociologists, and all those who take an interest in the administration of the criminal law and the welfare of their less fortunate fellow citizens.

Other important duties of the Home Secretary are:

(5) The taking of evidence in criminal cases pending in foreign courts, at the request of foreign governments, under s. 5 of the Extradition Act, 1873. Such requisitions for evidence to be taken are known as *Commissions Rogatoires*. The number of such cases in 1912 was 36.

(6) The care and supervision of criminal lunatics (see p. 164). The total number of criminal lunatics under detention at the end of 1912 was 1180. Of these 492 were accused of having committed murder, and 448 had been detained upwards of ten years.

(7) The production of prisoners in courts of justice when their presence is required (see p. 109).

II. HABEAS CORPUS

In this connection it may not be out of place to refer shortly
to the writ of *habeas corpus*, particularly as the Home Secretary
now represents the Crown (whose authority, within a given
sphere, is delegated to him) and it was principally against the
Crown that this writ was originally directed.

The days of arbitrary government are happily long past, and
the era of constitutional government well established, but this
writ remains as a convenient means of testing the legality of
the detention of any person who is alleged to be illegally
imprisoned by any other person. Ever since Magna Charta
(A.D. 1215) the personal liberty of an Englishman has been a
well recognised right, but in the centuries of practically despotic
government which followed, it was not always easy to provide
adequate safeguards for this right. The writ of *habeas corpus* is
said to exist at Common Law, and to be as old as the Common
Law itself, but the royal power, which claimed to be superior to
the Common Law, so long as the judges were subservient to that
power, could either withhold the issue of the writ or obtain an
unjust decision upon it, when issued; and it was not till 1641
(by the same Act as abolished the iniquitous Court of Star
Chamber) that it was finally declared by statute (16 Car. I.
c. 10), that the King had no "jurisdiction, power or authority"
over any man's lands or goods, "but that the same ought to be
tried and determined *in the ordinary courts of justice, and by the
ordinary course of the Law*" (s. 3), and that "every person committed by the Council," or "by the King's special command"
should, on application to the judges, have granted unto him
without delay on any pretence whatever a writ of *habeas corpus*;
that in the return to the writ the gaoler should certify the true
cause of commitment; and that the court which had issued the
writ should within three days examine and determine whether
the cause were just and legal or not, and "thereupon do what
to justice should appertain, either by delivering, bailing or
remanding the prisoner" (s. 6). Important as are these declarations this Act was found to be defective in several points; and

it was not till the Habeas Corpus Act, 1679 (31 Car. II, c. 2; which is *par excellence*, *the* Habeas Corpus Act) was passed, that the required remedy was found. It enacts that "on complaint and request in writing by or on behalf of any person committed and charged with any *crime*" (unless committed for treason or felony plainly expressed in the warrant, or unless he is convicted or charged in execution by legal process) "*the Lord Chancellor or any of the judges*[1] *in vacation*, upon viewing a copy of the warrant, or affidavit that a copy is denied," shall (unless the party has neglected for two whole terms to apply for his release) "award a habeas corpus for such prisoner returnable immediately before himself or any other of the judges." And upon service thereof the officer in whose custody the prisoner is shall bring him before the said Lord Chancellor or other judge, with the return of such writ and the true cause of the commitment. The writ must be returned and the prisoner brought up within a limited time according to the distance (of the place where he is imprisoned) not exceeding in any case twenty days after the service of the writ. A gaoler who refuses or neglects to obey the writ incurs heavy penalties.

When the prisoner is brought up in pursuance of the writ, the question whether his detention is legal or not is argued, and if it is decided that it is not, the prisoner is at once discharged out of custody. The Crown Office Rules, 1906, r. 226, provide that when a prisoner is brought up by *habeas corpus*, the procedure at the hearing shall be as follows:

1. Counsel for the prisoner is first heard.
2. Then counsel for the Crown, to justify the imprisonment.
3. Then *one* counsel for the prisoner in reply.

But the Habeas Corpus Act, 1679, not only protects against illegal imprisonment, it also insures that an accused person shall have a speedy trial, by providing that if any man, who has been committed for trial on a charge of treason or felony, is not

---

[1] If the Lord Chancellor refuses to grant the writ, application may be made to any of the other judges of the King's Bench Division. In fact the applicant may "go the round" of these judges until he finds one who will grant the writ. Such applications have precedence over all other business, as affecting the liberty of the subject.

indicted at the next assizes after his commitment, he must be released on bail, unless the witnesses for the Crown cannot be produced at that time; and if he is not indicted and tried at the next subsequent Assizes he must be discharged.

The Habeas Corpus Act of 1679, as it will be observed, applied only to persons committed upon criminal charges, all other cases of illegal imprisonment being left to the operation of the Common Law. Accordingly an Act was passed in 1816 (56 Geo. III, ch. 100) which declares that a writ of *habeas corpus*, returnable immediately, may be issued to bring up the body of any person restrained of his liberty other than for some criminal cause or matter. This Act enables parents to obtain the custody of their children, and husbands of their wives, and applies in the case of alleged lunatics.

There are other Habeas Corpus Acts, *e.g.* those of 1803 and 1804, which enable prisoners to be brought up out of prison if their presence is required as witnesses.

There are also several different kinds of writs of *habeas corpus*, but the principal one is that referred to above, *viz. the habeas corpus ad subjiciendum* (that you may have the body to answer).

Parliament alone can suspend the operation of the Habeas Corpus Acts, and this has been done only in circumstances of great national danger, when it is absolutely necessary for the Government of the day to seize any political leaders who are threatening rebellion and treason, and keep them safe under lock and key till the danger is past. When this course is taken Parliament only gives expression to the public opinion of the majority of the nation, to the effect that the circumstances justify such strong measures. Otherwise these Acts still remain in force, and provide the great safeguard of personal liberty and freedom for all law-abiding citizens. Thus is protected "the right of personal liberty—the most precious of all rights," without which life itself would scarcely be worth living.

For a person to send another out of the kingdom in order to evade the protection of the writ of *habeas corpus*, constitutes that vague and mysterious crime known to the Common Law as *praemunire*, and is one of the few offences which the Crown cannot pardon. It is the one legal "deadly sin." This provision is said to have been inserted in the Act of 1679 in order to prevent the Crown kidnapping obnoxious politicians, who were opposed to it, and sending them out of the country, and pardoning the agents it employed for the purpose. It is another instance of a provision which was originally intended only as a safeguard against an arbitrary order of the Crown, but which has become in course of time and by change of circumstances a means of protection for a general right.

III. THE POLICE

Perhaps no feature strikes a student of our institutions more forcibly than the exceedingly modern character of our system of police. It is so complete in its organisation, it covers every part of the country, it is so efficient, and it fits in so well with the established order of things, that it seems to be a permanent institution which has existed for a great length of time. Yet it is comparatively speaking but a thing of yesterday. It is indeed a fact no less curious than true that for several centuries England, a rich and prosperous country, was almost without any organised system of police and lay almost entirely at the mercy of the criminal classes. This fact accounts in no small degree for the extreme severity and cruelty of our older criminal law, until the beneficent reform of it was inaugurated by Sir Samuel Romilly little more than a hundred years ago. From the decay of the ancient Saxon system of frank-pledge (under which every free man was a surety for the good behaviour of nine of his neighbours, who were bound with him in an association to keep the peace and bring him to justice if he committed a crime), about the end of the fourteenth century, down to the establishment of our present police force at the beginning of the nineteenth century, the only protection and security against crime which the country possessed was the existence in most villages of a parish constable, frequently an old and decrepit man, to whom this office was given, in many instances, in order to keep him off the poor rate. The parish constable was elected by his neighbours, where the old local courts survived, or appointed by the Justices of the Peace, who were mostly village squires, and who, meeting in Quarter Sessions, ruled the county. In case of any serious crime, the "hue and cry" might be raised, and if it were on a grand scale, the Sheriff might call out the *posse comitatus* to assist him in dealing with it. In London there grew up a class of professional thief catchers, known as Bow Street Runners, but this was to a large extent a matter of private enterprise and private remuneration (by rewards, etc.) and not unfrequently they, as in the case of the notorious Jonathan Wilde, were in league with the criminals whom they professed to capture, and shared with them their unlawful gains. In the larger towns there was also a local system of watchmen, known as "Charlies," but the whole system of police throughout the country was unsatisfactory. It was either non-existent, or, where it existed at all, it was inefficient and incapable.

It was in these circumstances that our modern police system came into existence. Its initiation was really due to Lord Sidmouth, who was Home Secretary from 1813 to 1824, though Sir Robert Peel has received the greater share of credit and praise for it. The new Metropolitan Police force was created in 1829, and the City Police in 1839. In the same year (1839) an Act of Parliament enabled justices at Quarter Sessions to create a paid County constabulary, but this Act was permissive; some counties adopted it, and some did not; and it was not till 1856 that all counties which had not availed themselves of this Act were compelled to adopt it. The Municipal Reform Act, 1835, provided for the establishment of paid constables in boroughs. "Thus was England policed" (Maitland).

The police forces of England, as they exist to-day, may be classified as follows: (1) the City of London police; (2) the Metropolitan police; (3) County police; and (4) Borough police.

The area of the City Police district is 673 acres or little more than a square mile. It contains two police courts, *viz.* the Guildhall and the Mansion House, where the Lord Mayor and the Aldermen of the City of London sit as magistrates. The number of persons who sleep by night within this area is comparatively small, slightly under 20,000, but its rateable value is

rightly described as "enormous." The City Police force consists
of a Commissioner, an Assistant Commissioner, three Super-
intendents, five Chief Inspectors, 23 Inspectors, 23 Sub-Inspectors,
96 Sergeants, and 1029 Constables; also one Sergeant and 49
Constables on private service duty—a total of 1230. The Commissioner and Assistant Commissioner are appointed by the Lord
Mayor and Aldermen, but this appointment must be approved
by the Crown, expressed by the Home Secretary, who must
also approve of the police regulations made.

The Metropolitan Police district comprises an area of nearly
700 square miles, with a population of between seven and eight
millions. Within this area there are sixteen Police Courts,
the chief of which is Bow Street. The headquarters of this
force are at New Scotland Yard, S.W. This force on October 8,
1913, consisted of a Commissioner, four Assistant Commissioners,
six Chief Constables and their staff, 33 Superintendents, 617
Inspectors, 2789 Sergeants, and 17,468 Constables, making a
total of 20,907 men, with 344 horses. It is difficult to form
an accurate estimate of the actual value of the property under
police protection within this area, but the annual rateable value
of the real property only in the Metropolitan area (upon which
the police rate of 9*d*. in the £ for the year 1912–1913 was based)
was over £56,000,000. *Was für Plunderei!*

From the time of its establishment in 1829 the Metropolitan
Police has been under the direct and immediate authority of
the Home Secretary. The area, roughly speaking, covers the
district within a radius of fifteen miles from Charing Cross,
excepting the area of the City, and within this area the Home
Secretary exercises a close and constant supervision over the
maintenance of peace and order. "He advises the Crown as
to the appointment of the commissioner, the assistant commissioners and the receiver, or finance officer, of the police; the
regulations for the government of the force are made subject
to his approval" (Anson); and generally speaking all matters
relating to the pay and superannuation of the members of the
force, the erection of buildings for their use and other arrangements, are under his discretion.

The Criminal Investigation Department also has its headquarters at New Scotland Yard. It consists of two Super-intendents and a number of detectives, under the direction and control of one of the assistant commissioners. This Depart-ment (known shortly as the C.I.D.) forms a separate body, under an Assistant Commissioner, and the members of it as a rule wear plain clothes. A certain number of detectives are attached to each division of the Metropolitan Police, but the greater part of the work of criminal investigation in London is done by the chief office (Scotland Yard). The members of the higher ranks of this branch of the force are chosen for personal quali-fications, special aptitude for detective work, knowledge of foreign languages and other similar reasons. It is the duty of this department to obtain an intimate knowledge of the criminal classes and their habits. They also watch the seaports, both in England and abroad, for the purpose of obtaining information as to the movements of dangerous characters, either those coming to England from abroad or those attempting to leave this country. The department is in constant com-munication with the other police forces of the country and also with the foreign police, and members of it, in special cases, may be lent for the assistance of other forces. Attached to the headquarters of the C.I.D. is the Convict Supervision Office, under a Chief Inspector.

Every county and borough police force also has a certain number of detectives, or plain clothes officers, at its headquarters and various centres.

The Commissioner of the Metropolitan Police has the practical control of the force, but all general regulations made by him are subject to the approval of the Home Secretary, and the Home Secretary is responsible to Parliament for its efficiency and good conduct.

The Commissioner of Metropolitan Police is appointed by warrant under the sign manual, and acts under the immediate authority of the Home Secretary. He is a Justice of the Peace for London and the adjacent counties.

The Metropolitan Police is the only police force directly under the control of the Home Secretary. Consequently when-ever it is necessary to appoint police for imperial purposes they are the force chosen for such duties, *e.g.* the protection of dock-yards and railway stations at Woolwich, Devonport, Chatham, and Pembroke. They have full powers within an area of fifteen miles round these places, and they have certain limited powers with respect to Crown property and persons subject to military and naval discipline.

The Metropolitan Police district is divided into 22 divisions, 21 of which are distinguished by a letter of the alphabet, and the 22nd division is the Thames or river police. Division A is the Whitehall Division, where the Commissioner's office is situate.

The Home Secretary appoints the Chief Surgeon of the Metropolitan Police, and the divisional surgeons are appointed on his, the chief surgeon's, recommendation. To every police force there is attached at least one surgeon.

There are about 250 mounted police in London and a few in most large towns and some counties.

As regards the County and Borough police forces, it is impossible, within the limits of this work, to give particulars and statistics. It is sufficient to say that as regards the county constabulary the sanction of the Home Secretary is required to the appointment of Chief Constable, to any change in the numbers or pay of the force, and to its rules. In counties the police are under the immediate direction and control of the Standing Joint Committees, composed partly of Justices of the Peace and partly of members of the County Councils.

As regard borough police, they are governed in each borough by a committee of the Town Council, called the Watch Committee, which has certain statutory powers rendering it to some extent independent of the Council. The rules of each borough force must be approved by the Home Secretary, who is entitled to receive copies.

The Home Secretary appoints "H.M. Inspectors of Constabulary for England and Wales," of whom there are two. The duties of these officers are to make an annual inspection of all the county and borough police forces, and upon their report to the effect that such forces are in a satisfactory condition as to numbers, discipline and general efficiency, half the cost of pay and clothing is paid to the local authorities by the Treasury.

In this way the total cost of the police is shared between the local and the imperial authorities.

Police forces are governed by a large number of Acts of Parliament, beginning with the Special Constables Act, 1831, down to the Police (Weekly Rest-day) Act, 1910. The principal Act relating to the internal economy of the police (superannuation, pensions, allowances and gratuities) is the Police Act, 1890, with amending Acts of 1893 and 1908. The Police Act, 1909, is an act to amend the Metropolitan Police Acts, 1829–1899. By the Parish Constables Act, 1872, parish constables are no longer to be appointed unless Quarter Sessions deem it necessary.

The total number of police in England is about 55,000 and in Wales about 2000.

It would be very difficult to express the debt of gratitude which the country owes to its police, not only in regard to the security of life and property which it affords by night and by day to millions of peaceable and well-disposed citizens, the prevention of crime and disorder, and the detection and punishment of crime committed, but also in regard to many other matters, e.g. the regulation of street traffic, attendance at fires and accidents, the recovery of lost property, the giving of directions to wayfarers, etc., etc. With very rare exceptions these duties are performed with an amount of courtesy and kindness, combined with firmness, which has made the English police force as a whole the admiration of the world.

IV. PRISONS AND PRISONERS

Prisons are of various kinds, according to the class of prisoners intended to be confined in them. They may therefore be classified as follows:

1. *Convict establishments.* Of these there are six, *viz.* Dartmoor (989); Portland (700); Parkhurst, Isle of Wight (766); Camp Hill, Isle of Wight, for Preventive Detention (119; 4 females); Aylesbury (91) for females only; and Maidstone, which is both a convict establishment (255) and a local prison (207).

N.B.—The figures in brackets give the daily average number of convicts.

2. *Local or ordinary prisons.* Of these there are in all 56, situate in various parts of the country. They are for (*a*) those undergoing punishment, either with or without hard labour, and (*b*) those waiting trial, for custody only; and differ very much in size, according to the population of the area to be served.

Among local prisons are: Wormwood Scrubs (1342); Wandsworth (1240); Pentonville (1032); Holloway (710);—all these are in or near London;—Liverpool (1278); Manchester, Strangeways (1010); Birmingham (501); Leeds (487); etc. Bedford and Bodmin have only 55 each. *N.B.*—The figures in brackets give the daily average number of prisoners.

Again, some of these prisons are exclusively for females, *e.g.* Holloway, but the majority of them are for both sexes; the two sexes are, however, kept apart.

3. The principal criminal lunatic asylum is at Broadmoor in Berkshire, and accommodates an average of 830. There is another at Rampton, near Retford in Nottinghamshire.

4. Borstal Institutions, at Borstal, Canterbury, Feltham, and Aylesbury (for girls only).

5. State Inebriate Reformatories: Warwick (54) and Aylesbury (for females only) (60).

6. Reformatories and Industrial Schools for young persons.

7. Places of detention for children.

8. "Police custody." By s. 13 of the C.J.A. Act, 1914, "police custody" is substituted for imprisonment in case of short sentences, *i.e.* less than five days (see hereafter).

All these institutions are more or less directly under the control of the Home Secretary, acting through the Prison Commissioners, Lunacy Commissioners, and Inspectors, in pursuance of various Acts of Parliament.

The estimates for the years 1912–13 provide for 3400 convicts, 16,700 ordinary prisoners, 800 in Borstal Institutions, 110 in preventive detention, and 90 in state inebriate reformatories.

The total estimated cost of the prison service and upkeep in England and Wales in 1912–13 was £801,550, but this was

reduced by the proceeds of prison labour (£20,500) and the sale
of refuse, etc. (£4500) to £776,550, being a decrease of £4300 on
the net total for the previous year 1911–12.

As to the different classes of prisoners:

1. *A convict* is a prisoner who is undergoing a term of penal
servitude, the highest form of punishment known to our law
(except capital punishment), since it may extend from a minimum
sentence of three years to a maximum of penal servitude for life.
It was substituted in 1853 for transportation beyond the seas,
the practice which had previously prevailed. The name penal
servitude seems to have been taken from the *pœnæ servi* of
Roman Law; and the idea underlying it seems to have been
that the persons sentenced to it were in some sense slaves of the
state, since they were to be employed upon public works, and
Portland breakwater was constructed by such labour; but we
believe this idea has been to a large extent departed from now.
Convicts wear a distinctive dress marked with a broad arrow,
which is regarded as a mark of infamy; and though the work
to which convicts are set is usually hard, it has some com-
pensations, as they frequently work in gangs in the open air,
and conversation is permitted, while at Parkhurst, the prison
specially allotted to convicts of delicate health, the conditions
cannot be called severe. Indeed it is said that a sentence of
five years' penal servitude is much easier to undergo than one of
two years' imprisonment with hard labour. A considerable remission of the sentence may be earned by good conduct, and the
Home Secretary is empowered to grant licences or "tickets of
leave," upon such conditions as may be thought fit, to such convicts as have deserved them. Tickets of leave are revocable at
pleasure, and if the holder is convicted of any other indictable
offence he has to serve out the remaining portion of his sentence
of penal servitude. The holders of tickets of leave are subject
to police supervision (unless exempt by the conditions of their
licences) and have to report themselves to the police of the
district in which they reside *once* a month at least, and failure
to do so is itself an offence; they have also to report any
change of address. Police supervision may also be imposed, in
a strictly limited class of cases, as an addition to a sentence of

imprisonment. It is sometimes urged against this system that it operates greatly to the disadvantage of the holders of tickets of leave, since, if it becomes known that they are "ticket of leave men" it prejudices them in the eyes of employers and causes respectable working men to shun them; moreover it is said that the police sometimes act oppressively towards them, but on the whole we believe that the police act with forbearance and discretion. A certain amount of suspicion must inevitably attach to old offenders. A sentence of penal servitude is passed only for some very serious offence or after several previous convictions; and *convicts* are confined in "convict establishments."

2. Ordinary prisoners may be subdivided into (1) those imprisoned *with* hard labour; (2) those undergoing simple imprisonment, *i.e. without* hard labour. No sentence of hard labour can be imposed unless the Act of Parliament dealing with the offence expressly authorises it[1]; but a person sentenced to imprisonment without hard labour is not thereby exempt from all labour and allowed to pass his time in idleness. The maximum period to which a person may be sentenced to imprisonment with hard labour is two years. Indeed this sentence is seldom passed only in exceptional cases, such as robbery with violence.

(1) A prisoner sentenced to imprisonment *with* hard labour, according to the regulations now in force, serves the first 28 days "in strict separation," *i.e.* solitary confinement, and is employed during that time either in picking oakum, making heavy coal sacks, chopping wood or breaking stone. Oakum picking, as a rule, is enforced for 14 days only; after which the prisoner is employed, still in strict separation, on industrial labour till he has completed the 28 days. After the completion of the 28 days a prisoner is eligible for employment "in association," *i.e.* he is allowed to work along with others, either at his trade or at some suitable industrial labour, such as making hammocks, post bags, nose bags, ships' fenders, etc. During the first 14 days of his sentence a male prisoner sentenced to hard labour, who is between the ages of 16 and 60, and who is medically fit, is required to sleep without a mattress; but in all other respects his treatment differs little from simple imprisonment.

---

[1] But see now s. 16 (1) of the C. J. A. Act, 1914.

(2) A prisoner sentenced to simple imprisonment is employed from the first on some useful industry, and he may work either in his cell or "in association."

Prisoners sentenced to imprisonment *without* hard labour are now classed in three divisions (s. 6, Prison Act, 1898). These are known respectively as the First, Second and Third Divisions. Subject to some exceptions, it rests with the court which passes the sentence to decide in which Division a prisoner is to be placed.

The rules for the First Division are the same as those made for the treatment of first class misdemeanants under the Prison Act, 1865 (see p. 173). The number of prisoners to whom this special treatment is accorded has always been very small. Persons convicted of sedition, or seditious libel, and those committed to prison for offences under the Vaccination Acts, are placed by statute in this division.

The Second Division is an innovation introduced by the Prison Act of 1898. The rules made for persons placed in this Division constitute a considerable modification of the treatment accorded to ordinary criminals. They are kept apart from other prisoners, they wear a different dress, and they are allowed more frequent letters and visits. The criterion of a prisoner's fitness for this Division is not so much the legal character of the offence as the character and antecedents of the offender and the circumstances in which the offence was committed. It is important not to admit to it persons of criminal life or of bad character. But whenever it is clear to the court that a prisoner does not belong to the criminal class and has not been generally of criminal or disreputable habits, a special direction may properly be given for his treatment in the Second Division (see Home Office Circular of December 31st, 1906, and August 31st, 1908).

When no special order is made by the court a convicted prisoner is placed in the Third Division and treated under the ordinary prison rules.

All prisoners must obey the general rules of the prison and submit to discipline, upon pain of punishment. In every prison there is at least one surgeon and chaplain; one to attend to their physical, the other to attend to their spiritual needs[1]. There is no distinction between the treatment of prisoners in the different divisions in these respects; and a prisoner of bad character ought not to be placed in the Second Division simply on the ground of ill health.

As to *juveniles*, offenders under 21 are separated from other prisoners. If their sentences are long enough to allow of it they are located in selected prisons where special provisions can be made for their education and training.

All prisoners who have been sentenced to imprisonment for a term of more than one month (which by section 12 of the Prison Act, 1898, means "calendar month") may, by good conduct and industry in prison, earn a remission of the sentence to an amount not exceeding one-sixth. Misconduct in prison is punished by the forfeiture of a portion or the whole of this remission.

Prisoners imprisoned in default of entering into a recognizance, or of finding sureties to keep the peace, or sureties for good behaviour, are, in the ordinary course, unless they are *convicted* prisoners, treated in the same way as convicted prisoners of the Second Division. But if they are *convicted* prisoners (*e.g.* persons convicted of drunkenness and required to find sureties under s. 3 of the Licensing Act, 1902) they are placed in the Third Division, unless the court otherwise orders. The class of prisoners above referred to is known as "Surety Prisoners."

S. 16 of the C. J. A. Act, 1914, deals with hard labour and the classification of prisoners. It provides (*inter alia*) that "a court or visiting committee shall not direct an offender to be treated as an offender of the second division if his character and antecedents are such that he is likely to exercise a bad influence on *first* offenders." S. 17 deals with the commitment and removal of prisoners; and empowers the Secretary of State, by rule made under the Prison Acts, 1865 to 1902, to appropriate, either wholly or partially, particular prisons to particular classes of prisoners. It provides that "a prisoner shall not in any case be

---

[1] By the Prison Ministers Act, 1863, provision is made for ministration to prisoners other than those of the established church, *e.g.* nonconformists and Roman Catholics; and a prisoner is not to be compelled to attend the services of any other persuasion than his own.

liable to pay the costs of his conveyance to prison"; and that where a prisoner is suffering from disease and cannot be properly treated in prison, or where he ought to undergo and desires to undergo an operation which cannot be properly performed in the prison, he may be taken to a hospital or other suitable place for the purpose of treatment or the operation.

4. *Borstal Institutions.* These will be dealt with hereafter. See Part IV. (pp. 184–188).

6. *Reformatories and Industrial Schools.* "Reformatories" are institutions in which youthful offenders (between the ages of twelve and sixteen) are detained under the order of a court of justice for industrial training. They are under private management, but must be certified by the Home Office as fit for the reception of such offenders. "Industrial Schools" receive for the same purpose children (under the age of fourteen years) who are charged with various offences, *e.g.* with being mendicants, truants from elementary schools, whose parents are in prison, "or whose circumstances and surroundings are such as to make it probable that they will fall into criminal habits or modes of life or become the victims of criminal or immoral influences." Industrial Schools must also be certified by the Home Office.

The Home Secretary appoints the Chief Inspector of Reformatory and Industrial Schools and his staff. He is assisted by a Senior Inspector, four Assistant Inspectors and one Lady Assistant Inspector. They have their headquarters in the Home Office, Charles Street, S.W., and form another sub-department of that department. The Chief Inspector is under the supervision of the Home Secretary, and must make a Report to him every year, and this Report must be laid before Parliament.

Full particulars of these institutions, their inmates and management, are given in the Annual Report.

On December 31st, 1912, there were in existence 37 duly certified reformatory schools, of which 27 were for males and 10 for females; and 125 duly certified residential industrial schools, of which 78 were for boys and 47 for girls; and 11 day industrial schools for both sexes. Of the 78 boys' industrial schools 9 were "short-time" schools, mainly for offenders against the

Education Acts, whom it is the practice to release on licence after a short period of detention.

In 1912, 1273 youthful offenders were sent to reformatory schools, of whom 11 were sentenced at quarter sessions and 1262 by Courts of Summary Jurisdiction. The number of children admitted to ordinary industrial schools in the same year was 3015. Of these only 814 were charged with having committed crimes; the rest consisted of children found begging or wandering about without a home or not being under parental control or not attending elementary schools.

7. *Places of detention.* These are provided by police authorities for the temporary detention of children and young persons (under sixteen years of age) who are charged with offences where the circumstances are such as do not admit of release upon recognizances and it would otherwise be necessary to confine the child or young person in a police station or a prison; but the "imprisonment" of a child or young person (with some exceptions) is now abolished by the Children Act, 1908.

In 1912, 7212 persons were received into places of detention, *viz.* 5274 children and 1938 young persons. The children consisted of 4419 boys and 855 girls; the young persons of 1671 boys and 267 girls.

3, 5 and 8. The class of inmates for whom these institutions are intended is sufficiently indicated by the name of the institution and what is said above.

Down to the year 1877 local prisons were in the hands of local bodies, in most cases the Justices assembled in Quarter Sessions, and the cost was defrayed out of the county rate; but convict establishments were always vested in the Home Secretary, who controlled them through Directors of Convict Prisons. By the Prison Act, 1877, it was provided that all prisoners should be transferred to and vest in the Home Secretary and that the cost of maintenance of all prisons and prisoners should for the future be defrayed out of public funds, *i.e.* moneys provided by Parliament; and the Home Secretary should have the appointment of all prison officers, the control and safe custody of all prisoners, and all powers and jurisdictions relating to prisons and prisoners.

V. THE PRISON ACTS, PRISON RULES, PRISON COMMISSIONERS, ETC.

The principal Acts of Parliament now in force relating to prisons are the Prison Act, 1865, 1877, and 1898. The series extends from 1865 to 1902, and forms a complete code of prison management.

Schedule I to the Act of 1865 contained elaborate provisions as to the admission and discharge of prisoners; their food, clothing and bedding; their personal cleanliness; their employment, health and religious instruction; visits to and communications with prisoners; prison offences; the treatment of prisoners under sentence of death; prison officers who are to be constables and are not to sell or let to prisoners, to contract with them or to take gratuities (females are to be attended by female officers); the duties of the gaolers, *i.e.* governor, keeper or chief officer of the prison, matron, surgeon porter, etc. Among the duties of the gaoler are: to inspect the prison daily, to notify to the chaplain and surgeon prisoners requiring their attention, to report to visiting justices all insane prisoners, to be responsible for the safe custody of all books and documents, not to be absent without leave, to transmit lists of prisoners to the Secretary of State, to attend Quarter Sessions and Assizes, and to make reports.

Section 2 of the Prison Act, 1898, empowers the Secretary of State to make rules (called Prison Rules) for the government of local prisons and convict establishments, regulating thereby, among other things (*a*) any matter dealt with by the regulations in Schedule I to the Prison Act, 1865; and (*b*) any matter which under the Act of 1898 may be regulated by prison rules. The draft rules so made must be submitted to Parliament and the date when they are to come into force must be notified in the London Gazette. Under this power certain "Prison Rules" (313 in number) have been made, dated April 21st, 1899, and these are the rules (with some additions and alterations since made) now in force. It is sufficient to say that they carry out in still greater detail the matters formerly dealt with in Schedule I mentioned above.

As examples of the Prison Rules let us take the following:

"108. It is the duty of all officers to treat prisoners with kindness and humanity, to listen patiently to and report their complaints or grievances, at the same time being firm in maintaining order and discipline, and enforcing complete observance of the rules and regulations of the prison. The great object of reclaiming the criminal should always be kept in view by all officers, and they should strive to acquire a moral influence over the prisoners by performing their duties conscientiously but without harshness. They should especially try to raise the prisoners' minds to a proper feeling of moral obligation, by the example of their own uniform regard to truth and integrity, even in the smallest matters."

"109. An officer shall, without delay, inform the governor of any prisoner who desires to see him, or to make any complaint, or to prefer any request to him or to any superior authority."

"151. The governor shall hear the reports every day at such hour as may be most convenient"; and shall take care that every prisoner having a complaint to make, or request to prefer, to him, shall have ample facilities for so doing; and shall forward to the Commissioners without delay any report or complaint either by or against any officer of the prison. "The governor shall inform the Visiting Committee of the desire of any prisoner to see them."

"The child of a female prisoner may be received into prison with its mother, provided it is at the breast. In all such cases an authority from the committing magistrate for the child's admission should accompany the prisoner on reception. Any child so admitted shall not be taken from its mother until the medical officer of the prison certifies that it is in a fit condition to be removed" (19).

By Section 9 of the Prison Act, 1898, a prisoner who is committed for non-payment of a fine may obtain a proportionate reduction of his sentence on payment of a portion of the fine; but by the Rules no such payment can be made on Sunday. This right is now amplified by s. 3 of the C. J. A. Act, 1914 (see p. 56).

These regulations and rules strike one on the whole as very fair and reasonable considering their object, *viz.* the preservation of good order and discipline in the prison, combined with the carrying out of the sentence. The spirit which animates them is one of strictness but humanity, and the infliction of unnecessary pain and indignity is carefully avoided. The existence of these general rules and regulations which everybody in a prison must observe and obey secures uniformity of treatment of prisoners in all our prisons throughout England and Wales, from Berwick-on-Tweed to Land's End, and from London to Liverpool—an important consideration.

Male and female prisoners are now kept in separate prisons or at all events separately. The promiscuous herding together of the two sexes was one of the worst features of the old prison system, and gave rise to great evils.

Section 62 of the Act of 1865 imposes on gaolers of prisons the obligation to deliver, or cause to be delivered, to the Judges of Assize and to the Justices in Quarter Sessions a *Calendar* of all prisoners in custody for trial at such Assizes or Sessions, in the same way as a Sheriff of a county had hitherto been required by law to deliver a Calendar of such prisoners, and exempts the Sheriff from the duty of delivering such Calendar.

Section 67 of this Act (1865) provides that misdemeanants who are *not* sentenced to hard labour shall be divided into at least two divisions, one of which shall be called the First Division; and the Judge before whom he is convicted may order that a misdemeanant shall be placed in the First Division; the result of which is that he shall *not* be deemed to be a "criminal prisoner," but shall be treated as a "civil prisoner," *e.g.* a contumacious debtor. As we have seen above, under s. 6 of the Prison Act, 1898, these prisoners are now divided into three classes, the first of which corresponds with these first class misdemeanants. By the Act of 1865 a "criminal prisoner" means "any prisoner convicted of a crime."

There are certain offences in relation to prisons which are severely punished, *viz.* assisting prisoners to escape; carrying spirituous liquors or tobacco into a prison; and carrying letters either into or out of prison (see sect. 37, 38 and 39 of the Prisons Act, 1865). Notices setting forth the penalties which will be incurred by any person committing any of these offences are to be affixed in a conspicuous place outside all prisons (s. 40).

The Report of a strong Departmental Committee on Prisons, presented to Parliament in April, 1895, recommended (amongst other things): a larger margin of separate cell accommodation in London and certain provincial prisons; better organisation of Prisoners' Aid Societies; the abolition of unproductive labour; and the increase, as far as possible, of productive prison industries; a larger supply of books to prisoners; and the encouragement of any occupation which tends to elevate the mind and is consistent with order and discipline. It was largely in consequence of the report of this Commission that the Prison Act of 1898 was passed, and the Prison Rules of 1899 made, the number of such rules being increased from 111, as they existed before, to 313[1]. These Prison Rules have been framed with insight and sympathy, the result of long experience; they cover almost every detail of prison routine and administration; and together with the Acts of Parliament relating to prisons form a complete code of prison organisation and management.

There are separate Rules as to Convict Prisons also dated April 21st, 1899, and being 190 in number. Many of the rules are the same for both classes of prison.

THE PRISON COMMISSIONERS

The Act of 1877 also provided for the appointment by the Crown, on the recommendation of the Home Secretary, of Prison Commissioners (not to exceed five in number) and the appointment of Inspectors of Prisons, officers and servants to assist the Commissioners. All these officials receive such salaries, out of moneys provided by Parliament, as the Home Secretary, with the consent of the Treasury, may from time to time determine.

The Home Secretary appoints one of the Commissioners to be the chairman. It is under this Act that the Prison Commission, which is in effect a department of the Home Office, and

[1] Copies of these Prison Rules may be obtained from the King's Printer, price 4d.

has its abode in the same building, exists. By the Act of 1898, s. I, the Directors of Convict Prisons was amalgamated with the Prison Commissioners. The distinction between gaols and houses of correction has also been abolished, and several small prisons have been closed.

The duties of the Prison Commissioners are comprehensively defined as "the general superintendence of prisons under this Act (the Prison Act, 1877) subject to the control of the Secretary of State." Section 10 of that Act provides: "The Prison Commissioners shall, at such time or times as the Secretary of State may direct, make a report or reports to the Secretary of State, of the condition of the prisons and prisoners within their jurisdiction; and an annual report to be made by them with respect to every prison within their jurisdiction shall be laid before both Houses of Parliament." This report is to contain information as to the manufacturing processes carried on in prisons (s. 11). The Commissioners are also bound to make a yearly return to Parliament of all punishments inflicted within each prison and the offences for which such punishments were inflicted (s. 12). The Annual Report of the Prison Commissioners is a document full of human interest and the yearly return of punishments is a guarantee to the public that no oppressive or gratuitous cruelty goes on inside prisons.

VISITING JUSTICES

Section 13 of the Prison Act, 1877, provides for the appointment of a "Visiting Committee of Justices of the Peace" by Quarter Sessions; and s. 14 gives the Secretary of State power to make and publish, alter or add to, rules prescribing the duties of such visiting committee. In addition to this, s. 15 empowers any "justice of the peace, having jurisdiction in the place where the prison is situate, or having jurisdiction in the place where the offence, in respect of which any prisoner may be confined in prison, was committed," to visit such prison at any time he thinks fit and examine the condition thereof, but he shall not be entitled, in pursuance of this section, to visit any prisoner under sentence of death, or to communicate with any prisoner except in reference to the treatment in prison of such prisoner or to some complaint that such prisoner may make as to such treatment." This again is another protection to the prisoner and a guarantee of fair treatment.

EXECUTIONS IN PRISON

Before the year 1868 all executions took place in public and were generally attended with unseemly and deplorable scenes. Since that date they have taken place within prison walls, practically in private, greatly to the advantage of the community.

On the 20th July, 1840, the eminent novelist W. M. Thackeray was present at a public execution, and afterwards recorded his impressions, in very vivid and graphic terms, in an article which appeared in *Fraser's Magazine* entitled *Going to see a Man Hanged.* The man who was hanged on that occasion was a French valet named Courvoisier, a thorough-paced villain who had murdered his master, Lord William Russell, in circumstances of great atrocity, and afterwards endeavoured to throw suspicion upon a maid servant in the employment of the same master. He was a wretch who deserved no pity; but Thackeray ends his article with these words, "I feel myself ashamed and degraded at the brutal curiosity which took me to that brutal sight; and I pray to Almighty God to cause this disgraceful sin to pass from among us, and to cleanse our land from blood." Yet it took another twenty-eight years before public opinion and the public conscience, which move slowly even when stirred by so powerful a writer, were sufficiently aroused and the desired change was brought about.

It was finally brought about as the result of a recommendation made by the Capital Punishment Commission, which made its report in 1866.

By the Capital Punishment Act, 1868 (described as an Act to provide for the carrying out of Capital Punishment within Prisons) it is provided that judgment of death shall for the future be executed within prison walls. The Sheriff, who by his office is charged with the duty of carrying out executions, the gaoler (governor), chaplain and surgeon of the prison in which the execution takes place, *shall* (must) be present at the execution. And "any Justice of the Peace for the county, borough or other jurisdiction to which the prison belongs, and such relatives of the prisoner or other persons as it seems to the Sheriff or the Visiting Justices of the prison, proper to admit within the prison for the purpose, *may* also be present."

The prison surgeon is to examine the body of the offender, after the execution of the sentence, and ascertain the fact of death, and give a certificate thereof. The sheriff, gaoler, chaplain and justices (if any) present are to sign a declaration that the judgment of death has been executed upon the offender. The coroner is to hold an inquest on the body within 24 hours after the execution and the body is to be buried within the prison walls[1]. Power is given to "one of His Majesty's principal Secretaries of State" to make rules, etc., to be observed on all such executions, and such rules are to be laid before Parliament.

The powers and duties of the sheriff may, however, be performed by "his under sheriff or other lawful deputy acting in his absence and with his authority." Similar powers to delegate their duties to deputies are given to the gaoler, surgeon and chaplain.

The certificate of death and the declaration above referred to, and the duplicate of the coroner's inquisition, are to be sent to the Home Secretary "with all convenient speed," and printed copies of the same are to be exhibited for 24 hours at least on or near the principal entrance of the prison.

The object of these regulations is to ensure that the execution shall take place with propriety and to assure the public that everything shall be done with decency and order. No black flag is now hoisted or bell tolled.

The above-mentioned Act applies only to the execution of judgment of death on any person sentenced "for murder." If

---

[1] By s. 3 (2) of the Coroners Act. 1887, "When an inquest is held on the body of a prisoner who dies within a prison, an officer of the prison, or a prisoner therein, or a person engaged in any sort of trade or dealing with the prison, shall not be a juror on such inquest." This section applies to all inquests on prisoners, not only to those which follow executions.

therefore a person had to be executed for high treason, it is conceived that either a short amending act to the same effect would have to be passed or the execution would have to take place in public. This shows how difficult it is to draw a perfect Act of Parliament, and to provide for every contingency.

The Capital Punishment Commission, which reported in 1866, recommended that capital punishment should be retained for all murders deliberately committed, with malice aforethought, or in the perpetration of murder, arson, rape, burglary or piracy; but replaced by penal servitude for life in all other cases of murder.

PRISON REFORM

One of the most curious, and at the same time complete and interesting, parts of the British Section at the Ghent International Exhibition in 1913 was that which was devoted to prison life and the reformation of offenders in England. There were to be seen models of our convict establishments, a full-sized model of a cell in a Borstal Institution, and every accessory of punishment and reformation, including, by way of comparison, several gruesome relics of the severity and cruelty of our criminal law in the past. Many of these possessed considerable historic interest; and the section appeared to be popular and to be regarded as instructive. Yet strange to say there was a certain appropriateness in all this, for it was at Ghent (then in Austrian Flanders) that John Howard, the great prison reformer, when he visited various parts of Europe, in fulfilment of his self-imposed mission of mercy, found most to admire, and found the most enlightened principles prevailed, which he was moved to recommend for adoption in England.

The mention of John Howard reminds one that it was while serving the office of Sheriff of Bedfordshire, whose duty (as is mentioned above, p. 173) it then was to prepare the calendar of prisoners for trial at Assizes and Quarter Sessions, that his attention was first called to the subject of prison reform. He found that notwithstanding their acquittal by the jury prisoners frequently could not obtain their release from prison until they had paid certain fees to the gaoler. These facts affected him very deeply and led him to devote his life to prison reform. Howard found the prisons of England veritable infernos. They are not quite paradises now (and are not intended to be) but at least we have no reason to be ashamed of them. He died 1790; much has been done since then. The formation, in 1817, by that noble and heroic woman, Mrs Elizabeth Fry, of "The Association for the Improvement of the Female Prisoners in Newgate," marks another epoch in prison reform. Jeremy Bentham's favourite scheme of a Panopticon prison, where every prisoner could be seen by the warders, without the warders themselves being seen, is well known. The abolition of transportation, and the substitution of penal servitude, in 1853, were further steps in the right direction.

Side by side with the reform of prisons went the reform of the Criminal Law itself, through the untiring efforts of the philanthropic and enlightened Sir Samuel Romilly. The subject of prison reform, as well as that of the gradual improvement of the Criminal Law, is a very fascinating one; but it cannot be pursued further here.

If English prisons are not now all that prisons ought to be, it is not because of any lack of attention on the part of those interested in the subject, or of any zeal and enthusiasm on the part of public servants and officials. It would be idle to say that our prisons are perfect—finality has not yet been reached— but taking them as they are, they are not unworthy of a just and civilised nation, and looking upon them as a whole, one is proud to be able to say, with Milton,

> "Peace hath her victories
> No less renowned than war."

PART IV. RECENT LEGISLATION AND STATISTICS

I. RECENT LEGISLATION

FIVE Acts of Parliament have recently been passed which would do credit to any civilized nation, and which have done much to transform the administration of criminal justice, *viz.*: (1) the Probation of Offenders Act, 1907, which applies to children, young persons, and adults; (2) the Prevention of Crime Act, 1908, which applies to young offenders and habitual criminals; (3) the Children Act, 1908, which applies only to children and young persons; (4) the Mental Deficiency Act, 1913; and (5) the Criminal Justice Administration Act, 1914. It is impossible, even if it were desirable, to deal here with the details of these long Acts. All that can be done is to mention their objects and chief provisions.

1. THE PROBATION OF OFFENDERS ACT, 1907

This Act provides that "Where any person is charged before a court of summary jurisdiction, with an offence punishable by such a court, and the court thinks that the charge is proved, but is of opinion that, having regard to the character, antecedents, age, health, or mental condition of the person charged, or to the trivial nature of the offence, or to the extenuating circumstances under which the offence was committed, it is inexpedient to inflict any punishment or any other than a nominal punishment, or that it is expedient to release the offender on probation, the court may, *without* proceeding to conviction, make an order, either (i) dismissing the information or charge; or (ii) discharging the offender conditionally on his entering into a recognizance (bond) with or without sureties, to be of good behaviour and to appear for conviction and sentence when called on at any time during such period, not exceeding three years, as may be specified in the order." Such an order is known as a Probation Order.

In the case of a person convicted on indictment the court may "in lieu of imposing a sentence of imprisonment make an order discharging the offender" conditionally on his entering into a similar recognizance.

The court may at the same time order the offender to pay damages (not exceeding in the case of a Court of Summary Jurisdiction £10, unless a higher limit is fixed by the Act relating to the offence) and reasonable costs; and further it may make a Probation Order, placing the offender under the supervision of a specified person during such period, not exceeding three years, as may be specified in the order. This is a most valuable provision, especially in the case of wanton mischief by hooligans. It is a great mistake to let them off too easily, without any punishment at all. Nothing brings home to them the gravity of their offence so much as having to make restitution to the injured party. The recognizance entered into may contain conditions:

(a) For prohibiting the offender from associating with thieves and other undesirable persons, or from frequenting undesirable places.

(b) As to abstention from intoxicating liquor, when the offence was drunkenness or an offence committed under the influence of drink.

(c) Generally for securing that the offender shall lead an honest and industrious life.

By s. 8 of the C. J. A. Act, 1914, the following condition of probation is substituted for that marked (b) given above: "A recognizance under this Act may contain such additional conditions with respect to residence, abstention from intoxicating liquor, and any other matters, as the court may, having regard to the particular circumstances of the case, consider necessary for preventing a repetition of the same offence or the commission of other offences."

Section 9 gives the court power to vary the terms and conditions of probation.

The Act of 1907 provides for the appointment of Probation Officers (of either sex), and in particular of Children's Probation Officers, for offenders under sixteen.

Subject to the directions of the court, the duties of a probation officer are:

(*a*) To visit or receive reports from the person under supervision, at such reasonable intervals as may be specified in the probation order, or subject thereto, as the probation officer may think fit;

(*b*) To see that he observes the conditions of his recognizance;

(*c*) To report to the court as to his behaviour;

(*d*) To advise, assist and befriend him, and, when necessary, endeavour to find him suitable employment.

In case the offender fails to observe the conditions of his release, he may be re-apprehended and forthwith, without further proof of his guilt, convicted and sentenced for the original offence.

Before 1908 the enactments which dealt with the probation of offenders were s. 16 of the S. J. Act, 1879, and the Probation of First Offenders Act, 1887, both of which are now repealed. The power under the former section was limited to cases of summary conviction; but adults charged with indictable offences, who were dealt with summarily, were excluded from its operation. The latter Act, as its name implies, was limited to first offenders, and applied to them only in a certain limited class of cases. Moreover, under these enactments, there was no machinery for the supervision of those placed on probation. The Act of 1907 is much wider in its scope and provisions. It came into operation on January 1, 1908; and there was issued in 1910 a Report of a Departmental Committee on the first year's working of the Act, which contains some valuable suggestions for its improvement. Experience has since shown some defects; but the result of its working is to show that the Act is one of great value and utility.

This Act has now been in operation for five years and the numbers of probation orders made under it have been:

1908	..	..	.. 8,023
1909	..	..	.. 8,962
1910	..	..	.. 10,217
1911	..	..	.. 9,516
1912	..	..	.. 11,193

During the year 1912 these 11,193 probation orders were made in respect of

722 persons convicted on indictment;

7594 persons tried summarily for indictable offences; and

2877 persons charged with non-indictable offences.

Only 655, or 6 per cent., of the persons against whom probation orders were made were called up for sentence during the year. This fact also affords striking testimony to the success of the system.

The Home Office has issued three circulars on the subject of this Act, dated respectively 30th November, 1907; 21st April, 1910; and 3rd October, 1912. In the last it is stated: "It has long been recognised, in the administration of criminal justice, that numerous cases occur in which, though an offence against the law has clearly been committed, it is not necessary nor even desirable, that punishment should be imposed on the offender. It would be impossible to define these cases in precise terms. Sometimes a breach of the law may in itself be of a merely technical or trivial character; or there may be circumstances affecting the character of the offence which justify the court in holding that it will be effectively punished and its repetition prevented by a public reprimand and warning or by some form of probation. More frequently, however, a stronger ground for leniency will be found in the age, character or previous history of the offender than in the circumstances of the offence as proved by the evidence." The circular further states: "On the other hand the Secretary of State would strongly urge on the magistrates that no such order should be made unless there is a clear probability that such supervision as the Probation Officer is able to give, will be of real benefit to the offender." "In the case of a juvenile offender whose previous appearances in court show him to be of a persistently criminal disposition, it is not likely to be effective, especially if on any previous occasions it has been tried and failed...cases occur in which an offender has been put on probation three or even four times. This appears to the Secretary of State to be a misuse of the Act." Such cases are better treated in a Borstal Institution (see the Prevention of Crime Act, 1908).

The circular of 1907 lays stress on the character and qualifications of the persons appointed Probation Officers, and says that the success of the Act will largely depend thereon. "In all cases the Officers should be persons of good education and having some knowledge of the industrial and social conditions of the locality."

An excellent little book on *The Probation System* has just appeared (August, 1914) written by Mr Cecil Leeson, but it approaches the subject, and deals with it, from the sociological rather than from the legal and judicial point of view. It contains an introduction by Professor Muirhead, of the University of Birmingham, in which he says: "Probation is one of the most interesting of the signs of our times."

Speaking of the defects of the system, Mr Leeson says: "The defects of the probation system are the defects of administration, rather than of principle, and are traceable largely to misapprehensions of the nature of the system arising from its extraordinarily rapid growth. The defects consist chiefly in (*a*) unsuitable probation officers, (*b*) unsuitable cases, (*c*) too short probationary periods, and (*d*) inadequacy of organisation and control" (ch. VII, p. 175).

2. THE PREVENTION OF CRIMES ACT, 1908

The second of the Acts previously alluded to is that named above, the general scope of which is to make better provision for the prevention of crime by providing (1) for the reformation of Young Offenders, and (2) for the prolonged detention of Habitual Criminals. The Act is divided into two parts, each of which deals with one of these objects.

Part I provides that where a person is convicted on indictment of an offence for which he is liable to be sentenced to penal servitude, and it appears to the court (*a*) that the person is not less than sixteen nor more than twenty-one years of age; and (*b*) that, by reason of his criminal habits or tendencies, or his association with persons of bad character, it is expedient that he should be subject to detention, for such term and under such instruction and discipline, as appears most conducive to his reformation and the repression of crime; the court may, in lieu

of passing a sentence of penal servitude or imprisonment, pass
a sentence of detention under penal discipline in a "Borstal
Institution" for a term of not less than one year nor more than
three years. But before passing such a sentence the court shall
consider any report or representations which may be made to
it by or on behalf of the Prison Commissioners, as to the suitability
of the case for treatment in a "Borstal Institution," and shall
be satisfied that the character, state of health, and mental
condition of the offender and the other circumstances of the case,
are such that the offender is likely to profit by such instruction
and discipline. The Secretary of State may by order direct that
this provision shall extend to persons apparently under twenty-
three and not exceeding that age as may be specified in the order.

On the other hand power is given to transfer those who
are sentenced to detention in a Borstal Institution and prove
incorrigible, or exercise a bad influence over the others, to
prison; and also to release on licence suitable cases.

Similar powers are conferred on a Court of Summary Jurisdiction in regard to youthful offenders who have been previously
sentenced to detention in Reformatory Schools and have been
convicted of offences against the discipline of such schools.

The Secretary of State also has power to transfer from prison
to a Borstal Institution young offenders undergoing penal
servitude or imprisonment who may with advantage be detained
in a Borstal Institution, there to serve the whole or any part of
the unexpired residue of their sentences.

The Act provides for the establishment of "Borstal Institutions," in which young offenders may be detained, and whilst
so detained given such industrial training and other instruction,
and be subjected to such disciplinary and moral influences as
will conduce to their reformation and the prevention of crime;
and the Secretary of State may make regulations for the management of such institutions, and the temporary detention of such
persons, until arrangements can be made for sending them to
such institutions.

S. 10 of the C. J. A. Act, 1914, confers further powers on Courts
of Summary Jurisdiction in regard to the sending of youthful
delinquents to Borstal Institutions, by providing (*a*) that where

a person is summarily convicted of any offence for which the court has power to impose a sentence of imprisonment for one month or upwards, without the option of a fine, and it is proved that the offender has been previously convicted, or has enjoyed the benefit of probation, and it appears to the court that he is not less than 16 nor more than 21 years of age, and (*b*) that it is expedient he should be dealt with under the Borstal system, "it shall be lawful for the court, in lieu of passing sentence, to commit the offender to prison till the next Quarter Sessions," and leave Quarter Sessions to deal with him. (This procedure is analogous to the way in which "incorrigible rogues" are dealt with.) But where a person is referred to Quarter Sessions in this way and is committed to prison in the meantime, his treatment "in prison" shall, so far as practicable, be similar to that in a Borstal Institution; and every person sentenced to detention in a Borstal Institution by a Court of Quarter Sessions under this section may appeal against the sentence to the Court of Criminal Appeal. This section does not come into operation till September 1st, 1915.

S. 11 of the C. J. A. Act, 1914 provides that the term for which a person or youthful offender may be sentenced to detention in a Borstal Institution shall not be less than two years, and the period for which he is to remain under the supervision of the Prison Commissioners, after the expiration of the term of his sentence, shall be one year. The fixing of these minimum sentences is in accordance with expert opinion, which was practically unanimous as to the fact that the benefit of detention in a Borstal Institution was largely lost in some cases by the period of detention being too short. On the other hand, the section provides that if a person is re-called to a Borstal Institution the maximum period of his detention shall be one year. These periods of two years, one year and one year, are respectively substituted for the period of one year, six months and three months mentioned in the Prevention of Crime Act, 1908, in similar circumstances.

Four Borstal Institutions have been established (see p. 164). One is at Borstal, a village near Chatham (from which the institutions take their name); another is at Feltham, near

Twickenham; a third (for girls only) is at Aylesbury; a fourth is at Canterbury, where a wing of the prison is used for boys transferred thither from Borstal or Feltham for continuous misconduct. Mr McKenna (the Home Secretary), in introducing the Criminal Justice Administration Bill in the House of Commons said, speaking of the Borstal Institution: "It is not a prison. It is, or it should be, far more like a school under severe discipline, with a strict industrial training."

Sir Evelyn Ruggles-Brise, Chairman of the Prison Commission, recently wrote: "The object that the State has in view in establishing these Institutions is to give such training and teaching, alike of body and mind and character, as shall stop these young offenders in the downward course of evil doing on which they have already embarked, and transform them into honest, self-respecting, and self-supporting citizens; into men who both know the thing that is right, and desire to do it. It is a great and difficult transformation that the State is thus trying to effect. How does the State set about it? During the whole time that the inmate is in the Institution he is kept under strict discipline to teach him the necessity of obedience; he is worked hard to give him the habit of industry; and he is, if sufficiently capable, taught so much of a trade as the length of his detention admits. His bodily health and vigour, often very poor on admission, are restored by drill, gymnasium, and hard work. The defects of his school education are remedied by further teaching, and he receives, of course, careful religious and moral instruction. But of all the human factors making for reformation, the greatest is the personal influence of good and manly men. Everyone who has engaged in reformative work, or in any other kind of social work, knows this. All the machinery of gymnasium, school, and trade instruction fails if that is absent. It is on this factor, therefore, that, next to religion, the State places its reliance."

These words breathe the spirit of enlightenment and mark the writer as one who by sympathy and insight is eminently qualified to hold the difficult and responsible position he fills.

During 1912, 531 persons (481 boys and 50 girls) were admitted into Borstal Institutions, of these 520 were sentenced at Assizes and Quarter Sessions and 11 by Courts of Summary

Jurisdiction. This was an increase of 16 boys as compared with 1911. The figure 531 included 439 who had not been previously convicted. A period of detention of two years seems to be regarded as the appropriate one in most cases.

The Report of the Borstal Association, which has been formed to take care of boys and girls on their release from Borstal Institutions, shows that the system has been very successful. Records are kept, as far as possible, and these records show that over 75 per cent. of the boys released have not been reconvicted and that the conduct of over 40 per cent. of the girls released has been satisfactory.

By s. 7 of the C. J. A. Act, 1914, power is given to the Secretary of State to recognise and subsidise, out of moneys provided by Parliament, societies for the care of youthful offenders whilst on probation, or out on licence from a reformatory, industrial school or Borstal Institution, or under supervision after detention. No Probation Society has yet been formed, we believe, but possibly the work may be taken up by the Borstal Association and its branches.

A Home Office Circular, dated 8th July, 1914, calls attention to the fact that the Borstal system applies mainly to male offenders, "but it is very desirable that judicial authorities should bear in mind the fact that the system is equally applicable to girls as to boys." A Borstal Institution for females has been opened at Aylesbury.

The system forms an interesting and valuable experiment in sociology and criminology.

Part II of the Act provides that where a person is convicted on indictment of a crime, and the court passes on him a sentence of penal servitude (in respect of the offence with which he is charged on this occasion), and subsequently the offender admits that he is, or is found by a jury to be, an "habitual criminal," *if the court is of opinion* (in addition) that *"by reason of his criminal habits and mode of life it is expedient for the protection of the public that the offender should be kept in detention for a lengthened period of years,"* it may pass a further sentence upon him, ordering that, on the determination of the sentence of penal servitude passed in respect of the particular offence, he shall be "detained for such period, not exceeding ten nor less than five years, as the court may determine," and such detention is known as "preventive detention." A person on whom such a (double) sentence is passed shall whilst undergoing both sentences be deemed a "convict."

The Act, however, provides that a person shall *not* be found to be an "habitual criminal" unless the jury finds *on evidence* (or by his own admission)—

(*a*) That since attaining the age of sixteen years he has been at least three times previously, before the conviction charged against him in the indictment, convicted of a "crime," whether such previous convictions were before or after the passing of this Act, *and* "that he is leading persistently a dishonest or criminal life"; or

(*b*) That he has on such previous conviction been found to be an habitual criminal and sentenced to preventive detention.

Any person sentenced to preventive detention may appeal against the sentence, without leave, to the Court of Criminal Appeal.

This part of the Act contains similar provisions to those contained in the first part, *mutatis mutandis*, conferring powers on the Secretary of State in certain cases, if he thinks fit—

(1) To commute a sentence of penal servitude to one of preventive detention; and

(2) To discharge on licence, or absolutely; and provisions as to persons placed out on licence.

The sentence of preventive detention must in ordinary cases take effect immediately on the determination of the sentence of penal servitude, and in other cases, at such earlier date as the Secretary of State, having regard to the circumstances of the case, may direct. Ordinarily the sentence of penal servitude is determined and the convict goes to preventive detention at the time when he becomes due for discharge on licence under the penal servitude sentence. Persons undergoing preventive detention are to be confined in any prison or part of a prison which may be set apart for the purpose, and are to be regarded as if they were undergoing penal servitude, but "subject to such modifications in the direction of less rigorous treatment" as may be prescribed from time to time by the prison rules.

The Act came into operation on August 1, 1909. It makes a great change in our mode of treating criminals. Nothing but time can show whether the scheme will succeed or not, but it must be the earnest hope of every well-wisher of his country and his fellow men that this measure will eventually meet with the success it deserves and fulfil the benevolent anticipations of its promoters.

Perhaps, if one may offer a criticism, it seems rather unfair that the question whether a given person is or is not an habitual criminal, should be determined by the same jury which has just convicted him, and which therefore cannot fail, in many cases, to be somewhat prejudiced against him.

This view of the Act was apparently taken by Sir Rufus Isaacs (as he then was) L.C.J., in delivering the judgment of the Court of Criminal Appeal, in the cases of *Rex* v. *Crowley* and *Rex* v. *Sullivan* (L.J. Rep. vol. 110, at p. 130; J.P. Rep. vol. 78, at p. 144) on November 17th, 1913. After saying that it was necessary, when a prisoner is charged with being an habitual criminal, to see that his interests are jealously safeguarded, the learned L.C.J. proceded to give the reason why. It is, he said, "because he stands in a peculiar position, which is, to say the least of it, not a favourable one on his trial; that is to say, he is first of all convicted of the offence for which he is indicted, then he is put upon his trial as an habitual criminal. *It is enough to say that one must be scrupulously careful to protect him when this particular question, whether he is an habitual criminal or not, is being put to that same jury.*"

The same learned judge, in the same cases, said: "It is, however, of importance that judges in passing this sentence (preventive detention) *should bear in mind the policy of the Act.* No doubt the sentence of preventive detention must be punitive; it deprives a man of his liberty, and imposes upon him against his will restrictions and rules of life which are only possible if he has committed an offence which justifies such restrictions; and then, according to the view of the legislature, he may be sentenced to this term of preventive detention. *But it is not intended to rank as, or be the same as imprisonment; it certainly is not the same as penal servitude.*"

Rules have been formed under the Act in regard to preventive detention. By these rules those undergoing such a sentence are separated into three grades, and special privileges are given if a man conducts himself properly; thus he may be employed at certain useful trades, in which he may earn money, and power is given for part of the money so earned to be applied for the benefit of his family, and canteens have been opened, where prisoners may purchase articles of food, at prices to be fixed by the directors, *i.e.* the Directors of Convict Establishments. Prisoners of the ordinary grade may be allowed to associate at meal times, and those in the special grade (after getting their second certificate) may be allowed to associate at meal times and also in the evenings.

Prisoners undergoing preventive detention may also be allowed such relaxation of a literary and social character as may from time to time be prescribed; and, in addition to this, advice and counsel will be given to them.

A Board of Visitors has been appointed by the Secretary of State, to hold office for three years; and there can be no doubt but that this Board has the power of doing much good and useful work.

The object of the Act is to keep under constant control and supervision those old offenders who have shown by their histories that they are clearly not fit to be at large. A constant succession of comparatively short sentences does them no good and only gives them periodical opportunities of preying upon society after every release. Yet it is not intended that they should be perpetually imprisoned. To every old offender, whatever his past may have been, there is still held out a *locus pœnitentiæ*, a hope of reformation and a chance of liberty.

During 1912, 89 persons were sentenced to preventive detention. The offences of which they were found guilty, previous to this sentence being passed upon them, were: felonious wounding, 3; house-breaking and similar offences, 44; robbery, 2; larceny, fraud and receiving, 35; arson, 1; and coining and uttering counterfeit coin, 4.

The procedure under this part of the Act is very technical. The consent of the Public Prosecutor to this course being taken has to be obtained, and notice has to be given to the prisoner and to the court by which he is tried, and such notice must specify the grounds on which it is intended to rely as showing that the prisoner is an habitual criminal. The result is there have been a considerable number of successful appeals against the sentence.

In 1913, according to his Annual Report, 148 applications were made to the Public Prosecutor for his consent to prisoners being charged with being habitual criminals under s. 10 (4)(*a*) of the Prevention of Crimes Act, 1908. Of these applications 47 were refused and 101 granted. The results were: 67 were convicted of the offence charged against them and also of being habitual criminals; 28 were convicted of the offence charged but acquitted of being habitual criminals; five were acquitted of the first charge, and therefore the second charge was not proceeded with, and one absconded.

3.   THE CHILDREN ACT, 1908

Recognising that the youth of a nation is its most valuable asset, Parliament in 1908 amended and consolidated the whole law relating to children and young persons.

The third Act, therefore, provides (*inter alia*) that a *child* shall not be sentenced to imprisonment or penal servitude for any offence, or committed to prison in default of payment of a fine, damages, or costs; and that a *young person* shall not be sentenced to penal servitude or imprisonment for any offence, or committed to prison in default of payment of a fine, damages, or costs; *unless* the court certifies that he is of so unruly a character that he cannot be detained in a "place of detention," or is of so depraved a character that he is not a fit person to be so detained (s. 102).

Part V of the Act relates entirely to Juvenile Offenders and Part IV to Reformatory and Industrial Schools.

By "child" is meant a person under the age of fourteen years; and by "young person," one who is fourteen years of age or upwards and under the age of sixteen years. It may here be explained that a child under the age of seven years is by English Law considered *doli incapax, i.e.* incapable of committing any crime whatsoever; above the age of seven, and under fourteen, he or she is considered *doli capax*, on proof that he or she had *mens rea*, *i.e.* a guilty knowledge that he or she was doing wrong. Above the age of fourteen years, a person is fully responsible for his or her actions, unless and until it is proved that he or she is of unsound mind or subject to some disability, *e.g.* coercion, coverture, etc. The Act abolishes the death sentence in the case of children and young persons, and decrees that they shall be detained during His Majesty's pleasure. Cases are on record of children ten and even eight years having been hanged, but not, be it said for the credit of English Law, for many years past.

Generally speaking, the Act substitutes "custody in a place of detention" for imprisonment, as a punishment for children and young persons; and in no case can such detention exceed one month (s. 106). It makes provision for the establishment of such "places of detention," and the custody of children and young persons therein, and the expenses of their maintenance. It provides that a superintendent or inspector of police, or the officer in charge of the police station to which such person is brought, may, on arrest, admit children and young persons to bail, on the parent or guardian entering into a recognizance, with or without sureties, so as to secure their attendance upon the hearing of the charge. It also provides for the custody of children and young persons, who are not admitted to bail after arrest, in a "place of detention" instead of a prison, until they can be brought before a Court of Summary Jurisdiction; and directs police authorities to make arrangements for preventing, so far as practicable, the association of children and young persons with adult offenders, while being detained in a police station.

The Act contains power to compel the attendance at court of the parent or guardian of a child or young person charged with an offence, and the expression "guardian" *includes* any person who in the opinion of the court has for the time being the charge of or control (or lack of control) over the youthful offender.

It further provides that "where a child or young person charged with any offence is tried by any court, and the court is satisfied of his guilt," the court may deal with the case in **any** of the following methods:

(*a*) By dismissing the charge; or

(*b*) By discharging the offender on his entering into **a** recognizance (bond); or

(*c*) By so discharging the offender and placing him under the supervision of a probation officer;

(*d*) By committing the offender to the care of a relative or other fit person; or

(*e*) By sending the offender to an industrial school; or

(*f*) By sending the offender to a reformatory school; or

(*g*) By ordering the offender to be whipped; or

(*h*) By ordering the offender to pay a fine, damages, or costs; or

(*i*) By ordering the parent or guardian of the offender **to** pay a fine, damages, or costs; or

(*j*) By ordering the parent or guardian of the offender to give security for his good behaviour; or

(*k*) By committing the offender to custody in a place of detention provided under this Act; or

(*l*) Where the offender is a "young person," by sentencing him to imprisonment but only where he is of an unruly or depraved character; or

(*m*) By dealing with the case in any other manner in which it may be legally dealt with (s. 107).

The Act confers on any court, before which a child or young person is charged with an offence for the commission of which a fine, damages or costs may be imposed, if the court is of opinion that the case may be best met by the imposition of a fine, damages or costs, *power to order the parent or guardian to pay the fine*, etc., *instead of the child or young person*, unless the court is satisfied that the parent or guardian cannot be found or that he has not conduced to the commission of the offence by neglecting to exercise due care of the child or young person. But if the child or young person is himself ordered by a Court of Summary Jurisdiction to pay costs, in addition to a fine, the amount of the costs so ordered to be paid shall in no case exceed the amount of the fine. In the case of a child or young person it removes all the disqualifications attaching to felony.

This provision is a very desirable one, particularly in cases of mischievous and malicious damage to property by children and youths, and has long been advocated (see also s. 14 of the C. J. A. Act, 1914, as to Malicious Damage).

Where a child or young person is convicted on indictment of certain grave offences, *viz.* attempt to murder, manslaughter, wounding with intent to do grievous bodily harm, etc., and the court is of opinion that no punishment which it is authorised to inflict under this Act is sufficient, the court may sentence the offender to be detained for such period as may be specified in the sentence, and thereupon such child or young person is liable to be detained in such place and on such conditions as the Secretary of State may direct, and whilst so detained shall be deemed to be in legal custody. The Act also contains provisions as to the discharge of children and young persons so detained, in accordance with the directions of the Secretary of State, upon licence. This provision is obviously intended to apply to special (and it is to be hoped rare) cases. It does not appear that any such case has yet occurred.

Finally the Act provides for the establishment of what are known as " Juvenile Courts," by enacting that a Court of Summary Jurisdiction when hearing charges against children or young persons, or applications for orders or licences relating to them at which their attendance is required, shall sit either in a different building or room from that in which the ordinary sittings of the court are held, or on different days, or at different times. Moreover, it confers power to clear the court whilst a child or young person is giving evidence in certain cases, and a prohibition against children being present in court during the trial of other persons. The general object of these provisions is to prevent the contamination of children and young persons by association with old offenders, or (as old Lambard puts it) to see that they do not "suck corruption" thereby.

In 1912 the total number of juvenile offenders brought before criminal courts was 39,348. 21,177 children and 18,171 young persons. This total is little more than 5 per cent. of the whole number of persons against whom proceedings were taken for criminal offences during the year, but the figure, nearly 40,000, affords ample justification for the establishment of such courts; and in the opinion of experts the results have fully justified their establishment.

The statistics confirm the opinion generally received that "juvenile delinquency is mainly confined to the male sex." The 38,351 children and young persons brought before juvenile courts in 1912 included only 2135 of the female sex, or less than 6 per cent.

It is indeed a remarkable fact that the number of female criminals is out of all proportion to that of men, although in this country the number of the female population is slightly in excess of the male. The adult female defendants dealt with by ordinary courts of summary jurisdiction in 1912 amounted to 113,943, or say 16 per cent. of the whole; and if drunkenness and vice be excluded, only 12 per cent. Moreover, most of the offences committed by juvenile offenders fall under very few headings, *e.g.* petty thefts, acts of mischief, disorderly behaviour in the streets, and offences against police regulations, begging, gambling in public places, etc.

A Home Office Circular of March 9th, 1909, adverts to Juvenile Courts and draws attention "to the distress that is caused to modest girls by having to appear as witnesses in cases of indecency," and states that "in some cases the strain of a severe cross-examination has resulted in permanent injury to the witnesses' health," and that, "especially when indecent exposure is charged, the fear of undergoing such an ordeal is so great as to prevent the witness offering evidence." The Home Secretary therefore recommends magistrates, as far as they may properly do so, to prevent any abuse of the rights of an advocate in regard to cross-examination; and adds further: "It is very desirable that where a girl appears as a witness in a case of the nature now in question, she should not be examined without the presence of a woman, either her mother or some relative or friend."

On July 30th, 1914, in the House of Commons, in reply to a question by Mr Edmund Harvey, M.P., the Home Secretary, Mr McKenna, stated that the number of children charged with offences by the police within the Metropolitan Area in 1911 was 3051, and the number of those who were allowed to return at once to their own homes, under s. 94 of the Children Act, 1908, was 1834. In 1912, the numbers were 3553 and 2177 respectively, and in 1913, 3494 and 2175 respectively. These figures require no comment.

4. THE MENTAL DEFICIENCY ACT, 1913

By this Act (which came into force on 1st April, 1914) further powers and duties are conferred on (some) justices of the peace and other judges, in relation to "defectives," (*a*) idiots, (*b*) imbeciles, (*c*) feeble-minded persons, and (*d*) moral imbeciles, as defined in the Act, four classes of unfortunate persons more to be pitied than punished, from which, however, the criminal class has in the past been largely recruited. It is estimated that there are in England and Wales, including children, over 66,000 defectives.

By s. 19 the "judicial authority" under this Act is defined to be "any judge of county courts, police or stipendiary magistrate, or specially appointed justice who is a judicial authority for the purposes of the Lunacy Acts, 1908 and 1911," and the number of justices specially appointed shall be such as may be considered necessary to exercise the powers conferred by this Act. Every judicial authority is to have the same jurisdiction and powers as if he were acting in the exercise of his ordinary jurisdiction and shall be assisted by the same officers.

Under this Act idiots and imbeciles, and defectives under the age of 21 years, may be placed in an institution or under guardianship by their parents or guardians subject to certain safeguards, *viz.* upon two certificates in a prescribed form signed by two duly qualified medical practitioners, one of whom must be "approved" for the purpose; but where the defective is not an idiot or imbecile an additional certificate signed, "after such enquiry as he shall think fit," by a judicial authority for the purposes of this Act, is required. Thus the duty of making and holding such enquiries is imposed on the judicial authority.

A defective subject to be dealt with under this Act, *otherwise* than at the instance of his parent or guardian, may by s. 4 be so dealt with (*a*) under an order made by a "judicial authority" on a petition presented under this Act. (Such petition may be presented by any relative or friend of the alleged defective or by any officer of the local authority under the Act); (*b*) *under an order of a court*, in the case of a defective found guilty of a criminal offence punishable in the case of an adult with imprisonment or penal servitude, or liable to be ordered to be sent to an industrial school; or (*c*) under an order of the Secretary of State (Home Secretary) in the case of a defective already detained in a prison, criminal lunatic asylum, reformatory or industrial school, place of detention, or inebriate reformatory; but no order must be made except in the circumstances specified in the Act.

The Act sets out the requirements as to the making of orders, the presentation of petitions, the procedure on hearing petitions, and the variation of orders; but the only part that concerns the administration of justice is the procedure in case of persons guilty of offences, etc.

By s. 6 (2) it is provided, as regards the hearing of petitions, "Proceedings before the judicial authority may, in any case, if the judicial authority thinks fit, and shall, if so desired by the person to whom the petition relates, be conducted in private." Although as a rule publicity is very desirable, few people, considering the nature of the proceedings, will find fault with this provision. It must be remembered that these proceedings, though judicial, are not criminal, and the subject of the enquiry is the *status* of the alleged defective, not his punishment.

As to procedure in cases of defectives found guilty of offences, s. 8 provides that *on conviction by a court of competent jurisdiction* of any person of any criminal offence punishable as above, or, on a child brought before the court under s. 58 of the Children Act, 1908, being found liable to be sent to an industrial school, the court, if satisfied on medical evidence that he is a "defective" within the meaning of this Act, may either (*a*) postpone passing sentence or making an order for committal to an industrial school, and direct that a petition be presented to a judicial authority under the Act with a view to obtaining an order that he be sent to an institution or placed under guardianship; or (*b*) in lieu of passing sentence or making an order for committal to an industrial school, the court itself may make an order which shall have the like effect as if it had been made by judicial authority on a petition under this Act.

If the court is a Court of Summary Jurisdiction, and the case is one which it has power to deal with summarily, and it finds that the charge is proved, the court may give such directions or make such order, *without proceeding to conviction*, but such person shall for the purpose of the Act be deemed to be a person found guilty of an offence.

The court may act either on the evidence given during the trial or other proceedings, or may call for further medical or other evidence.

From what is said above it will be seen that this Act, in dealing with criminal offences committed by "defectives," proceeds on much the same lines as the Probation or Offenders Act, 1907.

On June 11, 1914, at the London Sessions, Mr Robert Wallace, K.C., Chairman, drew attention to what he considered to be a serious defect in the Act, saying that hundreds of prisoners of weak intellect could not be dealt with under its provisions, because they had not been so afflicted "from birth or an early age." In other words the mental deficiency which involves confinement by legal process must be constitutional and congenital. Any other mental weakness is not recognised by law unless it amounts to insanity.

By s. 41 of the Act the Secretary of State may make regulations as to the management of institutions for defectives.

5. THE CRIMINAL JUSTICE ADMINISTRATION ACT, 1914

This long promised Act at last received the royal assent on August 10th, 1914; part of it came into operation on December 1st, 1914, and part will come into force on April 1st, 1915. It is an "omnibus" Act, and deals with a large number of somewhat disconnected matters about which the law and practice have long stood in need of amendment. It deals under general headings with fines, court fees, probation, committals to Borstal Institutions, new power of dealing with offenders, imprisonment, bail and remand, and several miscellaneous and general matters, such as police supervision, the issue of warrants of arrest, evidence, the power of justices to order production of documents, costs, the recovery of rates, corporal punishment, right of appeal from justices, charges of drunkenness, convictions on indictment, etc. Some of these provisions are new, and some merely amendments.

Among the provisions as to *evidence* is the very useful one that "the wife or husband of a person charged with bigamy may be called as a witness either for the prosecution or defence, and without the consent of the person charged" (s. 28 (3)). As the law stood before, it not infrequently caused considerable difficulty in proving cases of bigamy and sometimes resulted in the escape of a guilty person.

It is obvious that it is impossible within the scope of a work like this to deal with all these matters. The principal changes made by the Act, so far as possible, have been incorporated or referred to in the previous pages; but magistrates, and all who have to do with the administration of justice, are strongly advised to peruse and note with great care all the provisions of this very important Act. One of the main objects of this book has been, while explaining, or endeavouring to explain, the working of the whole system, to call attention to the principles which underlie these changes and which have rendered them desirable.

II. THE STATISTICS OF CRIME

In 1892 the criminal statistics were revised and rearranged by a Departmental Committee appointed by the Home Secretary, and the recommendations of that Committee were carried into effect the following year. They have, therefore, now been compiled "on uniform principles and in substantially the same form" for twenty years, and the figures for 1912 enable us to institute comparisons for that period. The valuable *Introduction to the Criminal Statistics for the year* 1912, written by Mr W. J. Farrant, the superintendent of the Statistical Department of the Home Office, states that "advantage has been taken of the opportunity to review the progress of a few of the most important figures during the two decades."

The principal object of collecting and compiling statistics is to enable us to make comparisons and so to ascertain whether crime as a whole, or any particular form of it, has increased or decreased. If they do not show this, it is difficult to see what useful purpose they serve. The tables in the *Judicial Statistics, England and Wales,* 1912, *Part I, Criminal Statistics,* are admirably adapted for this purpose and full of interesting information. Yet it is somewhat difficult to say what is the best test to apply as to whether crime is on the increase or not. Mr Farrant thinks that "the number of persons tried for indictable offences has been found to be, on the whole, the best criterion of the amount of criminality." He adds, "owing to changes in procedure and practice trustworthy evidence as to the increase or decrease of crime cannot be based upon the figures of persons convicted or persons imprisoned." Another influence which affects the figures is the number of new offences created.

Taking therefore the number of persons tried for indictable offences during a given period of sufficient length (say 20 years) Mr Farrant is of opinion, and his opinion is of great weight as that of an expert, that during the last 20 years (1893–1912) "relatively to population criminality has diminished." During the period in question the population rose from about 29,760,000 to 36,540,000, an increase of 23 per cent.; in 1893 the number of persons tried for indictable offences was 192·7 per 100,000 of the estimated population; in 1912, the proportion was only 184·8. During this period there have been considerable variations. The lowest figures were in 1899; since then there has been an increase, which is very discouraging. The highest figures were in 1908.

1893, Proportion per 100,000 of population 192·7
1899,　　　 ” 　　 ” 　　 ” 　　 ” 　　 158·4
1908,　　　 ” 　　 ” 　　 ” 　　 ” 　　 194·3
1912,　　　 ” 　　 ” 　　 ” 　　 ” 　　 184·8

About fifteen-sixteenths of the indictable offences are acts of dishonesty, and consequently the rise and fall of this class of offences determine the annual fluctuations of the total of all crimes. It is, therefore, worth while to consider separately a few of the chief classes of offences other than dishonesty. The figures show that while offences of violence against the person have considerably diminished, sexual offences have considerably increased. The quinquennial average of offences of violence for 1893–7 was 1601; in 1908–12, it sank to 1471. On the contrary, the quinquennial average of sexual offences for 1893–7 was 1167; in 1908–12, it rose to 1389. Again, the quinquennial average of burglary and housebreaking for the period 1893–7 was 1762; for 1908–12, it was no less than 3875. These figures show how difficult it is to draw any general conclusions as to the increase or decrease of crime. There are many factors to be taken into consideration, amongst which are the state of trade, the weather, the influence of example (good or bad), police activity, the creation of new offences, education, morality, religion, etc. We can only hope that all the forces for good now at work will in due time have their effect. It certainly cannot be said that the criminal has not received sufficient attention from the legislator, the philanthropist and the sociologist. Society has tried to realise its responsibility for crime and to fulfil its duty in regard to it.

As to the distribution of indictable offences between the different courts, there has been very little change during the last 20 years.

	1893	1912
Tried at Assizes	8 per cent.	6 per cent.
Tried at Quarter Sessions	14 per cent.	14 per cent.
Tried by Courts of Summary Jurisdiction ..	78 per cent.	80 per cent.

But in regard to the results of the trials there has been a great change.

	1893	1912
Acquitted or discharged	18 per cent.	12 per cent.
Convicted and sentenced	77 per cent.	60 per cent.
Charge proved, but order made without conviction	5 per cent.	28 per cent.

These figures show that the provisions of the Probation of Offenders Act, 1908, are already bearing fruit.

If the cases dealt with by Courts of Summary Jurisdiction are also taken into account the difference of the figures in regard to this mode of dealing with offences is even greater. The increase is then from 6 to 32 per cent.; that is to say a very large number of cases, nearly one-third of the whole, are now dealt with in this way (by order, without conviction) whereas formerly the prisoners would have been either acquitted and discharged absolutely or convicted and sentenced. This mode of dealing with offenders, particularly first offenders, is indeed the most marked characteristic of modern criminal practice and legislation and gives us great hope for the future.

During 1912, 670,109 persons were charged with non-indictable offences of a criminal character, of which 299,586 were apprehended by the police, and 370,523 were proceeded against by summons. The number of non-indictable offences of a non-criminal character (see Appendix A) has steadily decreased, from 113,887 in 1893 to 73,917 in 1912. The decrease falls almost entirely under the heading of assaults, the average number of which during the years 1893–7 was 73,049, but only 44,389 during 1908–12.

The statistics as to the number of cases tried in each of the different criminal courts have been mentioned in connection therewith. More than twice as many prisoners are tried at Quarter Sessions than at Assizes, the numbers in 1912 being 9233 and 4053 respectively. During the same year 54,244 persons were tried and convicted of indictable offences by Courts of Summary Jurisdiction. In 1893, 14 cases were tried in the King's Bench Division of the High Court, in 1912, only 2.

In 1912 the number of persons under police supervision was 3463, nearly half of whom lived in London. More than 25 per cent. were reconvicted during the year, but about 50 per cent. were reported to be living honest lives. It was estimated that on the first Tuesday in April, 1912, there were 3885 habitual criminals at large, including 3270 thieves, 433 receivers of stolen property, and 182 others.

The number of criminal lunatics received into asylums during 1912 was 272. Of these 65 were found to be insane by the verdicts of juries, 8 were certified as insane while awaiting trial, and 199 were certified as insane while serving sentences in prison. Of the 272, 101 were received into Broadmoor or Parkhurst Criminal Lunatic Asylums, the remainder, mostly serving short sentences, were received into county and borough asylums. During 1912, 305 persons were received into inebriate reformatories, including 245 women and 60 men, and 300 were discharged therefrom, 40 on licence.

Bearing in mind what is said by Mr W. J. Farrant, that "trustworthy evidence as to the increase or decrease of crime cannot be based upon the figures of persons convicted or persons imprisoned," a good deal of interesting matter is to be derived from the *Annual Report of the Commissioners of Prisons and the Directors of Convict Prisons for the year* 1913–14 which has just been published (Oct. 1914). The first fact that strikes one's attention is that the number of persons in prison during the last twelve months shows a decrease, whatever its causes, of no less than 14,420 as compared with the previous year. The details are shown in the following table:

	1912–13	1913–14
Sentenced by Ordinary Courts:		
(a) To penal servitude	871	797
(b) To imprisonment	149,522	135,140
(c) To detention in Borstal	571	487
Sentenced by Court-Martial:		
(a) To penal servitude	10	11
(b) To imprisonment	288	263
Imprisoned as Debtors or on Civil Process	13,941	14,138
Imprisoned in default of sureties	820	767
TOTAL	166,023	151,603

The Commissioners themselves state (p. 7) that there is "need for caution in drawing deductions from statistics of imprisonment, but the remarkable decrease in the number of prisoners received after conviction for indictable offences (chiefly under larceny) during the last ten years, being no less than 7209, *is a most favourable symptom,* for it is crimes of this character, *i.e.* larcenies and the various acts of dishonesty, which make up about fifteen-sixteenths of the total number of indictable offences, and may be generally regarded as an index to the law-abiding instincts of the community." After referring to the manifold causes operating outside and independently of prisons, in restraint of criminal tendency, the commissioners go on to say: "We believe that some credit may be given, and is justly due, to the efforts of those working at the prisons themselves, of which the reports of governors and chaplains produce such gratifying evidence" (p. 7).

Amongst these reports may be mentioned the opinion of the chaplain of Knutsford prison, who states that prison officers of long service affirm that prisoners are now much quieter and more amenable to discipline than in the past. "This," he says, "is no doubt due to education and the higher level of conduct prevailing in the general community to-day; but it is also due to the humanity[1] of the modern prison system." "The greatly improved conditions of prison life and labour impress upon offenders that their welfare is desired, and their reformation hoped for, by the community" (p. 8).

The same gentleman remarks: "The average drunkard believes that he cannot exist without strong drink, and many moderate drinkers consider alcohol necessary to efficiency. Prison life dispels these and many similar fancies, and gives practical demonstration of the advantages of a simple life. Men are surprised to find, as their sentences proceed, that they are healthier, more vigorous, and in every way in improved condition. They begin to set a higher value on the quieter joys of life, such as reading, and to appreciate as never before the meaning and value of religion" (p. 8).

May it not be that the true criterion of criminality is not to be found after all in mere figures, but in such opinions as these as to the effect upon national life and character of all the moral, social and religious forces now at work, some of which are of a negative rather than a positive nature, and do not appear upon the surface? Since the outbreak of the war with Germany and Austria, judging by the accounts of the small number of prisoners

---

[1] According to an interesting and somewhat pathetic article in *The Times* newspaper for Tuesday, Feb. 9th, 1915, headed "Patriotism in Prison," a wave of patriotism seems to have swept over the inmates of our prisons, which is, perhaps, the best testimony that could be given to the humane treatment of our prisoners.

for trial at the various Quarter Sessions and Assizes, there
appears to be a great falling off in crime. How far this is due
to the increased sense of national unity and personal responsibility
is a difficult psychological problem. Low water mark in regard
to crime was reached in 1899, just before the Boer war. The
present war is a sad but stern necessity, and it has to be fought
out to a successful issue. War, however, has always a brutalising
and demoralising effect upon a nation, in spite of the great
qualities it evokes. We can only hope that when peace is
restored, there will be no recrudescence of criminality.

N.B. For the statistics of crime in 1913 see Notes, etc.,
hereafter (pp. 224–226).

*   *   *   *   *

Nothing whatever has been said throughout this book as to
the purity of the administration of justice in this country, and
for good reason, *viz.*, that it is always assumed, and therefore
there is no need to mention it. Mistakes are always possible in
human affairs, but happily they are comparatively few and far
between in the administration of the criminal law in England;
and when they do occur, it will invariably be found that they
are due to wrong headedness and not to corrupt motives. It
may safely be asserted that the standard of honour on the part
of all concerned in the working of our system of criminal law is a
very high one and that all feel keenly their responsibility.

*   *   *   *   *

Our legal system is not one of recent growth. It has been
built up by the best minds of the nation over a period of nearly
a thousand years, as the result of their experience of the needs of
society, and it is part of our civilisation. The English institution
of trial by Judge and Jury has been spread over a large portion
of the world, as part and parcel of the Common Law, which has
been transplanted into the United States of America and our
colonies as part of one common heritage. Comparing our system
of criminal law and its administration with that of other civilised
countries, we have just cause to be proud of it. It is one that is
worthy of a great, free and enlightened nation, which has taught
lessons of liberty and good government to the world, and has generally been in the vanguard of political, legal, and social progress.

APPENDIX A [see pp. 19, 51]

THE CLASSIFICATION OF OFFENCES

OFFENCES may be classified as follows:

I. Indictable.

II. Non-indictable.

    1. Of a criminal character.

    2. Of a non-criminal character.

The latter class, "though technically criminal, cannot be regarded as criminal in the most serious sense of the term. They consist mainly of contraventions of municipal regulations established in the interests of the public safety, health or comfort, and not involving violence, cruelty, or gross dishonesty" (*Introduction to the Judicial (Criminal) Statistics for the year* 1912, p. 9, note).

Another classification of offences (according to the mode of trial) is:

I. Those triable at Quarter Sessions and Assizes, by ordinary procedure, *viz.*

    1. Indictable, *e.g.* murder.

    2. Non-indictable, where the accused has elected to be tried by a jury, on being charged before a Court of Summary Jurisdiction with an offence punishable with more than three months' imprisonment (see s. 17 (1) S. J. Act, 1879) (Appendix C).

II. Those triable by Justices at Petty Sessions in the exercise of their summary jurisdiction.

    1. Non-indictable offences.

    2. Indictable offences which may be dealt with summarily, *viz.*

        (*a*) Offences committed by children.

        (*b*) Offences committed by young persons.

        [1](*c*) Certain offences committed by adults, where the value of the property in question is less than £20, and the accused consents.

        [1](*d*) When the accused pleads guilty.

---

[1] See List of Indictable Offences Triable Summarily (Appendix B).

APPENDIX B [see p. 48]

LIST OF INDICTABLE OFFENCES TRIABLE SUMMARILY

1.	Simple larceny and offences punishable as simple larceny, viz.	Larceny Act, 1861, s. 4.
(i)	stealing oysters from fisheries;	„ „ „ s. 26.
(ii)	stealing or destroying valuable securities;	„ „ „ s. 27.
(iii)	stealing metal, glass, wood, etc., affixed to houses or land;	„ „ „ s. 31.
(iv)	stealing trees, etc., in pleasure grounds, etc., to value of £1, or if elsewhere, to value of £5;	„ „ „ s. 32.
(v)	stealing trees, etc., to value of 1s. (third offence);	„ „ „ s. 33.
(vi)	stealing plants, fruit, vegetables, etc., growing in orchards, gardens, etc. (second offence);	„ „ „ s. 36.
(vii)	stealing by a partner . . .	Larceny Act, 1868.
(viii)	Fraudulently abstracting electricity	Electric Lighting Act, 1882.
2.	Larceny from the person . . .	Larceny Act, 1861, s. 40.
3.	Larceny by a servant . . .	„ „ „ s. 67.
4.	Embezzlement	„ „ „ s. 68.
5.	Obtaining goods, etc. by false pretences.	„ „ „ s. 88.
6.	Receiving stolen goods . . .	„ „ „ s. 91.
7.	Endangering the safety of railway passengers.	Offences against the Persons Act, 1861, ss. 32, 33.
8.	Destroying railways	Malicious Damage Act, 1861, s. 35.
9.	Setting fire to commons . . .	Malicious Damage Act, 1861, s. 16.
10.	Certain offences against the Post Office Laws.	
11.	Libel	Newspaper Libel and Registration Act, 1881, s. 5.
12.	Habitual drunkenness . . .	Inebriates Act, 1898, s. 2.
13.	Indecent assault on Juveniles . .	Children Act, 1908, s. 128.
14.	Indictable offences (except homicide) by children.	
15.	Indictable offences (except homicide) by young persons.	

Those offences numbered 1 to 9 inclusive may be tried summarily only where the property in question does not exceed £20 in value, and the accused *consents* to be tried summarily (see C. J. A. Act, 1914, s. 15).

To this list must be added *attempts* to commit any of the offences numbered 1 to 4 inclusive, whatever the value of the property in question.

Where the value of the property exceeds £20, the accused can be dealt with summarily, in the same cases, only *if he pleads guilty*.

APPENDIX C [see p. 52]

LIST OF OFFENCES (OTHERWISE TRIABLE SUMMARILY) IN RESPECT OF WHICH THERE IS A RIGHT TO TRIAL BY JURY, AND THE DEFENDANT MUST BE ASKED, *BEFORE THE CHARGE IS PROCEEDED WITH*, WHETHER HE DESIRES TO BE TRIED BY JURY

1. Purloining, embezzling, etc., of material entrusted to them by workmen in certain factories (*second offence*).

   Frauds by Workmen Act, 1777 s. 1.

2. Offences under the Night Poaching Act, 1828 (*second offence*).

3. Compelling, etc., minors to sweep chimneys; and frauds as to chimney sweepers' certificates (*second offence*).

   Chimney Sweepers, etc., Act, 1840, s. 2; and Chimney Sweepers Act, 1854, s. 19.

4. Charges under the Gaming Act, 1845, s. 4, and the Gaming Houses Act, 1854, s. 4.

5. Charges under the Betting Act, 1853, s. 3.

6. Dog stealing . . . . .

   Larceny Act, 1861, s. 18.

7. Stealing birds, beasts or other domestic animals not the subject of larceny at Common Law, *e.g.*, a cat. . . .

   „ „ „ ss. 21 and 22

8. Stealing or damaging trees, etc., wheresoever growing, when damage done is not less than 1s. (*second offence*).

   Larceny Act, 1861, s. 33 and Malicious Damage Act, 1861, s. 22.

9. Stealing or damaging fences (*second offence*).

   Larceny Act, 1861, s. 34 and Malicious Damages Act, 1861, s. 23.

10. Stealing or damaging plants, roots, etc., growing in gardens . . . . — Larceny Act, 1861, s. 36 and Malicious Damages Act, 1861, s. 23.

11. Stealing or damaging plants, roots, etc., growing elsewhere than in a garden (*second offence*). — Larceny Act, 1861, s. 37 and Malicious Damages Act, 1861, s. 24.

12. Maliciously killing or wounding dogs, birds, beasts or other animals (except cattle). — Malicious Damages Act, 1861, s. 46.

13. Certain charges under the Salmon Fishery Act, 1861 (*third offence*). — Salmon Fishery Act, 1873, s. 18.

14. Certain offences under the Prisons Act, 1865, s. 35.

15. Forging Pedlar's Certificate (*second offence*) . . . . . . — Pediars Act, 1871, s. 12. „ „ 1881, s. 2.

16. Certain offences by ticket-of-leave men and those under police supervision. — Prevention of Crime Act, 1871, ss. 3, 5, 7 and 8.

17. Forging certificate for a Pawnbroker's licence. — Pawnbrokers Act, 1872, s. 44.

18. Master neglecting to provide servant or apprentice with food, medical aid, etc. — Conspiracy and Protection of Property Act, 1875, ss. 6 and 9; and Employers and Workmens Act, 1875, ss. 6 and 10.

19. Certain offences under the Army Act (1881, renewed annually), s. 53 (aiding deserters, etc.) and under the Reserve Forces Acts, 1882 and 1907.

20. Summary proceedings for the suppression of brothels (*second offence*). — Criminal Law Amendment Act, 1885, s. 13.

21. Forging trade marks and other offences under the . . . . . — Merchandise Marks Act, 1887.

22. Exposure of unsound meat. . . — Public Health (London) Act, 1891, s. 47.

23. Offences under the . . . . — Merchant Shipping Act, 1894, s. 680.

24. Offences under the . . . . — Fertilizers and Feeding Stuffs Act, 1906, s. 7.

25. Offences under the . . . . — Prevention of Corruption Act, 1906, s. 1.

26. Knowingly making false statements in order to obtain an old age pension. — Old Age Pension Act, 1908, s. 9 (1).

27. Offences under Part I, ss. 1–11 (Infant Life Protection) of the . . . — Children Act, 1908.

28. Charges of cruelty to children under Part II, ss. 12–16, of the . . . — Children Act, 1908.

29. Gambling in Marine Insurances . . — 9 Edward VII, c. 12.

30. Forging a Justice's licence granted
under the Licensing (Consolidation)
Act, 1910, s. 44 (ii).
31. The making of false returns under the   Finance, 1909–10, Act, s. 75.
32. Contravention of Order, prohibiting
navigation over prescribed area,
made under the   . . . .   Aerial Navigation Act, 1911.

In most, if not all, of these above-mentioned cases the right
to trial by jury is the result of s. 17 (1) of the S. J. Act, 1879.

33 and 34. Under the Explosives Act, 1875, s. 92, where
the penalty (exclusive of forfeiture) may exceed £100; and under
the Conspiracy and Protection of Property Act, 1875, s. 9, where
a penalty amounting to £20, or imprisonment, may be imposed,
the accused *may*, on appearing before the court, *declare that he
objects* to be tried for such offence by a Court of Summary Jurisdiction; and thereupon the court *may* deal with the case in all
respects as if the accused were charged with an indictable offence;
and in *Rex* v. *Mitchell and another* [1913] 1 K.B. 56, it was held
that *may* here means *must*. These two enactments preceded
s. 17 (1) of the S. J. Act, 1879, and appear to have served as the
model for it.

APPENDIX D [see p. 58]

LIST OF OFFENCES WHICH MAY BE DEALT WITH SUMMARILY BY *ONE* JUSTICE OF THE PEACE

1. Keeping a "little goe" or other lottery
under the   . . . .   Gaming Act, 1802.
2. Certain offences under the Poor Law:
(i)   Paupers refusing to work or guilty   Poor Relief Act, 1815, s. 5.
of misbehaviour.
(ii)   Out-paupers misbehaving   . .   Poor Law Amendment Act,
1866, s. 15.
(iii)   Absconding from workhouse or   Pauper Inmates, etc., Act,
refusing to do task work.   1871, s. 7.
(iv)   Injuring clothes or property . .   Pauper Inmates, etc., Act, 1871,
s. 7.
(v)   Obtaining relief by giving false   Pauper Inmates, etc., Act, 1871,
name or making false statement.   s. 7; Divided Parishes, etc.,
Act, 1876, s. 44; Casual
Poor Act, 1882, s. 5.

3.	All offences under the . . . (Idle and disorderly persons, rogues and vagabonds, etc.).	Vagrancy Act, 1824.
4.	Certain offences under the . . .	Game Act, 1831; Larceny Act, 1861, s. 7.
(i)	Trespassing in pursuit of game in daytime.	Game Act, 1831, s. 30.
(ii)	Trespassing in pursuit of game (5 persons together).	„ „ „
(iii)	Trespassing in pursuit of game (not giving name, etc.).	„ „ s. 31
(iv)	Taking hares or rabbits in warren in daytime	Larceny Act, 1861, s. 17.
5.	Offences under the . . .	Bread Act, 1836.
6.	Certain Railway offences:	
(i)	Misconduct of servants of Company.	Railway Regulation Act, 1840, s. 13.
(ii)	Obstructing offices of company .	Railway Regulation Act, 1840, s. 16.
(iii)	Trespassers refusing to quit premises.	Railway Regulation Act, 1840, s. 16.
7.	Improperly conveying animals .	Cruelty to Animals Act, 1849, s. 12.
8.	Non-indictable (first) offences under the (except dog-stealing which requires two Justices)	Larceny Act, 1861.
9.	Non-indictable (first) offences under	Malicious Damage Act, 1861.
10.	Charges of drunkenness on highway, etc., under Licensing Act, 1872, s. 12.	Criminal Justice Administration Act, 1914, s. 38.

In all these cases the penalty is limited to a fine of 20s., including costs or imprisonment not exceeding 14 days. S. J. Act, 1879, s. 20 (7).

APPENDIX E [see p. 135]

CASES IN WHICH THE CONSENT OF THE ATTORNEY-GENERAL[1] (OR SOLICITOR-GENERAL) IS NECESSARY TO A PROSECUTION

1. Town Police Clauses Act, 1847 (certain offences under).
2. Larceny Act, 1861, s. 80 (2) (Frauds by Trustees).
3. Newspaper Printers, etc., Report Act, 1869.

[1] In some of the above cases an alternative consent may be obtained, *e.g.* under the Lunacy Act, 1890, the consent of the Commissioners in Lunacy is equivalent to that of the Attorney-General.

4. Public Health Act, 1875, ss. 251–253.
5. Explosive Substances Act, 1883, s. 7.
   [see *R.* v. *Bates* [1911] 1 K.B. 694].
6. Public Bodies Corrupt Practices Act, 1889, s. 4.
7. Lunacy Act, 1890 (certain offences under s. 325).
8. Moneylenders Act, 1900, s. 2 (3).
9. Prevention of Corruption Act, 1906, s. 2.
10. Punishment of Incest Act, 1908.
11. Marine Insurance (Gambling Policies) Act, 1909.
12. Official Secrets Act, 1911, s. 8.
13. Geneva Convention Act, 1911.

Under the Law of Libel Amendment Act, 1888, s. 8, no criminal prosecution may be commenced against any proprietor, publisher, editor, etc., of a newspaper for any libel published therein without the order of a Judge at chambers being first had and obtained. Notice of such application must be given to the person accused who must have an opportunity of being heard against the application; and the order (if made) being in a criminal matter, there is no appeal against it, *ex p. Pulbrook* [1892] 1 Q.B. 86; 56 J.P. 293.

APPENDIX F

CRIMINAL PROCEDURE AS IT WAS

The following verses show, in an amusing way, the great changes that have taken place in our criminal procedure in modern times. They are from the pen of Mr John William Smith, the learned author of Smith's Leading Cases (see *Law Magazine*, 1846, p. 191).

> "No tribe, with rusty camlet gowns
> And shabby horsehair wigs,
> Harangued the upper gallery
> In favour of the prigs.

> "No troops of venal witnesses,
> Inured to perjury,
> Were ever brought by knaves who sought
> To prove an *alibi*.

"For sundry wise precautions
        The sages of the law
Discreetly framed whereby they aimed
        To keep the rogues in awe.

"For lest some sturdy criminal
        False witnesses should bring—
His witnesses were not allowed
        To swear to anything.

"And lest his wily advocate
        The Court should overreach,
His advocate was not allowed
        The privilege of speech.

"Yet such was the humanity
        And wisdom of the law,
That if in the indictment
        There appeared to be a flaw,

"The Court assigned him counsellors
        To argue on the doubt,
Provided he himself had first
        Contrived to point it out.

"Yet, lest their mildness should, perchance,
        Be craftily abused,
To show him the indictment they
        Most sturdily refused.

"But still, that he might understand
        The nature of the charge,
The same was in the Latin tongue
        Read out to him at large."

LIST OF PRINCIPAL AUTHORITIES

The Encyclopaedia of the Laws of England, 2nd Ed. (Sweet and Maxwell.)
The Statutes of Practical Utility. (Chitty's Statutes.)
Lambard's Eirenarcha, 1602.
Blackstone's Commentaries, 1793.
A General View of the Criminal Law of England, by J. F. Stephen, 1863.
A History of the Criminal Law of England, by Sir J. F. Stephen, 1883.
A History of Police in England, by Capt. Melville Lee, 1901.
Outlines of Criminal Law, by C. S. Kenny, LL.D., 5th Ed., 1911. (Camb. Univ. Press.)
The Spirit of Our Laws (Anonymous), 1906. (Sweet and Maxwell.)
The Expansion of the Common Law, by Sir F. Pollock, 1904. (London, Stevens & Sons, Ltd.)
Maitland's Justice and Police. (English Citizen Series.)
Atkinson's Magistrate's General Practice, 1914.
Stone's Justices' Manual, 1914.
Archbold's Quarter Sessions Practice, 6th Ed. 1908.
Archbold's Criminal Pleading and Evidence, 1910.
Anson's Law and Custom of the Constitution.
Taswell-Langmead's English Constitutional History.
Gneist's History of the English Constitution (trans. Ashworth).
Dicey on Law and Public Opinion in England.
Maine on Popular Government.
Paley's Moral and Political Philosophy.
Bentham's Principles of Morals and Legislation. (Clarendon Press.)
Bentham's Theory of Legislation (par Dumont) (trans. Hildreth).
Publications of the Selden Society.
Judicial Statistics, England and Wales, 1912. (Part I—Criminal Statistics.)
Judicial Statistics, England and Wales, 1913. (Part I—Criminal Statistics.)
Report of the Royal Commission on the Selection of Justices of the Peace 1910.
Report of the Departmental Committee on Coroners, 1910.
Report of the Departmental Committee on Juries, 1913.
Report of the Commissioners of Prisons, etc., 1914.
Report of the Howard Association for 1914.
Home Office Circulars, 1914.
The Law Times (L.T.).
The Justice of the Peace (J.P.).

NOTES: ADDENDA ET CORRIGENDA

Lords Lieutenant of Counties (p. 8).

By the Army Regulation Act, 1871, they were deprived of their military command and duties, which were revested in the Crown and declared to be exercisable through a Secretary of State, or any officer to whom His Majesty, with the advice of a Secretary of State, might delegate such command and powers. But the right of appointing Deputy Lieutenants and their jurisdiction and powers in relation to the raising of the militia by ballot (if and when that course may be adopted) were reserved to the Lords Lieutenant. And now, by the Territorial and Reserve Forces Act, 1907, the Lord Lieutenant has been placed in his former position of military responsibility as President of the County Association (which he has the opportunity of becoming) and the first appointment to the lowest rank of officer in any unit of the Territorial Force is to be given to persons recommended by him as such President.

Deputy Lieutenants (p. 8).

The qualifications of these officers are set out in s. 32 of the Militia Act, 1882. These qualifications are not restricted either to magistrates or persons connected with the army or territorial forces. But His Majesty the late King Edward VII, by an order issued in 1907, announced that in the future he would not consent to the appointment as Deputy Lieutenant any gentleman who had not, in addition to the qualifications above referred to, held his military commission for a period of ten years or had not rendered signal service to the County Association formed under the Territorial Reserve Forces Act, 1907 (see the *Times* newspaper, November 22, 1907). Before this, for a long time, the office of Deputy Lieutenant had been confined almost exclusively to magistrates; and so far back as 1843, out of 3000 Deputy Lieutenants, no less than 2500, or five-sixths, were magistrates. The connection between the magistracy and the military power of the Crown through the Lords Lieutenant, Deputy Lieutenants and Home Secretary shows how intimately the civil power is allied at the top with the military, and that the ultimate basis of government is physical force, directed and controlled by public opinion. (See an article on *The Deputy Lieutenant* in *The Justice of the Peace* for March 13, 1915.)

Poor Man's Lawyer (p. 19).

"A great organisation some years ago in their appeal for funds spoke as if they were the lawyers of the poor. For years, without any appeal, any advertisement, or any reward, the magistrates of London have been and are still the legal advisers of the poor" (*The London Police Courts*, by Mr Thomas Holmes, Secretary of the Howard Association). There are now several such organisations, not only in London but also in large provincial towns, *e.g.* Birmingham, Manchester and Liverpool.

Rex v. Amendt (p. 68).

This decision was reversed on appeal by a Divisional Court of the K.B.D. on March 5, 1915, the Court holding that rule 21 of the Crown Office Rules, 1906, did *not* apply to the case of a writ of *certiorari* issued at the instance of the Attorney-General on behalf of the Crown. (See W. N., March 13, 1915, p. 122.) Apparently the maxim *Nullum tempus regi occurrit* applies to these proceedings as to others.

Kates v. Jeffery (p. 69).

This rule is considerably relaxed in the Court of Criminal Appeal, which had laid it down that that Court may give effect to a point of law which might have been taken at the trial; see *Rex* v. *Wicks* (*Thos.*), 10 Cr. App. R. 16. But the Court of Criminal Appeal will not entertain a defence (on facts) which might have been set up at the trial, but was not. **Rex** v. **Deane** (7 Cr. App. R. 69).

Advisory Committees as to the Appointment of Magistrates (p. 71).

Following the Report of the Royal Commission on the Selection of J.P.'s, and as the result of a certain amount of dissatisfaction and agitation, Lord Loreburn, L.C., in 1911 appointed Advisory Committees, consisting of magistrates with special local knowledge, both in counties and in boroughs, to assist the Lords Lieutenant and the Lord Chancellor for the time being in the selection of suitable persons as magistrates.

Clerks of the Peace (p. 78).

In counties (except in the county of London) the Clerk of the County Council is also the Clerk of the Peace; but in boroughs the Town Clerk is not always the Clerk of the Peace.

Summing up (p. 78 and p. 114).

The Court of Criminal Appeal has held that an inadequate summing up may be a sufficient ground for quashing a conviction, but it is not so in all cases, *e.g.* if the court is satisfied that the jury appreciated the question for them; see *Rex* v. *Wolff (Victor)*, 10 Cr. App. R. 107; and *Rex* v. *McGill (Thos.)*, 10 Cr. App. R. 267. Again the same Court has held that a mis-statement by the Judge in a summing up which is likely to influence the Jury is a ground for quashing a conviction; see *Rex* v. *Corrigan*, 8 Cr. App. R. 4. A short and hurried summing up is therefore dangerous.

Trial by Jury (pp. 101–116).

Under the Defence of the Realm Consolidation Act, 1914, apparently by oversight, civilians were deprived of their right to trial by jury in many cases, and were practically put under military law and made liable to be tried by courts martial. But by an amending Act the Government has restored this right (which is one of the first importance from a constitutional and legal point of view) subject to certain conditions.

No finer eulogium was ever bestowed on trial by jury than this: "Of all the devices for good government which the genius of the English people has evolved, of all those institutions which they reverence as the chief safeguards of their liberty, none perhaps has been more deeply cherished at home nor more widely imitated abroad than the system now known as Trial by Jury." (*Report of the Departmental Committee on the Law and Practice of Juries*, 1913, par. 4.) Everything must, however, yield to military necessity, *nam silent leges inter arma.*

Prisoners' Plea (p. 105).

There must be no ambiguity or mistake about the prisoners' plea. In *Rex* v. *Golathan* [1915] W.N. 45, the Court of Criminal Appeal held that "where there was any ambiguity in a prisoner's plea it must be taken as one of Not Guilty." And in *Rex* v. *Rhodes (James Wm.)* (11 Cr. App. R. 33) it was laid down by that court that in an appeal on the ground that the appellant had pleaded Guilty by mistake, the court will satisfy itself on the facts whether he really did, or did not, understand the effect of his plea. See also *The King* v. *Ingleson* [1915] 1 K.B. 512.

Separation of Jury (p. 115).

After the summing up the jurors are not allowed on any account to separate or to talk with anyone. In the very recent case of *Rex* v. *Ketteridge* (decided by the Court of Criminal Appeal on December 14th, 1914), W.N. 1915, p. 11; J.P. vol. 28, p. 604; it was laid down that "If a juror, after the judge has summed up in a criminal trial, separates himself from his colleagues, and not being under the control of the court, converses, or is in a position to converse, with other persons, it is an irregularity which renders the whole proceedings abortive, and the only course open to the court is to discharge the jury and commence the proceedings afresh." In this case the conviction was quashed and it was held that the irregularity was one that could not be sanctioned by the court itself; it was not necessary or relevant to consider whether the irregularity had in fact prejudiced the prisoner.

When once the jury has retired to consider its verdict no one is permitted to interfere with them or to influence them in any way, or to use any pressure to induce them to come to a speedy decision, not even the Clerk of Assize; see *Rex* v. *Willmont* (1914), C.C.A.; 10 Cr. App. R. 173; 78 J.P. 352.

In murder cases there is a rule that the jurors must not separate after the trial has begun. But this does not mean that they must not in any circumstances physically part from one another. Thus in *Rex* v. *Crippen* [1911] 1 K.B. 149, a juror was temporarily absent from the court for a short time, two medical men and an usher having been sworn to take charge of him; and the Court of Criminal Appeal held that that fact was not of itself sufficient to vitiate the verdict and quash the conviction.

Nor will the Court hear evidence to prove misconduct on the part of a jury or an individual juror unless the allegation is of a serious kind. *Rex* v. *Syme* (1914), 10 Cr. App. R. 284.

Sentences (pp. 119–121).

It is not the policy of the Court of Criminal Appeal to interfere with a sentence if its members are of opinion that they themselves would have given a less sentence, but only if the sentence appealed from is manifestly wrong; *Rex* v. *Wolff* (*Victor*), 10 Cr. App. R. 107. But the Court will correct a sentence due to a mistake in the record; *Rex* v. *Malory* (*Peter*), 10 Cr. App. R. 52.

Previous convictions (pp. 119–121).

In treating of the Court of Criminal Appeal it is difficult to avoid trespassing upon the Law of Evidence, which is bound up so closely with our system of procedure. The cardinal rule of the law of evidence is that the accused must be tried upon facts relevant to the issue, and not upon suspicion and prejudice. Accordingly the fact that the accused has been previously convicted should never be mentioned to a jury, except in those cases where it is permitted by law. In *Rex* v. *Hemingway* (8 Cr. App. R. 17) the Court of Criminal Appeal held that if evidence of a *previous conviction* is improperly given, the Court will quash a conviction which may be due to the jury knowing that fact. And in *Rex* v. *Barron* (9 Cr. App. R. 236) it was held by the Court of Criminal Appeal that it will quash a conviction when evidence even of a previous *accusation* of an offence similar to that charged has been given, though the Judge warn the jury to disregard such evidence.

After the jury has returned its verdict the fact of a previous conviction may be mentioned to the Judge to assist him in considering what sentence to pass.

In some cases the prisoner is charged with the previous conviction as a substantive offence and pleads to it. If he denies it, the conviction must be proved by calling evidence, generally that of a detective or prison warder, who was present at the previous conviction and can prove the identity of the prisoner.

Archdeacon Paley on Punishment and the Administration of Justice (pp. 120–1 and 124–5).

Paley declares: "The proper end of human punishment is not the satisfaction of justice, but the prevention of crimes" (*Moral and Polit. Philos.* Bk. vi. ch. ix).

Prof. A. V. Dicey says of this writer that he was "an acute and liberal thinker" (*Law and Public Opinion in England,* first ed. 1905, p. 49). "Paley stands in spirit nearer to Bentham. His theology and his moral philosophy are avowedly utilitarian. His writings betray a keen interest in legal problems. He possessed the intellect of an enlightened lawyer" (*ib.* p. 142). It is remarkable that more than a century after Archdeacon Paley wrote the English system of judicature should conform so closely to his ideal of what such a system should be.

A propos of the recent death of Mr H. J. Roby, the eminent scholar and jurist, *The Law Times* of February 6th, 1915 (p. 318), contains an interesting note on the number of English jurists who have *not been professional lawyers*, and remarks: "Legal studies are a source of intellectual strength and recreation, as in the case of Mr Roby, and many who have never been members of the Legal Profession and never had legal careers." To these there must be added the name of Archdeacon Paley.

"Trial at bar" in the K. B. D. (p. 123).

The cases which were most frequently tried in this way formerly were libel, or seditious libel, assault, conspiracy, perjury and nuisance, all misdemeanours at Common Law, and they were tried with some of the incidents of civil procedure. Thus a special jury may still be had at the instance either of the prosecutor or the defendant; and a new trial might formerly be obtained, usually at the instance of the defendant, if necessary in the interest of justice, *e.g.* when the verdict was contrary to the weight of evidence. But this right of a new trial was taken away by the Act which established the Court of Criminal Appeal, as being no longer necessary; see s. 20 (1) Crim. App. Act, 1907.

The Court of Criminal Appeal (pp. 125–129).

The chief reason of the existence of this court is to see that the accused has had a fair trial according to law and that the sentence is a proper one. Accordingly, in a proper case, this court will order enquiries to be made for its information; *Rex* v. *Hughes* (*Arthur*), 10 Cr. App. R. 10; if the court considers that there was no case to be put to the jury, it will quash the conviction, see *Rex* v. *Jackson* (*Annie*), 10 Cr. App. R. 28; and it has held that the disagreement of the Judge with the verdict of the jury is ground by itself for quashing a conviction; *Rex* v. *Smith* (*Josiah*), 10 Cr. App. R. 232.

The Court of Criminal Appeal and power to order a new trial (p. 127).

For a strong argument *against* the granting of a new trial in criminal cases see *The Law Times* for December 19th, 1914, p. 195. The writer, whose name is not given, incidentally remarks: "It may be said that the criminal law of England approaches more nearly to an exact science than any other branch of our law."

The Privy Council (p. 133).

As to "the amplitude of the criminal jurisdiction of the Privy Council," see an article on *The Legal and Political Unity of the Empire*, by Prof. J. H. Morgan, in the *Law Quarterly Magazine*, for October, 1914, at pp. 393 and 394.

Secretaries of State (p. 142).

By the Interpretation Act, 1889, s. 12 (3) the expression "Secretary of State" shall mean *one* of her (his) Majesty's Principal Secretaries of State for the time being.

Writ of Error and Court for the consideration of Crown Cases Reserved (p. 147).

The Writ of Error was applicable only to errors of law which appeared on the face of the record. The Court for the consideration of Crown Cases Reserved considered only points of law raised at the trial, which the Judge thought fit to reserve. With these two exceptions there was no appeal in "criminal proceedings" before the Criminal Appeal Act, 1907, was passed (see Judicature Act, 1873, s. 47); and this rule still prevails except as to matters coming under that act, *viz.* convictions "on indictment." Thus in *ex p. Pulbrook* [1892] 1 Q. B. 86 (see p. 213) it was held that there was no appeal against the order of a High Court Judge made under the Law of Libel Amendment Act, 1888, giving leave to commence criminal proceedings for libel, it being "a preliminary step in a criminal matter." And apparently there would be no appeal against the order of a High Court Judge admitting a prisoner to bail. (See the query of A. L. Smith, J., in the above case on p. 87.)

The Criminal Investigation Department (p. 161).

Lieut.-Col. L. W. Atcherley, M.V.O., chief constable of the West Riding has made an excellent attempt to reduce *Criminal Investigation and Detection* to a system, and has established at Wakefield a sort of "clearing house for crime," which has worked very successfully. The principles on which it is worked are set out in a little book entitled M(*odus*) O(*perandi*) which may be obtained on application to him, price 1s.

County and Borough Police Forces (p. 162).

Full particulars and details of these forces as to areas, *personnel*, strength, etc., are given in *The Police and Constabulary Almanac*, published by the Manchester Courier, Ltd.: which, however, is obtainable only from the publishers, and not through any bookseller.

The annual cost of the prison service (p. 165).

On February 16, 1915, the Home Secretary (Mr McKenna) in answer to a question in the House of Commons stated that the total estimate for the prison service for the years 1904–5 and 1914–15 was respectively:

1904–5 .. £735,762   1914–15 .. £783,890

being an increase, in ten years, of £48,128.

The daily average prison population (p. 204).

On February 16, 1915, the Home Secretary (Mr McKenna) in answer to a question in the House of Commons gave the following comparative figures showing the daily average number of persons in prison in 1904–5 and 1914–15 (up to date):

	1904–5	1914–15
In local prisons	18,169	12,651
In convict prisons	3,191	2,552
In State Inebriate Reformatories ..	68	65
In Borstal Institutions	—	870
In Preventive Detention	—	245
	21,428	16,383

being a decrease of 5045.

CRIMINAL STATISTICS FOR 1913.

The Criminal Statistics for 1913 have appeared somewhat earlier than usual, while this book was passing through the press.

As to Courts of Summary Jurisdiction, no less than 731,048 persons were tried by these tribunals in 1913, of whom 50,758 were charged with indictable, and 680,290 with non-indictable, offences. Of these 75,291 were acquitted and discharged; 85,810 were dealt with after the charge was proved, without conviction; and 569,947 were convicted. Of those convicted 58,198 were sentenced to imprisonment without the option of a fine; and 502,554 were sentenced to pay fines, but 75,152 of these went to prison in default of payment, a state of affairs which it has been the policy of the legislature for some years past to prevent, but apparently so far without very satisfactory results. A great improvement in this respect is looked for in the future.

The number of juvenile offenders brought before Juvenile Courts in 1913 was 37,220 (about 5 per cent. of the total number of persons charged with criminal offences) of whom 4358 were acquitted; orders without conviction were made in 17,648 cases, and 15,214 (about 40 per cent.) were convicted.

As to appeals from Courts of Summary Jurisdiction, there were, in 1913, only 127, and in 54 cases the conviction was quashed, 3 were abandoned, and in 70 cases the conviction was affirmed, but in 24 cases there was a variation of the sentence.

These figures apparently do not show the number of appeals to the High Court by way of Case Stated, and of virtual appeals by *certiorari* and *mandamus*, but only those to Quarter Sessions.

At Quarter Sessions and Assizes 12,511 persons were brought up for trial, having been committed by Justices and Coroners, and 12,284 were actually tried. In 194 cases the bills were ignored by the Grand Jury and in 4 cases the charge was not proceeded with; 29 prisoners were found to be insane and unfit to plead. Of these tried (12,284) 10,165 were convicted, 2084 were acquitted by the petty jury, and 30 were found to be guilty but insane.

The total number of persons tried for indictable offences in 1913 (both summarily and on indictment) was 63,269 (50,758 plus 12,511), being a reduction of more than 2000 in the five years' average. On the other hand the total number of persons tried for non-indictable offences by Courts of Summary Jurisdiction (680,290) is 27,000 above the five years' average.

As to the work of the Court of Criminal Appeal in 1913, there were 608 applications for leave to appeal, and leave was granted in 111 cases. The total number of appeals was 157, as against 114 in 1912. In 73 cases the conviction or sentence was affirmed, in 79 it was quashed (in 47 cases the sentence was reduced) and in 5 cases the appeal was abandoned.

During the year 1913, no less than 139,060 convicted prisoners were received into prison; 90,188 were sentenced to hard labour, and 47,280 were not so sentenced, the bulk of the latter being treated as offenders in the third division, 31 only being ordered to be placed in the first division, and 1609 in the second division. A considerable number of the 139,060, however, were no doubt persons who had been convicted of petty offences, *e.g.* drunkenness, and sentenced to short terms of imprisonment (in lieu of paying fines) several times perhaps during the course of the year.

In 1913, there were 28 capital sentences, and 815 sentences of penal servitude; 519 persons (471 males and 48 females) were committed to Borstal Institutions; 1224 youthful offenders were sent to Reformatory Schools, and 2933 to Industrial Schools. The number of criminal lunatics received into asylums during the year was 218, and the total number of inmates at the end of the year was 1164, of which 478 had been charged with murder.

The total number of Probation Orders made in 1913 was 11,057, as against 11,193 in 1912.

*   *   *   *   *   *

The Annual Report of the Howard Association (an association for the promotion of the best methods of Treatment and Prevention of Crime, Pauperism, etc., named after John Howard, the philanthropist and prison reformer) for 1914, in referring to a decrease of 61,000 prisoners from 1903—1904 to 1913—1914, ascribes it to three causes or factors, *viz.*: "(1) a growing habit of obedience to law and order throughout the country; (2) a growing disinclination to send people to prison; and (3) improved methods of dealing with prisoners."

The proportion of persons received into prison per 100,000 in 1914 was 369, which was 43 below the figure of the previous year.

Along with this report is published a letter from Prof. Lublinsky, of the Law Department of the University of Petrograd, warmly commending the Criminal Justice Administration Act. He says: "The folly of short sentences is so fully exposed in this Act, that I think other countries will soon follow with a similar reform."

Commenting on the figures last given, the *Justice of the Peace* for December 19, 1914 (p. 605), says: "Even this record will be surpassed when the feeble minded are properly cared for and the Criminal Justice Administration Act becomes operative." The full title of this Act is: "An Act to diminish the number of persons committed to prison, to amend the law with respect to the treatment and punishment of young offenders, and otherwise to improve the administration of Criminal Justice"—which well expresses its objects.

*   *   *   *   *   *

The Probation of Offenders Act, 1907, s. 2 (3) provides: "The court by which a probation order is made shall furnish to the offender a notice in writing stating in simple terms the conditions he is required to observe." R. 59 of the S. J. Rules, 1915, further provides: "The notice required under s. 2 (3) of the Probation of Offenders Act, 1907, shall, before the offender leaves the precincts of the court, be read over to him (by the probation officer if practicable) in the presence of a third person, with such explanation as may be thought desirable." The object of these provisions is to bring home clearly to the mind of the offender the exact conditions which he has to observe, so that he cannot afterwards, in case of a breach, plead that he did not know or understand them.

*   *   *   *   *   *

The whole trend of thought for some years past, and the whole policy of the legislature, has been to prevent young persons going to prison for the first time. That is the fatal step, from which there is no drawing back. When once a conviction is recorded against a young person and he enters a prison his character is gone, his *moral* is destroyed by the degrading associations of prison life, he is a "gaol-bird," and the stigma attaches to him for life. In few cases is it possible to retrieve the character and *moral* so lost; in still fewer is any attempt made to do so. The result is, another recruit is added to the criminal class. It has at length been seen that a constant succession of short sentences for petty offences does no good whatever to the offender and harm to the community. Many youths commit such offences from yielding to temptation, from want of thought, and from high spirits; and to treat them as criminals for one lapse is futile and little short of cruelty. It is now recognised in regard to criminal offences that "Prevention (in the form of Probation) is better than cure." No doubt there are some cases of confirmed criminals even amongst the young; for such cases there is little hope; for the others, a brighter day has dawned. But Probation is not now restricted to young offenders. Everyone, whatever his age, who has yielded to temptation, may have a chance of redeeming himself.

INDEX

Borstal Associations, 188
Borstal Institutions, 164–169; sentence of detention in, under penal discipline, 185; in what cases applicable, 184; further powers in regard to, conferred on Courts of S.J. and Q.S. by C.J.A. Act, 1914, 185, 186; Mr R. McKenna, Home Secretary, on, 187; Sir E. Ruggles-Brise on objects of, 187; statistics as to, 187, 188
Burglary, simple cases of, now triable at Quarter Sessions, 76

Case stated, what it is, 68, 80, 123
Caution, upon arrest, 23; statutory, before committal, 28
Central Criminal Court, 87, 88
Certificate of dismissal by J.P.'s, 59
Certiorari, what it is, 68, 123
Chairmen of County Councils and Urban and Rural District Councils are ex officio Justices of the Peace, 6
Chairmen of Quarter Sessions, and their duties, 78, 79; have to take notes and sum up, 78; grant certificates of appeal and send reports of trials, 79, 127; may certify that prisoner ought to have legal aid, 79
Chancellor, Lord, his position in regard to Criminal Law, 131, 132; in regard to Habeas Corpus, 156; head of our judicature, 131
Chaplains, prison, 168, 177
Charge, Judge's, to Grand Jury, 83
Charge read over to accused by Magistrate or clerk, 27
Child, what, 45, 192
Children, summary jurisdiction as to, 45, 46
Children Act, 1908, 192–197; modes of dealing with children and young persons under, 193, 194
Circuits, judicial, 83; system, 84; officials of, 85; results of circuit system, 85; power of Crown to regulate, 83
Circulars, Home Office, 70, 146
Classification of offences, 19, 51, App. A, 207
Clerk of Assize, 85; Notes, 219; of the Peace, 78
Clerks to Justices, see Justices' Clerks, 14

Commissions of Assize etc., 84; Commission Day, 82
Commission of the Peace, 7, 8; Prof. Maitland on, 7
Commissions rogatoires, 154
Commitment for trial, 29
Complaint or Information, 19
Consecutive sentences (see Sentences), 57
Consent of Attorney, or Solicitor, General, sometimes necessary to a prosecution, 135; list of such cases, App. E, 212
Constabulary (see Police); H.M.'s Inspectors of, 162; their duties, 163
Constitutional Law and Criminal Law, connection between, 145
Contempt of Court, 78
Convict, what, 165; police supervision, 166
Conviction, previous, provisions of C.J.A. Act, 1914, as to, 51; effect of, as to punishment, 55; must not be mentioned to jury, Notes, 220
Coroner and Coroner's Inquest, their functions, 97–101; different classes of coroners, 97; coroner's jury, 99; inquest as to cause of fire in City of London, 98; publicity in regard to, 101
Corrupt practice at election, a ground for removal of J.P., 10
County magistrates (see Justices of the Peace), 5
County Police Forces, 162; Notes, 223
Court-houses, by whom provided, 12
Court of Record, what it is, 78
Court of trial, 30
Courts of Law, organs by which State administers justice, 2
Criminal Appeal, Court of, 125–129; its establishment, 125; its constitution, 126; right of appeal thereto, in what cases, 126; its powers, 125–7; has no power to order a new trial, 127; notice of appeal thereto necessary, 127; results of its establishment, 128,129; expenses of, 129; Notes, 222
Criminal Investigation Department, Scotland Yard, 161; Notes, 223
Criminal Justice Administration Act, 1914, 199–200; provision of, as to bail upon arrest, 24; as to

ERRATUM

The last line of the scale of fines and imprisonments on page 55 should read:

Exceeds £20   .   .   .   .   3 cal. months.

But it is submitted that the practical effect of s. 15 (1) of the C. J. A. Act, 1914, is to give the Justices power to inflict a fine of £50 with the alternative of six months imprisonment.

Moreover, by s. 53 of the S. J. Act, 1879, in the case of offences against the laws relating to the Inland Revenue and Customs, where the penalty exceeds £50, the imprisonment on non-payment, or default of distress, may exceed three, but must not exceed six, months.

SUPPLEMENT
1919

DURING the great European War, now happily over, several important changes in the administration of our criminal law have taken place. Some of these were of a temporary character, due to the exigencies of the war itself; with these it is not proposed to deal, except incidentally. But some others are of a far reaching character and permanent. Others again, *e.g.* the Bill for the Appointment of a Public Defender and the Police Bill, are still before Parliament, but will probably pass into law as Acts before the appearance of this Supplement.

PUBLIC DEFENDER.

A Bill is now before Parliament having for its object the appointment of a public defender. This Bill carries further the policy of the Poor Prisoners' Defence Act, 1903 (v. supra, pp. 35–38[1]). The following summary of its provisions is taken from the *Law Times* of July 19, 1919 (vol. 147), p. 214.

"The second reading of this Bill has been adjourned, but it is on the papers for an early resumption. It proposes that a Public Defender should be appointed to institute, undertake, and carry out, or to assist in so doing, the defence of every person charged with an indictable offence. This is to apply alike to the Court of Criminal Appeal, Sessions of Oyer and Terminer, or of the Peace, before magistrates or otherwise. A person is still to be allowed, if he desires it, to provide for his own defence, but must bear the cost of so doing. The Public Defender is to be a barrister or solicitor of not less than ten years' standing, and his assistant must be of not less than seven years' standing. The Bill proposes that all persons charged with indictable offences are to receive a copy of the depositions gratis[2]. The discretion of the Court to direct payment of the costs of the prosecution or defence under the Costs in Criminal cases Act 1908 is untouched and these payments

---

[1] N.B. These pages refer to the pages in the book.

[2] This is really unnecessary as it is already provided for. (See rule 13 of the First Schedule to the Indictments Act, 1915.)

are to apply in respect of the costs of the Public Defender as they do to the case of a private defendant. Regulations are contemplated to carry out these proposals. The Bill applies to any offence punishable on summary conviction when that offence is under the Summary Jurisdiction Acts deemed to be, as respects the person charged, an indictable offence, but it is not to apply to offences in relation to the non repair or construction of any highway, public bridge, or navigable river. It is to apply, however, to persons committed as incorrigible rogues under the Vagrancy Act 1824."

This Bill has been rendered desirable by the practical failure of the Poor Prisoners' Defence Act, under which the assistance given is uncertain and frequently comes too late. In many cases it is as important that the accused should have advice and assistance in the earlier stages of the proceedings (in the getting up of his case, in knowing what witnesses to call, how to take their evidence in proper form, and how to secure their attendance at the trial, and in knowing what to plead) as that he should have assistance at his trial in the presentation of his case to the jury. The best of advocates can do little with a case that has been badly got up, or not got up at all, and especially, as is often the case, where the brief is put into his hands almost at the last moment. The office of Public Defender has been described as "the antithesis to that of Public Prosecutor." We should prefer to describe it as the complement. It is the logical and inevitable completion of a proper scheme for the administration of justice.

CHAIRMAN OF QUARTER SESSIONS (v. supra p. 78).

Tennyson, in *The Princess*, describes the typical chairman of Quarter Sessions in these words: "A great, broad-shouldered, genial Englishman....A quarter-sessions chairman, abler none."

It has been remarked that the one pre-eminent intellectual quality which has been acquired by the average English country gentleman is the power to marshal the facts of a case as given in evidence. The acquisition of this faculty (by no means an easy one to acquire) is due to their constant attendance as magistrates at Quarter Sessions and the fact that so many of them have been called to the bar and have practised for a time at the Assizes and Quarter Sessions.

THE CEREMONY OF OPENING THE ASSIZES (v. supra pp. 82–86).

The Judge comes into court and all present rise and remain standing.

The Clerk of Assize: "I have received and now produce H.M.'s Commission of Assize and by virtue hereof the Right Hon. Bernard John Seymour Baron Coleridge and The Hon. Sir Henry Alfred McCardie, two of the Judges of H.M.'s High Court of Justice are appointed to hold this Assize of General Gaol Delivery in the West Riding of the County of York."

(He then reads the Commission.)

"*GEORGE the Fifth*, by the Grace of God of the United Kingdom of Great Britain and Ireland and of the British Dominions beyond the Seas, King, Defender of the Faith, *TO OUR* well-beloved and faithful Counsellor, Robert Bannatyne, Lord Finlay, Lord High Chancellor of Great Britain; Our Most dear Cousins and Counsellors, George Nathaniel Earl Curzon of Kedleston, Lord President of our Council, David Alexander Edward, Earl of Crawford, Lord Keeper of Our Privy Seal; Our Most dear Cousin and Counsellor, Henry George, Duke of Northumberland; Our most dear Cousin, Henry Ulick, Earl of Harewood; Our most dear Cousin and Counsellor, John George, Earl of Durham; Our well-beloved and faithful Charles Henry Wellesley, Lord Nunburnholme; Our beloved and faithful Sir Thomas Hugh Bell, Baronet; Our well-beloved and faithful Counsellor Rufus Daniel Viscount Reading, Lord Chief Justice of England; Our Judges for the time being of our Supreme Court of Judicature[1]; such of our Counsel learned in the law as are for the time being authorised by our Royal Warrant or by the Warrant of Our Lord High Chancellor to be on the Commission; and the Clerk of Assize and Circuit Officers of the North Eastern Circuit,—

"*GREETING, KNOW YE* that *WE* have assigned you and any two of you of whom one of our Judges of Our Supreme Court of Judicature or one of our said Counsel learned in the law, shall be one, *OUR JUSTICES*, to enquire more fully the truth by the oath of good and lawful men of Our Counties of Northum-

[1] The names of all these are given in a printed Schedule accompanying the Commission.

berland, Durham and York, and in Our Counties of the Cities of York and Newcastle-upon-Tyne, of all offences and injuries whatsoever within our said Counties and Counties of the Cities, and to hear and determine the premises, and to deliver the Gaols of our said Counties and Counties of the Cities of the Prisoners therein being, and to take all the Assizes, Juries and Certificates before whatsoever Justices arraigned within our said Counties and Counties of the Cities—

"*AND THEREFORE WE COMMAND* you that, at certain days and places which you shall appoint for this purpose, you and any two of you as aforesaid, shall make diligent enquiries about the said injuries and offences, and hear and determine the same, within our said Counties and Counties of the Cities, and deliver the Gaols of our said Counties and Counties of the Cities, of the Prisoners therein being, and take all those Assizes, Juries and Certificates, within our said Counties and Counties of the Cities, Doing therein what to justice does appertain according to the laws and customs of England, saving to us the amerciaments and other things from thence to us accruing—

"*AND WE COMMAND AND EMPOWER* you to do in the execution of this Commission all things which have heretofore been lawfully done in obedience to Our Commissions of Oyer and Terminer, General Gaol Delivery, Assize and Association and our Writs of Association and *Si non omnes*: *AND WE WILL* that this Commission shall be deemed to be a Commission of Oyer and Terminer, a Commission of General Gaol Delivery and a Commission of Assize.

"*In witness* whereof we have caused these our letters to be made patent. Witness Ourself at Westminster, the twenty fifth day of April in the seventh year of Our Reign.

Seal

"SCHUSTER[1]."

The Judge's Clerk: "God Save the King and my Lords the King's Justices."

---

[1] Sir Claud Schuster, Clerk of the Crown in Chancery, and Permanent Secretary to the Lord Chancellor.

"The High Sheriff of this County will now please return the several Writs and Precepts due and returnable here that my Lords the King's Justices may proceed thereon."

The High Sheriff produces them: they are handed to the Judge, and the business of the Assize proceeds.

Here followed formerly the Judge's Charge to the Grand Jury (v. p. 82), but as the Grand Jury is now suspended this charge is also necessarily suspended (see below as to the Grand Jury).

This is an abbreviated and comprehensive form of Commission issued in recent years, and as will be observed from the last clause it includes within itself, and has the force of, the Commissions of Oyer and Terminer, Gaol Delivery and Assize, formerly issued as separate documents. It is issued with and under the authority of the Privy Council, which is still the "formal executive" for the purposes of the administration of justice. I am indebted to Mr C. Milton Barber, Clerk of Assize for the North Eastern circuit, for the copy of this Commission, which is the actual Commission in virtue of which the Summer Assizes were held on the North Eastern Circuit in 1917.

By s. 16 (11) of the Judicature Act, 1873, the Courts of Oyer and Terminer and Gaol Delivery (i.e. the Assizes and Central Criminal Court) are made an integral part of the High Court of Justice. See also *Rex* v. *Dudley and Stephens* [1884] 14 Q.B.D. 273.

THE PASSING OF THE GRAND JURY (v. supra pp. 91–94).

By the Grand Juries (Suspension) Act, 1917, the Grand Jury system was suspended during the war. The Act provides, s. 1 (1) that no grand jury shall be summoned; and s. 1 (2) that

"In any case where a person has been committed for trial or where the consent or direction in writing of a judge of the High Court or of the Attorney-General or Solicitor-General for the presentment of an indictment against any person has been given, but in no other case, an indictment against that person may be presented in the appropriate court without having been found by a grand jury, but in other respects as heretofore; and where an indictment is so presented it shall be proceeded with in like manner as if a true bill had been found and presented in the court by a grand jury, and the statute and common law relating to such proceedings shall apply accordingly."

The Court itself may authorise the addition of other counts to the indictment or the presentment of any further indictment against the same person.

By s. 1 (3) where a person is bound by recognizance to prosecute a person not committed for trial (*i.e.* a person whom the magistrates have declined to commit for trial) he shall apply to a judge of the High Court or the Attorney-General or Solicitor-General for consent to present an indictment, and if such consent is not obtained the recognizance shall be void. This is to meet cases falling within the Vexatious Indictments Act, 1859.

Sect. 1 (4) provides that the Indictments Act, 1915 (q. v. infra) "shall apply to all indictments presented in pursuance of this Act, except that the words 'presentment of the grand jury' required by rule 2 of the First Schedule to that Act shall be omitted"; and s. 1 (5) provides that the rule committee established by the Indictments Act, 1915, shall make rules for making such variations in forms and instruments as they may think expedient for carrying this Act into effect—in other words so as to bring the two Acts into conformity and provide for their smooth working.

The expression "appropriate court " means the court to which the accused is committed for trial.

The Act came into operation on 2nd April, 1917; and s. 2 (4) provides that it shall "remain in force only during the continuance of the present war and for a period of six months after the termination thereof." Unless therefore it is renewed and made permanent it will expire six months after the official termination of the war.

It does not extend to Scotland and Ireland, where the Grand Jury system still remains in operation.

At present, therefore, the condition of the Grand Jury is one of "suspended animation," and the question now is, will this Act, which is of a temporary character, be allowed to expire, and will the Grand Jury be revived, or will the Act be removed and the Grand Jury be permanently discontinued? The answer rests with Parliament. More than two years' experience of the Act has shown that no one has suffered by the absence of the Grand

Jury; while, on the contrary, it has resulted in very great saving of time and expense, both to grand jurors and the country. Under the old system all the witnesses who had to go before the Grand Jury had to attend at the Assizes the first day or two, and then return to their homes, as it might be several days before their cases came on for trial. All the cost of this is now saved. The Act tends to the more speedy administration of justice; and the Law Officers of the Crown have recently (April, 1919) submitted a report advising the Government against the restoration of the Grand Jury.

One result of the suspension of the Grand Jury has been that the Judge no longer delivers his charge to the Grand Jury, and the Grand Jury have no opportunity of making presentments as to the state of the country, etc. This is in some respects a loss, but it must be borne for the sake of a greater gain.

THE INDICTMENTS ACT, 1915 (v. supra pp. 94–97).

By far the greatest and most important change made in the administration of our criminal law during the war is that made in the form and contents of indictments by the Indictments Act, 1915, which was the result of the labours of a commission that had been sitting on the subject for some time, and the object of which is to simplify and codify the law relating to indictments, and shorten the form of indictments. This it does in a somewhat roundabout way by enacting, first that the Rules as to Indictments contained in the First Schedule to the Act "shall have effect as if enacted in this Act, but those rules may be added to, varied, or cancelled by further rules made by the rule committee under this Act." It thus establishes a Rule Committee, and gives it "power from time to time, subject to the approval of the Lord Chancellor, to make rules varying or annulling the rules contained in the First Schedule to this Act, and to make further rules," etc.

For what these rules are, we must refer the reader to the Act itself, and the rules themselves since published by the Rule Committee. Most of them are of a very technical character.

For our purpose, the main provisions of the Act are contained in s. 3 (1) which enacts: "Every indictment shall contain, and shall be sufficient if it contains, a *statement of the specific offence* or offences with which the accused person is charged, together with such *particulars* as may be necessary for giving reasonable information as to the nature of the charge"; and in s. 3 (2) which enacts: "Notwithstanding any rule of law or practice, an indictment shall, subject to the provisions of this Act, not be open to objection in respect of its form or contents if it is framed in accordance with the rules under this Act."

Rule 2 of the *First Schedule* provides:

"The commencement of the indictment shall be in the following form":

"THE KING *v.* A.B."

"*Court of Trial*" [*e.g.* Central Criminal Court (or) In the High Court of Justice, K.B.D. (or) Durham County Assizes, etc.].

[*Presentment of the Grand Jury.*]

N.B. These words are omitted so long as the Grand Juries (Suspension) Act, 1917, is in force.

"A. B. is charged with the following offence" [offences]:

Rule 4 (1) provides: "A description of the offence charged in the indictment...shall be set out...in a separate paragraph called a count."

(2) "A count of an indictment shall commence with a statement of the offence charged, called the statement of offence."

(3) "The *statement of offence* shall describe the offence shortly in ordinary language, avoiding as far as possible the use of technical terms, and without necessarily stating all the essential elements of the offence, and if the offence charged is one created by statute, shall contain a reference to the section of the statute creating the offence." This rule is a valuable and important one. It goes to the root of the administration of justice.

(4) "After the statement of the offence, *particulars* of such offence shall be set out in ordinary language, in which the use of technical terms shall not be necessary." "Ordinary language" in this and the preceding rule means popular language, so that it can be understood by prisoners, many of whom are of very limited education.

Another important rule is 13 (1): "It shall be the duty of the clerk of assize [after a true bill has been found on any indictment[1]] to supply to the accused person, on request, a copy of the indictment free of charge." And by R. 13 (2) the cost of any copy so supplied is to be treated as part of the costs of the prosecution.

An *Appendix to the Rules* gives a large number of model *Forms of Indictments*, and more have since been issued.

The form of an indictment is therefore now as follows:—

THE KING *v.* A.B.

Court of trial: Durham County Assizes, held at Durham.

[*Presentment of the Grand Jury*] (*v. supra*).

A.B. is charged with the following offence.

Statement of Offence.

Murder.

Particulars of Offence.

A.B. on the...day of...1919, at...in the county of Durham, murdered J.S.

Or, to take another example:

[Commencement as above.]

Statement of Offence.

Burglary and larceny, contrary to S. 26 of the Larceny Act 1915.

Particulars of Offence.

A.B. in the night of the...day of...1919, at...in the county of Durham, did break and enter the dwelling-house of C.D., with intent to steal therein, and did steal therein one watch, the property of S. T., the said watch being of the value of two pounds.

As stated above the object of the Act was to simplify and codify the law relating to indictments and shorten their form. In the opinion of some older practitioners it has gone too far in this direction. But it works well in practice. It lets a prisoner know exactly with what offence he is charged, which, after all, is the chief purpose of an indictment. It carries out some of the reforms advocated by the late Mr Justice Stephen, which have long ago been adopted with success in some of the great self-governing parts of our empire, *e.g.* Canada and New Zealand.

[1] The words between the square brackets are inapplicable so long as the Grand Jury is suspended.

The Act came into operation on 1st April, 1916. It is a permanent Act, but the existence of the Rule Committee, with extensive powers, renders it flexible, and enables them to make such changes as from time to time may appear to be necessary or desirable.

THE ATTORNEY-GENERAL AND SOLICITOR-GENERAL (pp. 135-6).

Referring to the statement on p. 135: "But the English law officers (unlike the Scottish and Irish) are not usually privy councillors"—and that the Attorney-General is not a member of the Cabinet—these sentences crept in from the first edition by an oversight. It is true, however, that from Sir Francis Bacon's time no Attorney-General for England was sworn a member of the privy council until Sir Robert Finlay, as Attorney-General, was so sworn. The last four or five holders of the office, have also been members of the Cabinet. This appears to have been due to their eminence as politicians and strong personality rather than to any conscious and deliberate change in constitutional practice: and it remains to be seen whether future holders of the office will hold Cabinet rank. (See correspondence in *The Times*, Oct. 28 and 29, 1915, in which Sir H. Poland opposes, and Sir E. Clarke favours, the propriety of the Attorney-General being a Cabinet minister. See also Note on "The Attorney-General and the Cabinet," *Law Times*, Oct. 30, 1915, p. 545, and Note on "The Attorney-General," *Law Times*, Nov. 6, 1915, p. 14). There is much to be said on both sides of the question.

HOME OFFICE CIRCULAR (p. 70) AND THE
BORSTAL SYSTEM (pp. 184–188).

In *Rex* v. *Oxwade*, *L.T.* vol. 147 (July 19, 1919) p. 213, it was pointed out by the Judges on the bench that two circulars relating to the Borstal system, issued by the Home Office in 1909 and 1915 respectively, are inconsistent and have caused a good deal of confusion. Thus it appears that not even the Home Office is infallible.

CAPITAL SENTENCES AND YOUNG PERSONS (p. 119).

On June 22, 1915, the Home Secretary (Sir J. Simon) stated in the House of Commons that during the preceding ten years sentence of death had been passed on six male prisoners over 16 and under 19 years of age; and added: "In no case was the

sentence carried into effect, and there had been no case of a
female prisoner of that age being sentenced to death" (*J.P.*,
July 3, 1915, p. 321).

THE POLICE (pp. 158–163).

During the summer of 1919 there was a good deal of unrest
and dissatisfaction amongst the members of the various police
forces in England and Wales, which culminated in partial and
abortive strikes and lack of discipline. Into the causes and
merits of this state of affairs we do not propose to go in detail.
It was due partly to the greatly increased cost of the necessaries
of life, which affects the police as it affects other classes of the
community, and partly to the general unrest amongst the industrial classes, which is the aftermath of the war. But the police
who struck forgot their peculiar position, their obligation, and
their traditions. All honour to those who stood fast by their
duty! The first function of the State in internal affairs is to
preserve and enforce law and order, and the police who struck
forgot that they are specially charged with the execution of
this duty. *Quis custodiet custodes?* The immediate consequence
of this weakening in the discipline of the police was seen in
rioting and great destruction of property and some loss of life,
e.g. at Liverpool, where the criminal class, always on the lookout
for such a chance, took full advantage of the opportunity to
plunder and commit wanton destruction. Referring to this
regrettable event, the *Manchester Guardian* of Tuesday, August 5,
1919, very wisely says: "But there are some injuries which time
does not affect. One of them is the bringing of law into contempt.
Every time the forces of disorder prevail over the will of the
State respect for law is weakened and the path which leads
ultimately to anarchy is made easier. Whatever form of society
the industrial workers may finally establish, it will be maintained
by law, and a respect for law, or it will cease to be a society."

The Government, recognising that the police may have
legitimate grievances, have introduced a Police Bill[1], which was
considered by the Standing Committee of the House of Commons
on July 29th, 1919. It sets up a Police Federation for all police
below the rank of superintendent, as an organisation through

[1] This Bill was read a third time and passed, in the House of Commons,
on Friday, Aug. 8.

or by means of which the police may give proper expression to all such legitimate grievances; but it prohibits them belonging to any other trade union, and penalises the creation of disaffection in the force.

In introducing this Bill the Home Secretary (Mr Shortt) stated that the approximate total number of the various police forces in England and Wales, including the City of London, to be affected by the Bill, was 59,660.

CASES IN WHICH THE CONSENT OF THE ATTORNEY-GENERAL (OR SOLICITOR-GENERAL) IS NECESSARY TO A PROSECUTION.

To the List given on pp. 212–213, must be added:

4a. Public Health (Officers) Act, 1884, s. 2.

14. Trading with the Enemy Act, 1915.

But no formal proof is necessary at trial where consent had in fact been given. See *Rex* v. *Metz*, *L.T.R.* vol. 113, p. 464.

15. Larceny Act, 1915, s. 21 (*a*) (Conversion to his own use by a trustee).

16. Cases falling within s. 1 (3) of the Grand Juries (Suspension) Act, 1917, so long as that Act remains in force.

In all these cases the consent must be given in writing, which, if regular on the face of it, is accepted by the court as evidence of the fact.

By s. 18 of the Registration of Business Names Act, 1916, no proceedings under that Act shall be instituted without the consent of the Board of Trade.

CRIMINAL STATISTICS (v. supra pp. 200–6, 224–6).

The Criminal statistics have been published as usual during the war, in a somewhat abbreviated form, the comparative tables being omitted. Those for 1917 have just appeared (July, 1919). They are the last available.

The number of persons tried at Assizes and Quarter Sessions for indictable offences has been:

1913	...	12,511	1916	...	5011
1914	...	10,800	1917	...	5586
1915	...	6,010			

The number of persons tried for indictable offences at Petty Sessions and dealt with summarily has been:

1913 ... 50,758	1916 ... 53,606
1914 ... 47,759	1917 ... 57,419
1915 ... 49,525	

The number of persons tried for non-indictable offences at Petty Sessions and dealt with summarily has been:

1913 ... 680,290	1916 ... 610,218
1914 ... 626,765	1917 ... 445,758
1915 ... 532,444	

Many of these would be of a very trifling character, contraventions of police regulations etc., not worthy of being dignified with the name of crime.

The total number of persons prosecuted for indictable offences in 1913 was 63,269; in 1917—63,005.

The total number of persons proceeded against in Courts of Summary Jurisdiction in 1913 was 731,048: in 1917—503,177.

A remarkable circumstance is that the number of persons convicted, both by juries and justices, bears very nearly the same proportion to those charged. Roughly speaking there are about four convictions in five charges, or, stated in another way, one person out of every five charged is acquitted. The difference in the proportion between those convicted by juries and those convicted by justices is very small; but in fact it is rather in favour of the justices. That is to say, a person charged with an offence has a slightly better chance of acquittal with the justices than with a jury. The actual figures of convictions in 1917 were 4384 (1202 acquittals) on indictment, and 393,841 (109,336 acquittals) on summary procedure.

It is very difficult to draw any sound conclusion from these figures. Down to a point there appears to be a substantial and satisfactory decrease; then a strong tendency to rise. It is easy to suggest reasons for this during the war, and 1917 marks the middle period of the war. Too much reliance must not therefore be placed on mere figures.

In the Court of Criminal Appeal, in 1915 there were 287 applications for leave to appeal and 89 appeals were heard or otherwise disposed of. In 1917, there were 252 applications, and

91 appeals were heard; in 16 of which the conviction was quashed, and in 15 the sentence was reduced or altered. Many of the applications to appeal are virtually appeals and are argued as such.

The number of appeals against summary convictions to Quarter Sessions in 1915 was 132: in 1917, it was 232, in 75 of which the conviction was quashed, and in 43 of which the sentence was modified.

EMERGENCY LEGISLATION OFFENCES.

In view of the termination of the war it is interesting to note what has been the effect as regards crime of the special legislation necessitated by the war, which created a large number of new offences. The following table shows the Acts passed and the number of offences committed against them, down to the end of 1917.

Statute	Number of persons prosecuted			
	1914	1915	1916	1917
Defence of the Realm Acts ...	83	33,071	121,563	59,506
Aliens' Restriction Acts	3226	7581	14,279	13,606
National Registration Act ...	—	50	879	1192
Trading with Enemy Acts ...	3	37	27	16
Maintenance of Live Stock Act...	—	7	48	21
Price of Coal (Limitation) Act ...	—	—	—	3
War Charities Act	—	—	5	11
Special Constables Act	—	27	28	13
Other Statutes	—	—	12	18

At the present time (August, 1919) there is a Bill before Parliament, entitled the War Emergency Law (continuance) Bill, designed to continue these restrictions for a further period of twelve months "from the termination of the present war"!

Speaking generally, it is too early as yet to say what has been or will be the effect of the war as regards crime. The armistice was signed in November, 1918, but Peace has only just been signed. All former wars have been followed by a period of increased criminality, and it would appear that this war is not likely to prove an exception to the rule. The habits of mind that war begets and fosters, the recklessness of human life and wanton destruction of property, the ready resort to violence to attain one's personal ends, are the negation of the habits of law and order engendered by peace. Add to this, the grave dissatisfaction and nervousness which prevails in all ranks of society, owing to the strain, the losses, and the heavy burdens of the war, and the unrest and disappointment which prevails amongst the industrial classes, owing to the increased cost of living and the hope and desire for a better social order, and it must be confessed that the prospect is far from bright, in spite of the fact that we have won the war. One of the most ominous signs of the times is the resort to sudden strikes and the outbursts of mob violence. But there is no reason to fear that wiser counsels and saner methods will not still prevail, and that Law and Order, to which we are accustomed and upon which society and civilisation depend, will not emerge as strong as ever. Towards this end it is the duty of all good citizens, who love their country, to work and strive with courage and fortitude by all means in their power.

SUGGESTED REFORMS IN THE ADMINISTRATION OF CRIMINAL JUSTICE.

1. The appointment of a Public Defender (v. supra).

2. The appointment of more Stipendiary Magistrates. Admirable as is the work done by the unpaid justices of the peace, they are after all only amateurs. The administration of justice is not the business of their lives, for which they have received a proper training. Their attendance is voluntary, and the mere presence of a Clerk, or a Clerk's clerk, is not a sufficient guarantee of continuity. The result is that different benches often arrive at widely different conclusions and impose widely different sentences. and there is an absence of continuity. There should be at least one stipendiary magistrate in every centre of population of 50,000 and upwards.

3. The establishment of an Inferior Court of Criminal Appeal. The present appeal tribunal (Quarter Sessions) is not a satisfactory one. The cost and delay of an appeal render it illusory. If more stipendiaries were appointed, a much better tribunal might be constituted by (say) three of these meeting monthly at convenient centres to hear appeals from petty sessions, with power to revise sentences. The stipendiary against whose decision or sentence the appeal was brought should not be a member of the Court, i.e. he should not sit on the hearing of the appeal.

4. The Court of Criminal Appeal should have power to order a *new trial* in cases where the Court thinks it desirable. At present it has no such power (*v.* p. 127).

5. Habitual criminals ought not to be tried by the same juries as have just convicted them of an offence which gives rise to this charge (*v.* p. 190). It is contrary to all our ideas of justice and fairness that this should be done. A fresh jury ought to be impannelled.

6. The practice of recording sentence of death, instead of passing it, in certain cases, should be revived (*v.* p. 117). This was introduced by an Act of 1828 (4 Geo. IV, c. 48) at a time when our penal code was at its worst, as a means of mitigating the large number of death sentences. After the reforms effected by Sir S. Romilly and the consequent reduction in the number of such sentences, the practice was discontinued, but the Act is still in force.

The Capital Punishment Commissioners of 1866 unanimously recommended that this practice should be restored to the judges even in cases of murder. It is little short of gratuitous cruelty to pass sentence of death in cases, *e.g.* infanticide, where it is well known to everybody in court, including the judge himself, that it will not be carried out.

7. Generally speaking more use should be made, both by Justices of the Peace, Recorders and Judges, of the powers of putting upon Probation and making Restitution. In May, 1915, the Chairman of the County of London Quarter Sessions (Mr R. Wallace, K.C.) in binding over a prisoner said: "The operation of the Probation Act is having a wonderful effect. Over 90 per cent. of the prisoners bound over never see the inside of a police court again. Thus their character is retrieved and the public are spared the expense of prison treatment." As to Restitution, there is nothing the average thief dislikes so much as having to make good his depredations. At the same time it is a simple act of justice to the sufferer.